D0296711

The Art of Reading

Edited by MORAG HUNTER-CARSCH

BLACKWELL EDUCATION

To the children

VERITAS

Movement, the response to life,
Move in the spirit of the dance,
Dance to the music of the song,
Sing the spirit of the words
And paint the picture of the truth.
Read and write to re-create the pictures.

CMH–C

First published 1989

© UKRA 1989

Published by
Basil Blackwell Ltd
108 Cowley Road
Oxford OX4 1JF
England

British Library Cataloguing in Publication Data

The art of reading.
  1. Children. Reading skills. Development
  I. Carsch, Morag Hunter
  428.4'3

  ISBN 0-631-90331-3

Typeset in 10/12 pt Symposium
by Colset Private Limited
Printed in Great Britain
by Billing & Sons Ltd., Worcester

Contents

* indicates brief reports, notes or abstracts

Preface

On behalf of the United Kingdom Reading Association I would like
to thank all those who submitted papers for consideration for this
book. These constitute an extensive, informative and delightful collection, which, together with the delegates' and planning teams'
contributions, fittingly celebrated the Association's Silver Jubilee
Conference. The anthology includes notes, short reports and
abstracts as well as full papers. This is not only to permit mention of
a greater number of interesting sources of information, but also to
try to meet the range of preferences for different styles of presentation and to provide illustrations from the breadth of the conference. It is most unfortunate that all of the papers submitted cannot
be included in this volume; I hope that other avenues can be found for
their publication.

The arrangement of the papers in the book follows, to a large
extent, the organisation of the course – which was in five sections
(days) each with a theme. These daily themes were part of the over-
riding conference theme of *Reading and Re-creation*.

Each chapter is not only valuable in its own right, but constitutes
part of a larger picture to which all have contributed. In this way,
too, the nature of the Association's aims with regard to the 'open
forum' may also be exemplified, since there are conflicting views,
not, I hope, competing for space, but potentially collaborating to
contribute to 'the greater good'.

Personal acknowledgement

In thinking about reading and those who have influenced my understanding of reading and its vital relationship with education, I would
like to thank all those who assisted directly with the 25th UKRA
Conference. In addition, I would like to acknowledge my appreciation of my own teachers; my respected Tutors, in particular Sir
Henry Wood and Professor Stanley Nisbet; my UKRA colleagues
and friends, especially Professor Margaret Clark, Mr Doug Dennis,
Mr Keith Gardner, Dr Joyce Morris and Dr Derek Thackray; and all
the children with whom I have worked and who, like Robert Lailey,
taught me more about reading as 're-creation of meaning'.

Themes and headings

1 Reading and re-creation

The section begins with a brief Introduction explaining the Conference theme. The following paper by Helen McLullich and Sue Palmer illustrates the nature of re-creation of meaning by pointing out the extent of individual differences in ways of using 'the inward eye'. In the next chapter, the analysis of Aileen Lowndes' approach to art and language teaching points to the possible prerequisites for 'image holding' as well as 'image making' in the development not only of imagination as a way of building 'inward pictures', but of learning to see more keenly what is 'outside of oneself', especially with a view to sharing the relevant experiences. The poems by Emma Walton and Kevin Wiles speak for themselves.

Chapter 5 is a report of the guest lecture given by Dr Che Kan Leong of the University of Saskatchewan, Canada, who was invited to speak in memory of the late Professor John Downing.

2 Policy and practice

At such a gathering of people concerned, in one way or another, with the educational system, it seemed important to consider the current educational philosophy and its directions and constraints as these relate to classroom practice. The obvious and immediate concern about resources required, as a priority, deliberations on published materials, hence the immediate involvement in the Publishers' Exhibition.

At this time of major policy development in the provision of guidelines for the new national curriculum, there is much interest in, and speculation about, the relative emphasis to be placed on language, literacy and communication, across the curriculum as well as within the subject area of English.

The recently-released *Report of the Committee of Inquiry into the Teaching of English Language* (the Kingman Report) was described and discussed by Sir John Kingman as first guest speaker at the Conference.* Chapter 6 is a personal comment on the occasion from Keith Gardner, one of the members of the Bullock Committee and a past president of UKRA.

* Sir John graciously gave permission for his lecture to be videotaped. Copies are available from the University of Leicester Audio Visual Services, PO Box 138, Leicester LE1 9HN (Tel: 0533 522900).

UKRA's response to the Kingman Report and the Cox Report (English from 5 to 11) is *Communicating Cox and Kingman*, Blackwell Education (in press).

The two short chapters by Alexandra Dilks and June Hall both illustrate ways in which groups of teachers have set about developing their school language and reading policies. The route towards a clearly formulated written statement is one which takes time and depends on the direct contribution and goodwill of all concerned if it is to be effectively implemented as well as 'created'. Print can then assist in the re-creation of what was collectively given shape.

Chapter 9 contains some cautionary remarks, from the work of Dina Thorpe, Keith Gaines, Helen Pain-Lewins and Bobbie Neate. This will be of interest to readers who may wish to explore further the matters they raise with reference to choice of published resources.

No discussion of school language policy would be complete without consideration of the practical and aesthetic matters of handwriting as distinct from development of written language. Peter Smith's review of points of consensus in his conference workshop discussion on this topic provides an excellent opening for any school-based INSET discussion. The next chapter, by Pam Czerniewska, assists in illuminating the early stages of developing literacy with reference particularly to written language, and incidentally throws light on handwriting issues by sharing examples of children's attempts to re-create writing and messages they have seen encoded by others.

In chapter 12 John Beech examines component parts in the reading process from the psychologist's perspective. It would indeed be a pity if his message were to be discounted for his use of the currently unfashionable term 'skills' since, as Beech recognises, there is more to reading than that. He appears to support the view that closer examination of classroom practice is needed. It is thus interesting that Tony Martin and John Merritt's chapter provides a classroom perspective which, appears to reject the place of a 'skills perspective' (Merritt, 1978) even in the larger picture of relating research and practice. The issue is considered later in the context of research and practice with reference to children with specific learning difficulties (see the chapter by Snowling and Chasty in Part 5) where the suggested value for the class teacher of maintaining an awareness of individual children's cognitive profiles is underlined.

It might be further suggested that it is not only the cognitive profile which needs to be considered. There may be more to learning, and more to the motivation with which the learning establishes and maintains its own momentum. There are the intimately related areas of affective, emotional/personal/social and moral development, not to mention physical and physiological. Without entering the details of the debate on the differentiation between learning and development, it may be sufficient to mention the fact that memory, as a factor often considered in cognitive terms, may be crucially affected by attitudes, perceptions and apperceptions, and what are sometimes almost summarily dismissed as 'feelings' (an area often relegated to the realm of the mystical because it defies immediately discrete classification or 'controlling' in linguistic terms).

How reason and reasoning are related and dynamically develop from, or alongside with, sensations and feelings, constitutes the focus of concern of the kind of reading that is fostered through the work of Bruce (see Part 3.) and many of the 'creative teachers' who have an 'intuitive understanding' or apperception of what it is that reading does and can do. They can 'get children into print' as easily as they can get them to sing, move and dance.

It seems obvious that we should be looking at examples of 'good teaching' although this may tend to raise other questions and distractions, if the debate centres on possible penalties for those who are considered by some to be less effective teachers or if too much time is spent on deciding how to go about the task.

3 Communication in the classroom

This theme was chosen not only because policy requires to be communicated in order to become part of practice, but because it needs to be recognised that the Association's broader interests include 'communication'. The importance of clear communication as it relates to classroom practice provided a further endorsement of the desirability of the two ideas: 'classroom for learning' and 'communication' being linked and immediately following the previous topic.

All of the papers in Part 3 concern classroom practice and provide information and ideas which have been explored and 'tested'. The sequence of papers also presents, in itself, a small INSET course for those who wish to use it in this way in the context of the theoretical issues introduced in Part 2, with regard to development of written language, reading and independent or guided study.

In chapter 16, Richard Binns responds to the following questions, 'Why don't you correct the child's writing?' and 'Why work from imprecise language?'. He points out that it is necessary to recognise the child's knowledge and ownership of the picture which he or she is trying to convey through writing. To do this requires taking the child's language, however imprecise, as the 'sparking point' that permits the re-creation and eventual sharing of the picture through the written word. He states that 'it may become clearer if, and only if, the unvarnished text is the starting place'. His approach has been developed systematically over long years of classroom practice. It reflects in part the perspectives of the artist, and indeed his formal training was in the field of the visual arts, as well as in linguistics.

Vivienne Cato and John Trushell provide a delightful illustration of the way in which modern technology can be employed in the advancement of both oracy and literacy. Taken in dialogue with the previous and the following chapters, their contribution provides an appreciation of the parallel, intertwining and/or integrated developmental patterns across the areas of reading and writing, listening and speaking.

Muriel Bridge's paper was given a particularly warm reception at conference as it focused on an interesting and fashionable field of controversy, concerning the supposed superiority of story approach. The 'literacy-initiative' study investigated different approaches to the beginning stages in learning to read in school. As Bridge's paper concerned the early stages, it seemed appropriate to include, also, a paper which gave its attention to the later stages with particular consideration of reading comprehension. Morag MacMartin's chapter is built on a review of procedures including that known as propositional analysis of text; it introduces a mode of analysis of errors in comprehension which perhaps takes us into a new realm of 'miscues'.

4 International sharing: linguistics and learning

This is a stated aspect of the Association's aims. This part of the programme provided a reminder of links with the founder body to which UKRA is affiliated. The family of affiliates who together constitute the membership aim, through collaborative, co-operative exchanges, to achieve the greater ends of improving literacy and thus learning, and one hopes, understanding within and across nations.

Part 4 begins with a review of these links and the development of international sharing. The next chapter is an autobiographical contribution which honours, celebrates and shares the development of both the professional and personal involvement of Dr Joyce Morris, co-founder and second President of UKRA. The International Citation of Merit Award was presented to Dr Morris at conference. Dr Hans Grundin, as a member of the Board of Directors of the International Reading Association, presented the award, reading the citation which began, 'Teacher, psychologist, researcher and author, she works tirelessly and courageously to influence the professional practice of teachers in the cause of literacy . . .'. The lengthy citation referred to her research, which is internationally recognised, and to many aspects of her outstanding contribution to the language arts.

Dr George Young's chapter keeps speech and writing distinct for analytical purposes but emphasises the need to understand how they relate to one another and how both relate to reading. This of course touches the very kernel of the re-creation process.

The sub-heading *Linguistics and learning* was chosen not only for love of alliteration and indeed poetry, but because it reflects the current potentially healthy trend towards sharing a modern approach to the understanding of how language works. Taken at a fairly broad level, the idea of classroom teachers becoming more precise in their description and sharing of their own model for language cannot but assist in bringing about a clearer understanding for pupils, if only by giving them all equal access to ways of handling complex ideas in fairly simple and generally accepted terms which are descriptive, not prescriptive. If, in fact, the ideas do not prove to be very helpful, the fastest way of arriving at that conclusion (if that is the direction the exploration would take) is to open up the avenues for all to make informed judgement on the basis of understanding the evidence, and, of course, examining other models. Any theory of language comprehensive enough to be of lasting use in the classroom, should explain language and literacy (also oracy) difficulties, as well as their development and the nature of the relevant abilities. In that sense the topic of 'linguistics and learning' could have been attached to any part of the course and should permeate all of this book.

In chapter 22 Alison Littlefair introduces the concepts of 'genre and register', mentioned in Part 2, in the context of Neate's work employing these constructs in the analysis of children's information texts. In order to see the potential value of grasping these strategies developed from applied linguistics, the basic ideas themselves are briefly described. The work may have implications for educators at all levels. The implications for 'Study-skills' (if I dare use the word 'skill') are, I trust, not too difficult to discern. These are links also with the work of Morag MacMartin in Part 3 which may have some bearing on re-creation of meaning by the reader.

Frank Potter's paper, short and potent, embodies the modern routes to communication and sharing across and within national boundaries. It is interesting to speculate what would happen if, in response to Professor Sugano's paper, some Japanese children were to be 'paired-learner-communicators via microcomputer-technology' with English-speaking counterparts. This raises the question of whether developments which focus on the written (screen) printed words and 'programmes' towards sentence and paragraph construction might provide an appropriate transition strategy from textbook grammar-based work to 'language exchanges' of the kind that are based on sharing experiences.

5 Literacy difficulties

Here the intention is to look more closely at the processes of reading, communication and learning by examining them in terms of understanding what 'goes wrong' in some instances. Looking at the reverse side of the coin, it is suggested, might help with recognition of what the coin is and its worth, although we might not use any further monetary metaphors since the terms in which we deal are unlikely to be satisfactorily explained in the language of commerce.

The section begins with a sympathetic exploration of retelling stories as a way of recreating their messages and meaning. Professor Goodacre's paper eloquently illustrates the kind of stance that needs to be taken if we are to hear what children are telling us about the reading process. For others to learn how to listen in the way she does, may take special training as well as the predisposingly appropriate attitudes.

In the context of discussing literacy difficulties, Jean Palmer draws attention to the fundamental importance of being able to hear. She makes some suggestions about steps that might be taken to ensure that hearing difficulties are identified, more widely understood and more sympathetically treated in the sense of adapting teaching to meet individual needs.

John Bald's review introduces discussions in the field of specific learning difficulty. His seminar was found to be particularly helpful and stimulating by participants who have indicated a wish to extend the exchange of views and information.

The chapter by Margaret Snowling and Harry Chasty negotiates the mass of communication problems generated between and within professions which all claim to be concerned about the welfare and education of young learners. Dr Snowling quickly gets to the important practical point of what it is that appears to be going wrong, or is missing, in the case of those children with subtle and individual learning difficulties now generally described (since the Warnock Report's adoption of the term) as 'specific learning difficulties'.

Harry Chasty makes a plea to teachers to consider, in depth, the learning needs of those children whose problems require adaptation of usual approaches to teaching, and, essentially, individualisation as well as routines for helping them to tackle what are, for them, harder aspects of learning.

David Lloyd's lively chapter on the Puppet Theatre is not simply a commentary on the world as a stage. It also represents the links between the arts in the most delightful approach to building confidence as well as providing enjoyment while incidentally developing abilities to communicate in ways which include listening, speaking, reading and writing. Children with learning and literacy difficulties need to feel hopeful as well as to share a love of literature and life.

Finally, Norma Mudd's report brings together a group of people with a special interest in encouraging and assisting those who have the courage to ask, after school age, for support in developing their literacy.

Together, these papers constitute the proceedings of the recreative and re-creative 25th celebratory conference.

CM Hunter-Carsch

Acknowledgements

On behalf of the United Kingdom Reading Association, I wish to thank the following individuals and institutions for their assistance:

The Conference Committee in co-operation with the Committee of the Leicestershire Local Council of UKRA, Advisory Assistants and Secretarial Assistants:

Alan Beck, Rosemary Benn, Betty Blythe, Richard Brown, Henry Carsch, John Chapman, David Chesworth, Joyce Cooke, Inga Dobson, Val Fitzhugh, Carole Fitzpatrick, Marian Garratt, Betty Giddens, Ann Glenton, Jean Greaves, Mollie Hanger, Maureen Hardy, Colin Harrison, Sandra Hawkins, Jane Hislam, Roy Illsley, Roy Kirk, David Lloyd, Janet Moyles, Diana Potter, Sylvia Riches, Judith Schofield, Carolyn Skilling, Jayne Tansley, Neil Tansley, Angela White

The University of Leicester:

*The School of Education
The School of Education Library Staff
The Conference Office and Catering Department
The Staff of the Halls of Residence*

The City of Leicester

Leicestershire Education Authority

*Computer and Special Education Exhibition
Pauline Harrison
Leicestershire Libraries School-Services Department*

Northamptonshire and Buckinghamshire Education Authorities

Leicester Polytechnic:

*Brian Allison, Professor Emeritus for 'Children's Use of Works of Art' Exhibition by courtesy of R. Clements and Devon Schools
Colin Brookes for the Exhibition, 'Reading Images'
Rachel Mason for the Exhibition, 'Using Images to Increase Social Understanding'*

Exhibition of Leicestershire Children's Art, 'Do you read me?': Aileen Lowndes and Pedigree Petfoods

The Educational Publishers' Association, particularly Barbara Brookes, and:

*E.J. Arnold & Son Ltd
Basil Blackwell Ltd
Books for Students
Central Independent Television plc
Cranfield Press
East Midlands Arts Association*

*Hodder & Stoughton
Invicta Plastics
Ladybird Books
Pedigree Petfoods
Pergamon Press (Primary Source)
Russell Press (Special Children)
Stanley Thornes
Task Master*

I would also like to express my appreciation to Valerie Fawcett and Marion Casey (Basil Blackwell Ltd) .

C. Morag Hunter-Carsch, UKRA Administrative Office, Edgehill College of Education, St. Helen's Road, Ormskirk, Lancs. L39 4QP

A note on the contributors

Mr John Bald, Reading and Language Centre Educational Adviser, Colchester Institute, Marine Parade, Clacton, Essex CO15 6JQ

Dr John Beech, Psychology Department, University of Leicester, University Rd. Leicester LE1 7RF

Mr Richard Binns, Researcher/Consultant, 17 Montrose Gardens, Milngavie, Glasgow G62 8NW

Mrs Muriel Bridge, Literacy Support Service, (School Psychological Service), Collegiate House, College St. Leicester LE2 0JX

Dr Violet Bruce, Consultant/Lecturer, Corner Cottage, Skeffington, Leics

Ms Vivienne Cato, Department of Language, NFER, The Mere, Upton Park, Slough SL1 2DQ 2AJ

Dr Harry Chasty, Director, Dyslexia Institute, 133 Gresham Rd, Staines, Middlesex TW18

Ms Pam Czerniewska, National Writing Project, Schools Curriculum Development Council/Director, Newcombe House, 45 Notting Hill Gate, London W11 3JB

Mr Doug Dennis, Past President UKRA, Worcester College of Higher Education, Henwick Grove, Worcester WR26 HA

Mrs Alexandra Dilks, Teacher, Meadow County Primary School, Meadow Way, Wigston Magna, Leicester LE8 1QZ

Mr Keith Gaines, Castleford Area Reading Centre, Temple St. Castleford WF10 5RE

Mr Keith Gardner, Past President UKRA, 45 Hermitage St. Newcastleton TD9 0QE

Mrs Ann M Glenton, Head of English, Bushloe High School, Station Rd. Wigston Magna, Leicester LE8 2DT

Mr Martin Good, Cambridge Training and Development Ltd. 43 Clifton Rd Cambridge CB14 FB

Professor Elizabeth Goodacre, School of Education, Middlesex Polytechnic, Trent Park Site, Cockfosters Rd Barnet, Herts. EN4 2BA

Ms June Hall, Area Senior Teacher, Brent Learning Resources Service, London, c/o Sudbury Junior School, Perrin Rd, North Wellesley, Middlesex HA0 3EY

Ms Maureen Hardy, Teacher in Charge of Language Development, Sandfield Close Primary School, Sandfield Close, Leicester LE4 7RE

Mr Alastair Hendry, Past President UKRA, Craigie College of Education, Ayr KA8 0SR

Mrs Margaret Herrington, Distance Learning Base, John Ellis Community College, Corporation Rd Leicester LE4 5PW

Mrs Sue Houlton, Aylestone Adult Basic Education Scheme, Saffron Lane Estate, Leicester

Mrs Morag Hunter-Carsch, UKRA President, School of Education, University of Leicester 21 University Rd. Leicester LE1 7RF

Dr Kjeld Johansen, Educational Adviser, RØ Skolevej 14 DK 3760 Gudhjem, Denmark

Dr Che Kan Leong, Department of Education for Exceptional Children, University of Saskatoon, Saskatoon S7N0W0 Saskatchewan, Canada

Mrs Margaret Litchfield, Literacy Support Service Area 1, Knighton Fields Teachers' Centre, Herrick Rd Leicester LE2 6DJ

Mrs Alison Littlefair, Researcher, 56 High St, Harlton, Cambridge CB3 7ES

Mr David Lloyd, Special Educational Needs Teacher, Merrydale Junior School, Claydon Rd Leicester LE5 0JD

Mrs Aileen Lowndes, Teacher, Linden Primary School, Headland Rd. Leicester LE5 6AD

Ms. Morag Mac Martin, Teacher, Breadalbane Academy, Aberfeldy, Perthshire PH 152 OU

Mr Tony Martin, Tutor in Language Development and Children's Literature, Charlotte Mason College of Education, Ambleside, Cumbria LA22 9BB

Mrs Helen Mc Lullich, Consultant, 20 Rosefield Gardens, Uddingston, Lanarkshire GT17 AW

Professor Emeritus John Merritt, Past President UKRA, Honorary Research Fellow, Charlotte Mason College of Education, Ambleside, Cumbria LA22 9BB

Dr Joyce Morris, Co-founder and second President of UKRA, 33 Deena Close, Queen's Drive, London W3 0HR

Mr David Moseley, Reader in Applied Psychology, University of Newcastle upon Tyne Dept. of Psychology Bldg. 4th Floor, Clarement Place, Newcastle upon Tyne NE1 7RU

Dr Norma Mudd, Consultant/Lecturer, Arlon, Richmond Avenue, Burscough, Ormskirk Lancs L40 7RD

Ms Bobbie Neate, Consultant/Researcher/Lecturer, 133 Maze Hill, Blackheath, London SE3 7UB

Ms Helen Pain-Lewins, Department of Library and Information Studies, LoughboroughUniversity of Technology, Loughborough, Leics LE113TU

Mrs Jean Palmer, Department of Audiology, Education of the Deaf and Speech Pathology, The University of Manchester, Oxford Rd. Manchester M13 9PL

Ms Sue Palmer, Consultant, 11 St George's Rd Truro, Cornwall, TR13JE

Dr Frank Potter, Edgehill College of Education, St Helen's Rd Ormskirk, Lancs L394QP

Mr Peter Smith, Past President of UKRA, Consultant, 17 Freame Way, Gillingham, Dorset SP8 4RA

Dr Margaret Snowling, National Hospitals College of Speech Sciences, London

Professor Yoshihiko Sugano, Chuo University 742-1 Higashi, Nakano, Hachioji-city, Tokyo Japan

Ms Janet Swinney, 2(FL) Spottiswoode St Edinburgh EH9 1DG

Ms Dina Thorpe, Librarian, c/o Cranfield Press, Cranfield Institute of Technology, Cranfield, Bedford, KM43 0AL

Professor Marian Tonjes, Education Department, Western Washington University, Bellingham, WA USA

Mr John Trushell, Department of Language, NFER, The Mere, Upton Park, Slough SL12DQ

Dr George Young, School of Education, University of Leicester, 21 University Rd Leicester LE1 7RF

PART 1

Reading and Re-creation

1 Introduction: reading and re-creation

Morag Hunter-Carsch

> . . . in language alone the inner life of man finds its complete exhaustive and objectively intelligible expression. Hence the art of understanding focuses on interpretation of those remnants of human existence which are contained in written words.
>
> W. Dilthey (1923)

At the beginning of the planning for the conference the idea of reading for pleasure seemed to be a suitable theme, in the light of the celebratory nature of a silver jubilee conference. There was a happy note about it. This idea quickly developed into the concept of reading for recreation. Yet the idea of recreation with its connotations of refreshment, entertainment and amusement was somehow too narrow and almost 'irresponsible' – or at least not fully responsible – in that it did not adequately represent those aspects of its potential and direction which were implicit in the concept of reading. It was as if the messages the reader took in by one eye were immediately let out by the other. Yet for centuries reading has been known to be far more than this. For instance, Ben Jonson wrote of his 'early and invincible love of reading' which he would not exchange 'for the treasures of India' and Shakespeare thought that 'reading and writing were essential attributes of man' (A Midsummer Night's Dream) a sentiment echoed by Sir Richard Steele in the 18th century when he suggested that reading is 'to the mind what exercise is to the body' (Tatler, No. 147). A hundred years later Trevelyan (1942) warned that education had 'produced a vast population able to read but unable to distinguish what is worth reading . . .'.

On reflection, it seemed that the range of benefits that can accrue from reading, particularly the real pleasure that so many have derived from reading for so long, perhaps in the sense of lasting worth, required a closer and more penetrating examination of the process by which we attribute meaning to what is being read. In the first place, this seems to consist of a process of decoding, which, to be complete, requires the reader to attribute both meaning and value to what is being read.

These intimately interwoven concepts are usefully kept distinct for analytical purposes. For instance, people may share the 'meanings' of an object (the term is generic and may include persons, characters in novels, etc.) while they may differ markedly in their valuation of the object. These differences may in turn lead to differences in their respective readiness to accept or reject the object.

Generally, the meanings attributed to an object tend to be culturally patterned; generally, also, such meanings are taken for granted. That is, groups within the orbit of a given culture come to share such meanings, more or less unwittingly unless the meanings of the object involved are being publicly challenged (as in 'consciousness raising'). This process probably applied to the attribution of value in small homogeneous, pre-literate groups living in relative isolation from other groups. However, in contemporary societies: complex, heterogenous, competitive, 'open' and living in close rapport with other societies, the processes of valuation within a given culture tend not to be so unequivocal. For instance, children may agree that a given person is a 'teacher', but in Britain and other, comparable societies, they may differ as to whether that person is a 'good' or a 'bad' teacher. (In many totalitarian societies, children may not even dare to conceive of such qualitative differences.)

This raises the question of how differences in valuation may arise. An extensive body of literature on the subject seems to suggest that they are based primarily on self-referential materials: for instance on the basis of a perceived common quality, a resemblance, physical or otherwise including preferred forms of conduct and self presentation, or indeed whether the person involved would himself like to be that person or 'object'. Or again, does the object offer some kind service? Does it make one smile or laugh or feel happy? Does it offer protection or some reward? Such, it appears, are the circumstances leading to positive valuation, while their diametric opposites may be conceived of as leading to negative ones (Carsch, 1965).

To apply this model to reading, perhaps we should examine the relevant process in relation to the traditional melodrama, particularly useful because of its simplicity of structure. Essentially this consists of a dramatised conflict between 'good' and 'evil', traditionally exemplified by 'heroes' and 'villains'. Conventionally, the 'hero' is endowed with a wide range of qualities which are culturally perceived as 'good'. By contrast, the 'villain' is characterised by qualities which are culturally defined as 'evil'. In short, the hero exemplifies the culturally patterned system of values while the villain exemplifies the countervailing system or the negation of these values.

The hero's conduct benefits society while the villain's threatens its survival. Traditionally, the hero is conspicuously and generously rewarded, while, as the drama come to a close, the villain tends to be subjected to comparably heavy penalties.

This formula appears to be universal to human society (Murdock, 1945). It seems to have made its initial appearance in the oral idiom (folk and fairy tales) in remotest antiquity, was quickly adapted to print and now finds its most frequent expression on the screen (Riesman et al, 1950).

The reason for the success of this 'melodrama' stems, in part, from its flexibility, rendering it amenable to a wide range of contexts and perhaps an infinite variety of thematic variation and elaboration on virtually all levels of relative sophistication. Perhaps equally important to its success are the patterns of response it elicits: the 'hero's' struggles, although the outcome is certain, are followed with anxious attention and his ultimate victory is greeted with much enthusiasm. This not only because, conventionally, he is presented as an attractive individual, but precisely because the values he dramatises are those which are individually and collectively held dear and which are, to put it in more technical terminology, subjectively ego-involved. Conversely, the 'villain', in his negation of these values, promotes discomfort and mobilises high hopes for the hero's ultimate victory. Moreover, since the 'hero' is rewarded for the values he dramatises, it is the values of the entire society which are thus rewarded which conduces to the greater satisfaction of all involved. The resultant sense of well-being and strength affects both individuals and the group, and can, at times, spill over into anti-social conduct (Durkheim, 1954).

Under the circumstances, it may not be surprising that this formula is frequently employed with the purpose of retaining culturally-patterned values at their requisite strength of intensity, or, conversely, for the purpose of change. It may also be employed by individuals or groups within a society to flatter and to gain support. Ultimately, the focus in the discussion is the 'relationship' between the reader and the persons or objects about whom or which the reading materials revolve. Technically, the processes in question involve the identification of the reader with the hero or (surrogate) object. This process may lead to an actual introjection, in the course of which significant aspects of the hero are incorporated into the reader's self perception – to the point at which the reader may actually perceive himself as the hero. Conversely, the reader may conceive of the 'villain' as his 'not me' and onload onto the 'villain' descredited qualities which he does not possess or wishes he did not possess (projection). In both instances, it is the reader's imagination which is stimulated and which can be said to have been enriched by the experience, depending, of course on the quality of materials read. These processes, not the less complex for their wide distribution, constitute an essential and initial part of what is meant by re-creation.

It may be possible to explore these processes from the perspective of an artist accustomed to creating pictures, sculpture, music, dance, mime or drama. In this way reading is viewed as an art. Of course this does not deny the validity of employing scientific methods and measures. However, taking the stance of the artist requires us to explore perspectives in the various definitions of reading from those who have studied the process as psychologists, psycholinguists or sociolinguists, teachers, teacher-educators, librarians . . . Some of the pertinent questions involve:

1 *Perspective* – how does the artist's location influence his view?
2 *Selectivity* – what does the artist see and what does he fail to see?
3 *Reference* – to whom does the artist address himself and his work?

The conference theme attempted to broaden horizons and to provide a context within which delegates could explore their personal perceptions of reading and their feelings on being engaged in reading – not merely of graphic signs but also of a range of symbols such as pictures, art, dance, drama and music.

Personal engagement in these activities would, it was hoped, render explicit their connection with the basis of the reading process. In addition it would illuminate the relationship of reading to the writing process (and where it differs) and to speech and how these modes of message-making and receiving differ. The agility of the artist in moving from one perspective and stance to another, to stand back and to come closer to look more keenly thus comes into play. The facility of the actor also has to be employed; actors reveal some of their expertise in terms of how much they appreciate the character they are representing. That also can be considered as a matter of how clearly they can see the picture emerging as they 'read the person' not only the printed word.

Historical and current issues

The need to explore reading from this broader perspective can be traced to the third part of the helpful tripartite definition in the *Bullock Report* (DES 1975). Reading is defined as:

(i)   a response to graphic symbols in terms of the words they represent

(ii) (i) plus a response to text in terms of the meanings that the author intended to set down

(iii) (i)plus (ii) plus a response to the author's meanings in terms of all relevant previous experience and present judgement of the reader.

There has been substantial research on the reading process (see Downing and Leong, 1982; Chapman, 1987; Clark, 1987) much of which deliberates on the features noted in parts (i) and (ii) of the above definition. It is as if the process had become an entity and exploring what reading is may have obscured the fact that the third part, which concerns what reading **does**, is essentially and dynamically related. The spurious argument about 'top-down' or 'bottom-up' directions of the process must be seen in this connection and referred, from the point of view of its contributors, to the relationship between reading, thinking and knowing. These are ultimately involved in what becomes and includes the kind of reading development required, for example, in literary criticism.

In this context it may be useful to refer to Mathieson's (1985) discussion with respect to Steiner's tribute to Leavis (1967) in which Leavis is reported as having considered the demands of practical criticism as involving,

> the whole, the complete reader. . . . the ideal critic is the ideal reader. He realises to the full the experiences given in the words of the poet or the novelist. He aims at complete responsiveness, at a kind of poised vulnerability of consciousness in the encounter with text. He proceeds with attention which is close and stringent, yet also provisional and at all times susceptible to re-evaluation. Judgement arises from response: it does not initiate it.

Later in the discussion, Steiner comments on 'literacy of feeling' as 'a precondition to sane judgement in human affairs'.

The link here with the work of the specialist English teacher is pertinent to the current educational policy discussions in England

and Wales in the context of the shift from teaching *A Language for Life* (*Bullock* – DES 1975) to teaching *English* (*Curriculum Matters 1: English from 5–16* – *DES, 1984*) and the teaching of *English Language* (*The Kingman Report* – DES, 1988).

It might be suggested, however, that UKRA's interest in reading, language, communication and learning are at the same time both wider than some of its sister associations' foci of attention (eg National Association of Teachers of English (NATE); National Association for Remedial Education (NARE); or Scottish Learning Difficulties Association (SLDA)) and narrower (in the emphasis on 'reading'). Yet the Association's multidisciplinary, non-political and international perspectives, together with the nature and range of its interests, requires that its case is articulated from a stance as broad as that of the *Bullock Report*.

However, in accepting the challenge of going further down the 'Broader Bullock Road', there is the knowledge that the path involves the crossing of the 'Curricular Division Mountains' to take, en route, the 'Kingman Channel' to metalinguistic clarity and the calm 'Plains of Clearer Communication' of the case. The view from the peaks of the mountains can constitute an experience of a kind that is fast-moving in motivation and awe-inspiring in its capacity to re-create the energy to share their beauty. Their truth, seen from the top continues to illustrate the kind of 'dynamic knowing' that is the stuff of both living and learning in the holistic sense. For members to be able to articulate this, there will need to be pauses on the journey to observe and reflect on the ways in which the road, channel and peaks relate to each other. To 'read' the signs and symbols, situations and relationships they will need an awareness of how their understanding of learning and of reading is affected by their own re-creation of images from encoded messages.

References

Carsch, H.H. (1965) *Dimensions of Meaning and Values in a Sample of Fairy Tales* Doctoral Dissertation, Princeton University.

Chapman, L.J. (1987) *Reading from 5–11 years* Open University Press.

Clark, M.M. (1987) *New Directions in the Study of Reading* Falmer Press.

DES (1975) *A Language for Life* (The Bullock Report) HMSO.

DES (1988) *Report of the Committee of Inquiry into the Teaching of English Language* (The Kingman Report) HMSO.

[also Kingman: Videotape of Guest Lecture available from: University of Leicester Audio-Visual Services Dept].

Dilthey, W. (1923) 'Gesammelte Schriften' Vol. 5. V.B.G. Tenbner Leipzig.

Downing, J. and Leong, C.K. (1982) *The Psychology of Reading* Macmillan.

Durkheim, E. (1954) *The Elementary Forms of Religious Life* Glencoe The Free Press

Inglis, F. (1975) *Ideology and the Imagination* Cambridge University Press.

Mathieson, M. (1985) *Teaching Practical Criticism: An Introduction* (pp. 11) Croom Helm.

Murdock, G.P. (1945) 'The Common Denomination of Cultures' in Linton, R. (ed) *The Science of Man in the World Crisis* (pp. 123–125) New York Columbia University Press.

Riesman, D., et al. (1950) *The Lonely Crowd* (pp. 84) New Haven Yale University Press.

Trevelyan, G. (1942) English Social History D VIII

2 The inward eye: a personal investigation of mental imagery

Helen McLullich and Sue Palmer

When you read a passage, do you 're-create' pictures in your mind's eye of the people, events and ideas which it describes, or do you rely on the impact of the words alone?

An incident at the UKRA Conference four years ago led us to an informal investigation of our own processing strategies. Our findings suggest that there are considerable differences in the ways individuals respond to texts (and other stimuli) in terms of mental imagery. The following extracts from our correspondence on this subject provide information on two very different ways of thinking and 'seeing'

The correspondence

Letter 1

Dear Helen McLullich,

I hope you won't mind my writing to you out of the blue like this. It's about a point you raised during the lecture you gave at the United Kingdom Reading Association Conference last week – the part about imagery.

At one point, if you remember, you asked the audience to read a passage about fire engines racing to a fire. Then you asked us to raise our hands to show how we had responded to that passage in our heads – had we 'seen' the events described as we were reading? Had we 'heard' them? Had we 'smelt' them? I was sitting in the back row of the lecture hall, and was astounded to see the forest of hands that went up in response to each of these questions. My own hands didn't twitch at all until you asked the final question: *'Did we respond to the words?'*

That's what I want to ask about. Do you know whether the majority of people are able to do this *'seeing in their heads'* trick? I've never seen anything in my head in my life: all I ever have to respond to is words . . . You see, it seems a very important question if one is teaching young children. You tend to assume that your own brain works in much the same way as anybody else's, and that affects the way you teach. I'd be very grateful, therefore, if you could let me know more about the subject. Are there any good books about it? Has there been any research? Have you any idea of the proportions of *'visualisers'* and *'non-visualisers'* in the population . . .?

Sue Palmer

Letter 2

Dear Sue,

Many thanks for your letter and may I hasten to assure you that I'm delighted you wrote to me.

I remember seeing you at my talk at Reading University – I have complete visual recall of the occasion and can summon up an image of you sitting at the back of the lecture room. I distinctly remember my utter astonishment when I noticed you were among the minority who processed information entirely linguistically.

Recalling pictorially, and in colour, seems such a simple device – one which, for many years, I wrongly assumed to be a universal endowment – so it's really quite difficult for people like me (visualisers) to understand how people like you (non-visualisers) recall without the use of imagery. In fact, I appear to have as many questions to ask you as you've put to me, and for a start, I'd like to know how on earth you recognise people you meet after a lapse of time if there's no stored image to call up? And how do you set about finding mislaid car keys? I'd simply run an *'internal film sequence'* sparked off by internal monologue, eg *'When did I last use the car and what was I wearing?'* (Missing keys invariably turn up in a pocket!) Visual would immediately take over from verbal and visual imagery would be interspersed with auditory imagery (words) whenever analysis/logic was called for . . .

I realise that I use visual imagery very frequently and for many purposes:

1 *To recall – all sorts of things (images absorbed as well as consciously studied)*
2 *To enrich what I'm reading*
3 *When being given instructions/directions*
4 *To spot mis-spellings when words don't match my stored image*
5 *To recall or interpret music*
6 *To anticipate a problem*

Pressure of work has prevented my pursuing the imagery

phenomenon as widely as I'd have liked, but I've studied hundreds of children in the five to seven age-range whose education was my responsibility and I've discovered that non-visualisers seem to have the following in common:

1 *No response to a Look/Say method of teaching reading*
2 *Spelling not caught – had to be taught*
3 *Opting out of listening – even a story*
4 *Persisting problems with left/right*
5 *Inability to sing in tune or remember a simple tune*
6 *Difficulty with look-alike letters*
7 *Difficulty in naming colours*
8 *Difficulty in distinguishing between 41/14, 96/69, etc*
9 *Depending on home background, deceptively good command of the English language*

By present-day standards I estimate that 25 per cent of five-year-olds starting school have poor or no visualisation skill. I emphasise *'present-day'* because I think that the influence of television may have been underestimated. Television denies the use of visual imagery. It also stirs emotions by the skilful use of music and sound effects. It's not altogether surprising, therefore, that for some children (and possibly adults) an unillustrated page of print has something missing – the image and emotional input.

My professional experience of the adult population, although mainly with teachers, is also with adults who have failed to learn to read. With regard to the latter, almost without exception, these unfortunate souls were astonished by my claim that people could *'see in their head'*.

Some years ago I tried to find published research findings on the subject of imagery but references were mostly sporadic and it was invariably suggested that mental processes were too difficult to objectify. I've recently discovered, however, that some interesting work has been done in the Institute of Technology, California, and this seems a likely avenue to follow.

Helen

Letter 3

Dear Helen,

Thank you so much for your long letter, which was *fascinating*. Does your mind really work so differently from mine? I mean, can you really *'see'* me sitting in that lecture theatre? Can you remember what I look like, and what I was wearing and which hand I put up when I responded to your question? It seems impossible to me.

I can remember *facts* about the occasion, facts which for one reason or another I committed to memory at the time. The committing to memory was done in words, but I think it's stored in my brain in some other form – 'meaning' or 'thought' or something. When I want to re-summon the memory it turns into words again. There's a wonderful quote from Vygotsky's *Thought and Language* which sums up what I mean: *'A thought is a cloud, shedding a shower of words.'* Does that make sense to you?

You ask how a non-visualiser like me recognises people. The answer is, I'm afraid, that quite frequently I don't recognise people. I'm ashamed to admit, for instance, that I have no idea now what YOU look like. We could pass each other on the street tomorrow and I wouldn't remember you at all – or I might vaguely recognise your face but have no way of working out why I knew it. As to finding mislaid car keys, quite often I don't manage that either. Like you, I adopt the internal (or, in my case, muttered external) monologue system – *'When did I last use the car?'* – but there's no *'internal film sequence'* to go with it. If I can manage to remember enough to retrace my steps physically, there's a chance of finding the keys. But my general strategy with lost items is Wait Until It Turns Up. It's usually quicker.

I'm doing a little private teaching at the moment and one of my pupils is Steve, a young man of 28 who failed miserably at school, but has since taught himself to read and is coming to me to learn spelling. He's a very good pupil, learning extremely quickly, and I wondered, after reading your letter, how much of his failure at school may have been due to his being a non-visualiser. We had a long chat about it, and it seems he is as sadly lacking as I am. We discovered that, when he knocks on the door to come for a lesson, he has no mental image whatsoever of me; I, meanwhile, am on my way to answer the door with no mental image of him. When the door is open, we both have a momentary feeling of *'Ah yes, THAT'S what he/she looks like!'*

Your description of non-visualisers in the five to seven age-range is fascinating. Aren't *all* children dreadful at left/right? (I still am, incidentally. Absolutely dreadful. And I can't remember tunes either!) And does it mean that you would recommend different teaching methods for different children, depending on the extent of their visual imagery? In the light of it, I'm surprised I became literate: there were so many hurdles to overcome. Actually, I reckon I learned everything of importance about reading and writing from my mother. She is a brilliant intuitive teacher, as I now see when she's playing with my baby daughter, Beth. She lets Beth set the pace, but she's alert all the time for the sort of information she needs to go further. Mum had taught me the basics of literacy before I started school. (Without this, I could easily have ended up in the same boat as my pupil, Steve.) She also taught me to draw when I was tiny – to copy simple line drawings, cartoons of animals and so on. When I wasn't reading, I drew. But what about my spelling, Helen? One of my proudest boasts is that I'm an ace speller! I *love* spelling, and I really am good at it! From what you say, we non-visualisers shouldn't be able to spell very well . . .

Sue

Letter 4

Dear Sue,

Thank you indeed for your most interesting and informative letter. I have to confess to somewhat juvenile anticipation when I spotted your handwriting on the envelope, for suddenly having access to the mental processes of an adult non-visualiser is an exciting prospect.

You ask how a visualiser operates. Well, for me all thought seems to be based on visual and/or auditory imagery. I see and hear things in my head – usually simultaneously and, I'm afraid, continuously. Watching TV or live performances, where images are imposed, must be the only occasions on which I'm free of it. But, on reflection, even then association of ideas may spark off visual images so that I '*observe*' two completely different scenes at the same time and I'm pretty sure that when that happens, the imagined is actually stronger than the real. Yes, I'm pretty sure this is the case because I've been aware of having to jerk myself out of the imagined and back to reality. To a non-visualiser this must seem an incredible state of affairs . . .

And now spelling. At first glance it appears that my listing of identifiable traits of non-visualisers is not quite accurate, for your spelling is impeccable. (I rather expect mine to be also!) You say that the young man you are presently tutoring in spelling is a non-visualiser also. How fortunate for him that he found you! You are, of course, exceptional so I looked for clues in the two letters you've written to me and found the following:

1　'*One of my proudest boasts is that I'm an ace speller!*'
2　'*I remember facts.*'

3 *'Words (and meaning) are everything to me and along with them some sort of verbal reasoning.'*
4 *'I've always read voraciously.'*
5 *'I like playing word games – cryptic crossword puzzles.'*
6 *'I reckon I learned everything of importance about reading and writing from my mother.'*
7 *'My mother taught me to draw. . .'*

You've said it all.
Pride – a great motivator. Isn't that what motivates your young male student to seek spelling tuition?
Exposure to words – you read voraciously.
Facts/verbal reasoning – you've worked out that there is a sequential probability of letters in the English language.
Word games – they really force you to look carefully at words.
Parental involvement – a proven advantage.
Those drawing sessions – you learned to look at detail, so letter discrimination presented no problem. You also acquired good hand control (before you were required to think about spelling!) essential to fluent spelling . . .

Helen

Concluding comments

Our correspondence, which continued for many months, convinced us that different individuals think and remember in different ways. It seemed likely that visualisers were at an advantage in the early stages of literacy-learning, but that non-visualisers could be helped in two ways. They could be helped to develop their powers of imagery through, for example, the media of music and art; and/or they could be helped to develop and use learning techniques appropriate to their own methods of mental processing. With appropriate teaching there seems no reason why non-visualisers should not do well within the educational system, but appropriate teaching may not be forthcoming if teachers are unaware of the differences in the extent of individuals' powers of mental imagery.

Our informal researches among friends (mainly teachers) suggested to us that there is a continuum of visualisation skills, with Helen at one end and Sue at the other. There were problems in discussing what we meant by *'visualisation'*, as each individual tends to interpret terminology in terms of his/her own way of thinking.

Eventually we discovered the following rule-of-thumb test (Hunter, 1957).

Can you summon up an image of: *a glove, a house, a fire burning and a sunset?*

Perfectly clear and vivid as the actual experience	4
Very clear and comparable in vividness to the actual experience	3
Moderately clear and vivid	2
Not clear or vivid but recognisable	1
No image present at all	0

Most adults of our acquaintance seemed to be towards Helen's end of the continuum, with only a handful at the other end. Whether this would be reflected in the general population we cannot tell. We suspect that the incidence of non-visualisers among those who fail to learn to read and write might well be higher than average.

One disturbing finding so far had been the resistance felt by some teachers to the idea that other people may be able to visualise to a greater or lesser extent than themselves. One colleague refused to believe that anyone might be unable to summon up a mental picture of his/her own mother. As Sue bewailed in a later letter:

If it hadn't been for my mother I might well be unable to read and write – but I can't summon up a picture of her, no matter how hard I try!

References

Hunter, I.M.L. (1957) *Memory* Pelican. Reprinted 1968 and 1969.
Vygotsky L.S. (1932) *Thought and Language* MIT Press

3 Language and art: enhancing reading comprehension by re-routing words through creating visual images

Aileen Lowndes and Morag Hunter-Carsch

Art education is, we believe, an essential part of the education of the 'whole child'. Even an elementary education in art and the arts requires deliberation on the relationship between words and mental images, the revealing of our ideas. The image-making process in the course of reading constitutes one aspect of this larger process which is worthy of systematic exploration by educators. It is not just a matter of 'leaving it to the imagination to develop on its own', it can be developed with the assistance of informed and caring teaching. This chapter reports on work carried out in a multiethnic primary school in Leicester and offers an analysis of learning-teaching experiences there, with reference both to aspects of language learning and art education.

Reading comprehension as 'sharpening-up of images'

The word is the symbol; once a child can decode words, comprehension is a matter of understanding the referent. To discern what the child does understand, the teacher needs to be aware of what it is that the child thinks the word represents. Developing reading comprehension is then a matter of revealing, exploring and working together to gain a 'clearer picture'. Although the words 'represent', 'reveal' and 'picture' are often thought of in visual terms, they are not necessarily explored visually by teachers and children – in ways which actually heighten the visual imagery and flexibility of imagination of the individual child. There is, indeed, such a range of individual differences in experiencing images that it soon becomes evident that developing reading comprehension must take this diversity into account (see also McLullich and Palmer, Chapter 2. and Chasty, Chapter 30. regarding cognitive profiles and Mac

Martin, Chapter 19, for categories of reading comprehension difficulty).

Jaqueline Goodnow puts it differently, with reference specifically to drawing. She writes:

> *A large part of our learning consists of coming to know that one thing may 'stand for' another or be called 'the same as' another: photographs reflect people, words stand for objects . . . The learning that words and various squiggles on paper 'stand for' or 'correspond to' other objects or events is called the learning of equivalents. Within this broad area of equivalence learning we may talk about the perception of equivalents . . . We learn to know what certain words stand for; and we learn to read photographs, pictures and music.*

Using picture-making and picture-reading as a part of developing reading comprehension requires one to become involved with exploring this kind of knowledge of equivalence. It quickly brings to the fore the function of imagination in the development of knowledge. The idea of knowing is to be differentiated from the idea of knowledge in the sense that so often knowledge is considered to be 'fixed' or perceived as a 'body'. The body of knowledge is then treated much as if it were a 'dead body'. By contrast 'knowing' is more readily pictured as dynamic and continuing. The appreciation of the body of knowledge (seeing its potential) is then an integral part of the knowing. It is as if the creative element extended and gave life to the otherwise non-dynamic box of component parts ('the body').

This bringing together of the learning process and the product – through increasing awareness, by systematic study, of image-making – is 'natural' and 'automatic' for many good teachers. What is not always clear is the extent to which they are conscious of what they are doing and of how it can be built on and explicitly developed in and through art and language experience with children. For many teachers, it is an *'intuitively obvious point' that 'the way people represent conceptual categories is affected by what they know'.* (Roth and Frisby, 1986).

The following paragraphs explore this process of image-making as it was developed in a series of six lessons within a topic study on 'Space'. The summary chart on page 25 draws together different aspects of learning from the subject areas of art and language, with reference to cognitive and affective development.

Examples from a topic study on 'SPACE'

The topic of 'Space' was used to explore children's perceptions and their grasp of equivalence through the use of words as well as visuo-spatial representations. A series of 'lessons' in art were carried out with 22 seven- to nine-year-olds in a multiethnic city primary school over a period of about six weeks, on a roughly once-a-week basis. The lessons were formal only in the sense of including a pre-planned sequence of developmental steps. The lesson format was similar to many other lessons or activities in that it included group work, individual work and whole-class discussions.

Lesson 1: Holding on to an idea (attending and abstracting)

The children sat on the carpet in the reading area, around a mobile blackboard. They were asked to listen for the word the teacher would say and also to listen for the word they thought of as soon as they heard the teacher's word. The use of the word 'thought' was discussed and developed as synonyms were produced by the children. The ideas, 'reminded of', 'heard' and 'came into their minds' were explored. It was explained that they would need to hold on to their word and try not to forget it, and they were asked not to shout it out but to put up their hands until invited to say it.

The teacher wrote the word 'Space' and added the children's responses round it (Figure 3.1).

The initial reaction on the part of readers might be to wonder what this has to do with art. The language part is evident. There is no accident, however, in the fact that the starting point in this series of lessons is with the idea of Space. The teacher's first step in encouraging learning in the creative arts, as in other areas of the curriculum, involves catching and holding the child's attention. But, particularly in the creative arts, the emphasis must be on engaging their interest in such a way as to help them attend to their own

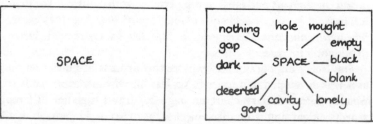

Figure 3.1

thoughts and feelings, not just what is happening outside of themselves or between themselves and others.

It is in this context that we might suggest there is a need to create a space 'inside' the child, before the child can do his own writing about the experience. It is preferable, therefore, if not prerequisite, to establish and maintain an atmosphere of calm and trust which permits concentration on the topic. Beginner teachers sometimes attempt first to 'establish attention' then to 'teach', instead of seeing attention as a part of the engaging of interest and thus, with the exception of the first moments spent settling into a comfortable and safe place (and space), an integral part of communicating with children about things of mutual interest and wanting to hear (and thus have suitable conditions for) their responses. More experienced teachers may take it for granted that they establish routines for settling down only as a means of leading immediately and directly to the real message which involves the invitation to work together on a topic of mutual interest.

In the lesson the assistance for the children to focus their attention on listening (more than hearing) was provided by the teacher's attention to the various alternative ways of expressing the ideas. The teacher was thus showing that she cared about what was expressed in words. This caring about the precise choice of words also affects discussions, once it is perceived as a matter of importance by the children. It is not necessary to be explicit about these issues of underlying attitude and respect for each other's expressions, whether in words or other forms. There is nothing sentimental about such a form of respect as it also alerts the participants in the discussion to any inappropriate contributions. In such an atmosphere the children as much as the teacher (or more so) control the tone and influence the pace and depth of the exchange.

Slowing down the pace at which words are experienced is another vital part of this work and indeed of all work involving attempts to assist children to 'catch on' to the form as well as the meaning of words. The chance to see the teacher write the words carefully (from left to right in clearly formed letters) is another step in this process. The involvement of the senses, perception, and cognitive (as well as affective) associations can thus be 'felt'. Watching (looking and seeing) and mentally tracing along the writing as the teacher writes, can be an avenue for practising (mentally) kinesthetic (motor/movement) memorising of how to write (spell) the word. If the words remain on the board for some time and the extended discussion returns to these familiar places (ie spaces the words take up), this all forms part of the learning that is so fleetingly carried out in 'real time'.

As the children generated the words in response to 'space', there soon erupted in some quarters a sense of frustration about ownership. One child exclaimed, *'You said my word!'* another muttered, *'Oh! I was going to say that'*. There was considerable difficulty in establishing their 'space' in the interaction. It took some discussion to accept that it was fair and reasonable that more than one person might think of the same word and that neither the word nor the individual's offering was thereby devalued. Clearly the exercise had to be extended to permit further exploration of the images which the children experienced in response to the word and to establish continuity, similarities and difference between the images.

Lesson 2: Reading and thinking about the words (decoding)

In the same situation around the board, the teacher and children discussed the word spellings and meanings. This also provided practice, especially for the slower readers, in reading the words aloud.

Lesson 3: Words, letters and shades (tones) of meaning (encoding)

A large display board was covered with silver paper – selected for its reflective qualities and the effect of space this created. The children, working in twos or threes, were given one of the space words (spoken to each group), large templates for making letters, and a choice of paper (black, grey or white).

Groups were quickly involved in discussing reasons for the choice of tones to represent the particular feeling they associated with the word. Other issues included how to spell the word, who should cut out which letter, which were 'hard' letters to cut, how to negotiate with the neighbouring group for the letters needed by both. The words were then stapled onto the silver board as they were completed and much spelling, reading and checking occurred spontaneously.

Lesson 4: Phrases and definitions (extending)

Sitting around the board, the children practised defining a word. As the first example they took the word 'happiness'. It had to be defined in personal terms. Returning to their tables they wrote their own definitions for the word 'SPACE'. A selection of the definitions was written in large print by the teacher and placed above the silver-covered display board.

Phrases included the following:

Space is a place with nobody there, a swimming pool with no-one in it, an apple when a worm has gone through it, a big empty place. (Keith, 7) (Figure 3.2)

Space is my plate when I have eaten my tea, the gap between us and God, when I'm away and there is nobody at my table, beyond our galaxy, an open window, in my glasses for me to see through. (Kathryn, 8)

Space is an empty jar, an empty playground without any people in it, a hole in my sock where my toe pokes through. (Sumiyah, 8)

Again discussion, enjoyment and reading accompanied and followed the work.

Lesson 5: Concept and contrast (differentiating)

A smaller display board between two large windows was covered in white paper, the paper again chosen deliberately to represent space. The children were asked which of the space words would be best to put on that board. Eventually it was agreed that 'blank, empty and nothing' were the most suitable and these were printed in very small letters on cards which were placed in front of the board and below it. The window sill area to the left of the board was deliberately filled with an array of books, plants and paintbrushes to demonstrate that it was not empty.

Lesson 6: Assimilating, communicating and translating

The word 'blank' was examined. Its meaning and use were explored. Phrases like, 'Don't look so blank!' and 'He had a blank cheque.' were discussed, along with 'blank cartridges' and 'blank expressions'. Trying to hold a blank expression was found to be difficult when everyone else laughed!

The children were then each given a sheet of paper, larger than A4 size. As it lay in front of them they were asked to look at it and think of any words that came into their minds. Not surprisingly, connections with the previous work on words were readily made and descriptive words for 'blankness' came freely. Up to this point the emphasis might appear to have been on 'English' (word study). At this stage, faced with the blank paper, the teacher explained that they were going to 'Take a line for a walk' over the surface of the empty paper. The idea progressed through a series of lessons linking work on line, space, shape, images and story creation/re-creation (Figure 3.3).

Independently of this series of lessons the class had been involved in much work on 'line' in their art sessions. They were confident in their experience of straight and curved line drawings and ranges of ways of 'scribbling'. There had also been extensive language work on 'English' independently of the linked language and art work described briefly above.

Discussion and analysis of teaching and learning

For the purposes of this chapter it is unnecessary to report further on the artwork which ensued except, perhaps to indicate that the children appeared to have moved naturally into a mode of relating to each other and to their own 'creations' on paper or in other media, whether in words or other representational forms. They were both appreciative and critical, constructive yet demanding while being tolerant of individual differences. They were not as readily tolerant of interruptions to their work and were more inclined to want to continue work on any one piece, than might have been expected initially. This would all appear to be part of the engagement with work from 'inside'. They had developed confidence and competence in exploring learning by being encouraged to experience their own feelings and reactions in such a way as to lead from the personal to the social, sharing through words.

This practice of 'translating' was not for specific, isolated exercises, but as a way of experiencing, 'knowing' and sharing. It valued their expression in whatever media and led easily to the will to go on further with the valued work which was shared. In this way, the experience generated its own programme of 'improving' and extending learning through both art and language. There was no difficulty about going on learning, nor was there a dependence on a series of isolated art experiences ranging over topics, materials and techniques. The development was integrated and systematic, with a firm framework of reference. Such developments have also been observed to take place amongst children using the Binns method of systematic drafting and redrafting (see Chapter 16) as a means of developing written language. Both depend to a large extent, for their success, on the child's developing appreciation of the concept of 'stance' as he experiences it and as it can be used to translate the messages the child wants to convey through art and language and to share what he

A PLACE WITH NOBODY THERE

A SWIMMING POOL WITH NO-ONE IN IT

KEITH SAYS SPACE IS

AN APPLE WHEN A WORM HAS GONE THROUGH IT

A BIG EMPTY PLACE

Figure 3.2

He flew as fast as he could, over the trees and roofs and through the clouds.......

Figure 3.3

understands through reading. Knowing where you are standing, and thus the perspective from which you view the experience, is helpful in achieving fluency of expression and for improving reading comprehension.

Although the following analysis chart (Figure 3.4) includes only a very small part of the topic study on 'SPACE' it is evident that the highly structured introduction to attending and perceiving as well as conceptualising, expressing and translating messages is valid not only for work in the subject areas closely related to the visual arts. From the teacher's point of view, knowing where you stand involves having an awareness of the pace at which your pupils can move, when they are learning, from a position which they feel is their own territory. It can take some time to establish confidence in exploring that territory, but once the 'sensory-motor-perceptual' process swings into action the pace, although varying from individual to individual, can be surprisingly fast. It is well worth letting learners enjoy words and meanings in this systematic way. It may lead into sharing images since they pay attention, with genuine interest, not only to the teacher's instructions and suggestions but to their own questionings and their friends' discourse. They read voluntarily to answer their own questions because they are allowed to make the decision to engage with learning and to continue the 'dialogue with themselves'. It is that dialogue which is essentially what goes on in 'reading comprehension'.

Within the extensive field of research on the relationship between reading and the written word (Chapman 1987) we are interested in the relative imbalance between recognition given to work from 'the arts' (particularly the visual arts) and work presented in the format of the scientific paper. The latter characteristically, and perhaps necessarily, employs stylised abstractions often so far removed from the classroom situation as to be barely recognisable to ordinary teachers. Among the researchers' statistically represented findings on techniques for propositional analysis or 'directed activities related to text' (DARTs, Lunzer & Gardener 1984) we rejoice in the clarity of Donaldson's 1978 suggestion (quoted by Chapman) that:

the very features of the written word which encourage awareness of language may also encourage awareness of one's own thinking and be relevant to the development of intellectual control with incalculable consequences for the development of the kinds of thinking which are characteristic of logic, mathematics and the sciences

ANALYSIS OF SIX LESSONS WITHIN A TOPIC STUDY OF 'SPACE' CARRIED OUT WITH 22 CHILDREN AGED 7–9 YEARS

LESSON	CURRICULAR DEVELOPMENT AREAS		CHILD DEVELOPMENT AREAS COGNITIVE AND AFFECTIVE
	ART	LANGUAGE	
1 Words for 'SPACE'	Becoming aware of (seeing) own thoughts (images) by looking inwards Stance: experiencer + self-observer	Listening and comprehending words and ideas (synonyms).	Attending and abstracting Appreciating and valuing self
2 Consolidating meanings for the word 'SPACE'	Examining the images Discerning patterns in them and between them Stance: observer of surface form of words	Reading and spelling words Graphological and phono-logical segmentation	Perceptual skill development. Decoding, sequencing Sharing with others
3 Making a wall-display of words for 'SPACE'	Selecting the media and expressing (giving form to) the images Designing, modelling, cutting Stance: observer of surface features	'Writing' given words by matching and constructing them from letter forms	Motor skill development Encoding (representing) Co-operating and controlling self and others and media
4 Defining 'SPACE' and making a display of phrases	Seeing more detail (background-foreground). Stance: participant/generater of messages (expressing)	Writing own phrases and definitions (prior to idea of simile and metaphor)	Extending understanding Enjoying own capacity to create
5 Labelling 'empty space' and 'filled space' (teacher's choice)	Finding another way of representing the message (2D–3D equivalence) Stance: participant + observer	Refining choice of words through paired discussion	Differentiating the concept (reasoning; developing the capacity to reject, to exclude) Negotiating with peers
6 Further word study of meaning of 'blank'	Exploring further dimensions of the images Stance: Participant + observer	Discussing and drama/mime	Assimilating, translating Part/whole relationship Communicating and relating to others

Figure 3.4

The reasons for our appreciation of Donaldson's statement are not only that it is in 'plain English' and hopeful in tone, but that it gives us a clue to thinking about priorities in the classroom, for how can children be guided to develop their appreciation of the features as well as the content of both the written and spoken word, if they are not first aware of and comfortable with their own knowledge that they *can* think and what, in fact, thinking, knowing and feeling are? We trust that, given the chance, the arts can assist children in this process and can put back the heart and 'warm' the will in teacher-researchers to share what they know and can learn from their everyday work with children reading, envisaging and giving form to their thinking.

References

Chapman, L.J. (1987) *Reading from 5–11 years* Open University Press.

Donaldson, M. (1978) 'Children's Minds' in Chapman, L.J.op cit. Fontana Collins.

Goodnow, J. (1977) *Children's Drawing* (Ch. 1. p. 25) Fontana Collins.

Hunter, C.M. (1982) 'Reading and Learning Difficulties, Relationships and Responsibilities' in Hendry, A. *Teaching Reading: The Key Issues* Heinemann Educational Books.

Lunzer, E. and Gardner, K. (1984) *Learning From the Written Word* Oliver & Boyd.

Roth, I. and Frisby, J.P. (1986) *Perception and Representation A Cognitive Approach* Open University Press.

Acknowledgements

UKRA Research Committee for a small grant to A. Lowndes to support classroom research; the Leicester local UKRA Teacher-INSET group with the University of Leicester School of Education; Mrs. T. Abbott and the staff and children of Linden Primary School; Mr. T. Mason and Mr. R. Illsley, Advisers, Leicestershire L.E.A.; Professor B. Allison and Leicester Polytechnic, also Mr. B. Michael, Jordanhill College.

4 'Images' and 'Prepositional thoughts': two poems

Images

You can try to pick up the silky shining water in your hands, but it finds a way out, almost uncatchable.
When you stir the water shrimps skitter to the safety of the burrows.

Emma Walton, aged 10

Prepositional thoughts

Within my head anguished thoughts are in a frenzy
to free themselves.
Inside my head sad thoughts of depression jump about.
Beneath my head blurred memories of happy times roam
like tigers.
Outside my head crying feelings are aroused to emotional
thoughts.
Above my head dejected thoughts lie, discontented and
grief striken.
Around my head happy thoughts bounce like bubbles.

Kevin Wiles, aged 10.

From: *Once upon a Celebration* by Children in Northamptonshire Schools, reproduced by kind permission of Northampton County Council, Education Department. 1988.
(ISBN 0 9507010 5 x)

5 Reflections on literacy and knowing

Che Kan Leong

Professor Che Kan Leong, joint author, with the late Professor John Downing, of The Psychology of Reading (1982) was invited to give a lecture in memory of UKRA's first President, John Downing.

In his introductory remarks Professor Leong thanked the UKRA, the University of Leicester and the University of Saskatchewan, acknowledged his appreciation of UKRA Conferences past and present and honoured those whom he called giants in the field of reading studies. He named amongst them Sir Fred Schonell, Professor Magdelene Vernon and Dr Joyce Morris.

His dedication of the lecture included a brief history of John Downing's contribution as a teacher, scholar, researcher and friend, active and respected director on the Board of the International Reading Association and founding editor of the Canadian Journal of Reading, Reading-Canada-Lecture.

Professor Leong commented particularly on two aspects of Downing's contribution to the psychology and pedagogy of reading: first, his research into comparative reading behaviour in different countries using different orthographies; second, his cognitive postulate in learning to read.

With reference to comparative reading research, Downing helped to rekindle the interest aroused by William Gray. Downing worked collaboratively with researchers in North America, Europe, the Soviet Union, Australia and elsewhere.

With reference to understanding what it is that children need to know to learn to read, Downing's work is in the tradition of Vygotsky (1934, 1962, 1978) and Luria (1979, 1981), Elkonin (1973) and Reid (1966). In their integrative works, Vygotsky and Luria have discussed the notions of the internalisation of higher psychological functions; the regulatory functions of speech in human cognition; the mediational role of language in thinking; and consciousness as affective and cognitive phenomena. These are among the core notions that Downing and others apply to the psychology and pedagogy of reading.

Downing's work also involved him in making two separate field trips to the interior of Papua New Guinea in 1982 and 1985 where, with his wife as research associate, he studied in situ some of the linguistic and cultural factors affecting literacy in schooled and unschooled PNG children.

Downing firmly believed that there is much that we in the 'developed countries' can give to the Third World from our wealth of knowledge on reading, just as there is much we can learn from the Third World.

It was in the spirit of International Sharing and to 're-create reading' that Professor Leong introduced what was a profoundly moving lecture, in a joyful celebratory memorial of John Downing, issued in to the words of John Milton in Samson Agonistes (1,1721):

> *Nothing is here for tears, nothing to wail*
> *Or knock the breast; no weakness, no contempt,*
> *Dispraise or blame; nothing but well and fair,*
> *And what may quiet us in a death so noble.*

Literacy and knowing

On literacy

To begin with, the key concepts of 'literacy' and 'cognition' need to be delimited, even if not exactly defined. Literacy as a static concept in terms of a number of years of schooling or the acquisition of the mere 'skills' of reading and writing, is now found to be inadequate. Literacy is much more dynamic and has different implications in different cultural contexts. It includes a whole range of cultural activities and is not necessarily constrained by reading and writing or even schooling (Olson, 1987). Furthermore, 'What matters is what people do with literacy, not what literacy does to people' (Olson, Torrance, & Hildyard, 1985, p. 14).

On cognition

If the preceding is a succinct statement of literacy, what about cognition? The philosopher Nelson Goodman (1984) in his book *Of Mind and Other Matters* has something very pertinent to say. Goodman explains:

> *Cognition includes learning, knowing, gaining insight and understanding by all available means. Developing sensory discrimination is as cognitive as inventing complex numerical concepts or proving theorems. Mastering a motor skill involves making subtle kinaesthetic distinctions and connections. Coming to understand a painting or a symphony in an unfamiliar style, to*

recognize the work of an artist or school, to see or to hear in new ways, is as cognitive an achievement as learning to read or write or add.

(Goodman, 1984, p 147)

Different modes of literacy and knowing

If cognition can be broadly equated with thinking in a cultural context, one can well ask whether thinking be in words or whether thinking can be without words. Goodman's notion of *knowing* can be illustrated with two examples of art. One is a Chinese painting portraying the Chinese poem *On Quietude* by Wang Wei (701–761) (see Figures 5.1 and 5.2). The brush painting conveys a great deal of the feeling of quietude. The poem [translated] is as follows:

> No one can be seen in the deserted mountain;
>   Only some random words are heard;
>   The evening sun strays into the deep forest
>   And frolics among the green mossy stones.

Figure 5.1   Chinese painting portraying the poem *On Quietude*.

Figure 5.2   The poem *On Quietude* in Chinese calligraphy.

The other is Henry Moore's *Two Forms* that I saw quite some time ago in the Museum of Modern Art. Even the Philistine in me could not escape appreciating the rhythm, the harmony and the beauty of the piece of sculpture. But the interplay of the artist's inner vision and thought escaped me until I read the works on visual thinking by Rudolf Arnheim (1969, 1974) and Sir Ernst Gombrich (1960). In particular, it was only when I saw Jean Baptiste Camille Corot's *Mother and Child on the Beach* in Philadelphia in 1986 that I realised more fully the subtlety and the complexity of Moore's carving. The larger form bending over the smaller form in Moore's figures embodies the same conceptual theme of the protective, loving mother bending over the small child in Corot's painting.

The suggestion here is that perceiving a work of art as gentle and compassionate is both emotive and cognitive. There are similarities and differences in *reading* pictures as in reading words. Pictures are semantically interpretable, but are syntactically amorphous. Pictures are not simply read holistically but also read over time, much as written words are. These characteristics are well explained by Kolers (1973, p. 38–39):

> *Pictures are freely open to many interpretations because they are rich in semantic information, but deficient in syntactic regularities; any part can be seen as 'modifying' any other. Sentences are more constrained by rules of syntax, and notations are even more constrained.*

The notion is that readers of pictures must develop an awareness that these words are not replicas of actual objects, but are representations.

Similarly, when I heard the Funeral March (Marche funèbre) from Chopin's Sonata No2, Op35 in B Flat Minor played by my daughter Daphne several years ago, and later by Murray Perahia, I understood much better the rhythm and the sombre mood of Ariel's ditty in Shakespeare's *Tempest*:

> *Full fathom five thy father lies;*
>   *Of his bones are coral made;*
> *Those are pearls that were his eyes:*
>   *Nothing of him that doth fade*
> *But doth suffer a sea-change*
> *Into something rich and strange.*
> *Sea-nymphs hourly ring his knell:*
> *Hark! now I hear them, – Ding-dong, bell.*

These comparisons are meant to underscore the much wider perspectives of literacy. It was within this broader scope that John Downing and I attempted to define reading as 'the interpretation of symbols' (Downing and Leong, 1982, p. 4) even though convention dictated that we should discuss reading in our treatise as interpreting print. My current definition would be:

> *Reading [literacy] is the interpretation, application, revision, and invention of symbol systems.*

The functions of literacy are thus: informing, re-forming and forming with different symbol systems.

Literate activities as discovery

This broader interpretation includes literacy in different modes (by ear and by eye) and different symbols or symbol systems (scripts, pictures, musical notations, mathematical notations and the like). For example, poems, plays are meant to be read orally, listened to, and enacted. Only thus will the gentle, gossamer-like quality of Portia's plea for mercy, which 'droppeth as the gentle rain from heaven' in Shakespeare's *The Merchant of Venice* be properly appreciated. So also in this 'performatory act' can we savour the sensuous quality of the passage in *Antony and Cleopatra*, describing Cleopatra gliding down the River Nile in a barge, and come to understand that 'age does not wither her, nor custom stale her infinite variety' in the subtle and variegated Cleopatra.

While reading and writing are cognitive activities and help us to advance further in our quest for knowledge, art and music are just as complex cognitive activities. 'Reading' art and music involves both appreciation and understanding, just as reading print and reading other notations do. All these are aspects of *knowing*. This viewpoint is well put by Goodman (1984, p. 4):

> *In art – and I think in science too – emotion and cognition are interdependent: feeling without understanding is blind, and understanding without feeling is empty.*

Furthermore, 'cognition of any kind involves discovery.' (Goodman, 1984, p. 85). What counts are the novel and subtle ways in which the discoveries are achieved.

The computer metaphor

Expanded technologies in the 1980s have a large role to play in literate and cognitive development. The wide-ranging and insightful book *Media and Symbols* (Olson, 1974) bears testimony to the diverse ways in which print and nonprint media are used in literacy and knowledge acquisition and development. The contributors to that volume have critically examined the potential of prose, pictorial, electronic and other media, and also direct experience, for improving children's learning and for different purposes. In a sense, this evolution was anticipated by Sir Karl Popper (1972, pp. 238–239) when he commented on the development of knowledge from the use of 'papers, pens, pencils, typewriters, dictaphones, the printing press and libraries'. Were Popper writing in the 1980s he might have added the mainframe, mini- and microcomputers. So also might Elizabeth Eisenstein in including computer technology as an agent of change in her treatise *The Printing Press as Agent of Change* (Eisenstein, 1979).

At the practical level with computer technology, educators are gradually moving from the use of computer software for 'drill and practice' to problem-solving. An oft-quoted work is Papert's (1980) LOGO language to help children to learn subjects like geometry and physics in enjoyable and informative ways. Other notable works are the Bank Street College of Education program in composing and the promotion of cognitive development (Webb & Shavelson, 1985); and the knowledge-telling and knowledge-transforming models of written composition by Bereiter and Scardamalia (1987). With all these and other developments, I am more sanguine of the potential and viabilities of the computer for developing mental functioning and reorganising higher-order cognition skills (see Webb and Shavelson, 1985).

Indeed, educators should on the one hand accept the ubiquitous presence of computers and encourage their use. On the other hand we should also ask some fundamental questions in our euphoria in embracing computer technology. These questions include: What is the educational value of computers as an informing, forming and reforming medium as separate from their contents? What are some of the social and cognitive consequences of the microchip evolution for learners?

'Man-machine' duality

The evolutionary aspect brings us back to the modern-day origin and the philosophical conception of mind and computing machines. Charles Babbage, a mathematician at Cambridge University from 1828 to 1839 is usually credited with planning his *Analytical Engine*, a digital computer which he never completed. It was A.M. Turing (1950) who put forth the automata theory and delimited the behavior of the computer. The Universal Turing Machine was supposed to be capable of executing cognitive functions, if algorithms could be written to describe such functions. This line of reasoning provided the framework for *knowledge* through an internally constructed and stored representation of it. This framework was consonant with the thinking at the time that the on/off binary system of computers was analogous to the 'firing' or 'not firing' of the neurons in the nervous system. Thus automata theory seemed to be in accord with brain theory.

The more humanistically inclined psychologists/educators could well raise a number of philosophical questions on the man-machine duality (the 'sexist' term derives from a major international journal with the same name). These questions relate to consciousness (can machines think their own thoughts?); to fallibility (can machines make errors as humans do?); to continuity of thought versus discrete thought. Some of these arguments were anticipated early on. For example, Jefferson (1949) asked similar questions:

Not until a machine can write a sonnet or compose a concerto because of thoughts and emotions felt, and not by the chance fall of symbols, could we agree that machine equals brain – that is, not only write it but know that it had written it.

Turing (1950) pointed out that the extreme form of the answer could be that one had to be a machine to know its 'feelings'. More to the point, he offered this dialogue between his 'investigator and 'witness' as arguments that the computer could command a range of thoughts:

Interrogator: In the first line of your sonnet which reads 'Shall I compare thee to a summer's day', would not 'a spring day' do as well or better?
Witness: It wouldn't scan.
Interrogator: How about 'a winter's day'? That would scan all right.
Witness: Yes, but nobody wants to be compared to a winter's day.
(p. 446)

Turing went on to point out that machines, like humans, also make mistakes. He distinguished between 'errors of functioning' which have to do with calculations and 'errors of conclusion' which pertain to propositional inputs. Thus machines do not go wrong in terms of functioning; but they can go wrong in terms of false premises leading to false conclusions. An anecdote is the machine translation from English into Chinese: 'Out of sight, out of mind' which became 'Invisible idiot'. Another anecdote of computer translation from English to Russian is 'The spirit is willing but the flesh is weak' which was rendered as 'The vodka is strong, but the meat is rotten!'

That computers have *some* thoughts with *some* subject matters do not seem to be impossibilities. Some current advances in the area of text-to-speech synthesis can be cited. Basic research at the Haskins Laboratories and the MIT Research Laboratory of Electronics, among others, has provided significant theoretical and empirical findings in speech perception and production. The MIT research group's sustained effort in the last 20 years has led to the development of the MITalk system of text-to-speech conversion (see Allen, Hunnicut, and Klatt, 1987, for details). The Digital Corporation has also devised a sophisticated DECtalk text-to-speech conversion system. In general, these textual analyses involve the analysis of phonemic, morphemic, syllabic and syntactic elements of the discourse together with the related semantic and pragmatic information. The text-to-speech conversion requires the successful integration of all the analysed linguistic information, high-fidelity speech waveform and sophisticated computer technology. These technological advances seem to validate some of Turing's arguments that, in a large measure, machines can think their own thoughts and that they could be like humans. The converse, of course, is not true. We cannot be machines.

This is the plea for caution in the man-machine metaphor. Grossly simplifying, the argument goes as follows. Cognitive activities can be simulated by discrete happenings in automata. But cognitive systems can be *indeterminate* and may not be dominated by boundaries and initial conditions (algorithms). Indeed, Turing (1950) himself discussed discrete-state machines and continuous machines. His argument foreshadowed the current thinking of the *discrete* mode (governed by rules) and *dynamic* mode (governed by laws of behaviour) of cognition. Thus the Zeitgeist of literacy and cognition brings us back to their philosophical and biological roots.

Summary

In the educational enterprise we as educators should help the child to develop knowledge in symbol systems, in reflective abilities and other areas. In all these tasks we need to keep in mind exactly what it is that we help the child to develop (Siegler, 1978). Is it domain-specific knowledge? Is it the generality of knowledge structure? Were we to assemble here again in the year 2013 on the occasion of the fifieth anniversary of the UKRA, the topic of literacy and cognition would no doubt show a much richer amalgamation of related disciplines. Education would tell us how different philosophies, different educational systems and curricula could bring about cognitive behaviour; psychology, about knowledge acquisition and development; social anthropology, about the cultural contexts of literacy and knowing; and computational science, about artificial intelligence in natural language processing. We are now at the intersection of these areas and must march forward.

I would like to end by adding to Sir Francis Bacon's aphorism: 'Reading maketh a full man, conference a ready man, and writing an exact man'. The revised aphorism should read: 'Reading makes a full person, discourse a ready person, writing [composing] an exact person, art and music an emotive person, and computing a logical person'. You may well ask: Where is the full person? But that is another story.

References

Allen, J., Hunnicutt, M.S., & Klatt, D. (1987) *From text to speech: The MITalk system* New York: Cambridge University Press.

Arnheim, R. (1969) *Visual thinking* Berkeley, CA: University of California Press.

Arnheim, R. (1974) *Art and visual perception* Berkeley, CA: University of California Press.

Bereiter, C., & Scardamalia, M. (1987) *The psychology of written composition* Hillsdale, NJ: Erlbaum.

Downing, J. (Ed.). (1973) *Comparative reading: Cross-national studies of behaviour and processes in reading and writing* New York: Macmillan.

Downing, J., & Leong, C.K. (1982) *Psychology of reading* New York: Macmillan.

Downing, J., & Downing, M. (1983) 'Metacognitive readiness for literacy learning'. *Papua New Guinea Journal of Education*, 19, 17–40.

Eisenstein, E. (1979) *The printing press as an agent of change* Cambridge: Cambridge University Press.

Elkonin, D.B. (1973) 'USSR' In J. Downing (ed.), *Comparative reading* (pp. 551–579) New York: Macmillan.

Goodman, N. (1984) *Of mind and other matters* Cambridge, MA: Harvard University Press.

Gombrich, E.H. (1960) *Art and illusion* New York: Pantheon Books.

Jefferson, G. (1949) 'The mind of mechanical man: Lister Oration for 1949' *British Medical Journal*, 1, 1105–1121.

Kolers, P. (1973) 'Some modes of representation' In P. Pliner, L. Krames, & T. Alloway (eds), *Communication and affect: Language and thought* (pp. 21–44) New York: Academic Press.

Luria, A.R. (1979) *The making of mind: A personal account of Soviet psychology* (Eds.: M.Cole, & S. Cole) Cambridge, MA: MIT Press.

Luria, A.R. (1981) *Language and cognition* (J.V. Wertsch ed.) New York: John Wiley.

Morris, J.M. (1966) *Standards and progress in reading* Slough, UK: NFER.

Olson, D.R. (ed.) (1974) *Media and symbols: The forms of expression, communication, and education* Chicago: University of Chicago Press.

Olson, D.R. (ed.) (1987) 'Understanding literacy' [Special Issue] *Interchange*, 18 (No. 1/2), 1–173.

Olson, D.R., Torrance, N., & Hildyard, A. (1985) *Literacy, language and learning: The nature and consequences of reading and writing* New York: Cambridge University Press.

Papert, S. (1980) *Mindstorms: Children, computers, and powerful ideas* New York: Basic Books.

Popper, K. (1972) *Objective knowledge: An evolutionary approach* Oxford: Clarendon Press.

Reid, J.F. (1966) 'Learning to think about reading' *Educational Research*, 9, 56–62.

Schonell, F.J. (1942) *Backwardness in the basic subjects* Edinburgh: Oliver and Boyd.

Siegler, R.S. (1978) *Children's thinking: What develops?* Hillsdale, NJ: Erlbaum.

Turing, A.M. (1950) 'Computing machinery and intelligence' *Mind, LIX*, 433–460.

Vernon, M.D. (1957) *Backwardness in reading* London: Cambridge University Press.

Vygotsky, L.S. (1962) *Thought and language* (E. Hanfmann, & G. Vakar, eds & trans) Cambridge, MA: MIT Press. (Original work published 1934).

Vygotsky, L.S. (1978) *Mind in society: The development of higher psychological processes* (eds: M. Cole, V. John-Steiner, S. Scribner, & E. Souberman). Cambridge, MA: Harvard University Press.

Webb, N.M., & Shavelson, R.J. (eds). (1985) 'Computers and education' [Special Issue] *Educational Psychologist, 20* (4), 163–241.

PART 2

Policies and Practices

6 A comment on the guest lecture by Sir John Kingman

Keith Gardner

The *Report of the Committee of Enquiry into the Teaching of English Language* has been published, comment has appeared in the press and the journals, the first reactions have been recorded. There has been agreement that the Report possesses the twin virtues of conciseness and clarity whilst most commentators also believe that within its closely argued pages a good deal of sound advice may be found. What then is there to add?

One advantage of hearing Sir John give some of the background to the recommendations of the Committee was that the gap between the experience of members of the Committee and the assumptions of a reader faced only with cold print was, to some extent, narrowed. For, however carefully the Report has been prepared, some misinterpretations will arise.

In my own case I came to Sir John's Lecture in general agreement with much that the Report contained. It appeared to provide a starting point for a useful professional debate and pointers towards needed changes in both the curriculum and classroom practice. However, one aspect of the presentation gave me reasons to pause and think again.

Sir John pointed out how the terms of reference put forward by the Secretary of State had influenced the shape and form of the model of the English Language which was eventually agreed. Immediately, I recalled my experience on the Bullock Committee in the early 1970s. That Committee rejected the terms of reference set by the Secretary of State on the grounds that they were too restricting. It then worked out its own terms of reference which were designed to maximise discussion.

I do not for one moment suggest that the Kingman Committee should have done the same. But it is important to remember that the model of the English Language detailed in the Report is the outcome of thinking constrained by the need to meet the demands of attainment targets and assessment procedures.

One can only speculate about the direction the thinking of the

Committee might have taken if the terms of reference had either been less specific or the contentious issue of defining language as a body of knowledge made more open. What is certain, however, is that the note of reservation sounded by Professor Widdowson takes on an added significance. If the recommendations of the Committee are a response to a set of constraints imposed by the Secretary of State, then the need for a clear rationale, as suggested in the 'Note of reservation', becomes crystal clear if a purposeful debate is to take place. The end result might be an agreement with the main proposals of the Committee, but at least the suspicion that the Report is only another means of justifying the National Curriculum and formal assessment would be removed. At the moment the question concerns the adequacy of the rationale for what is regarded as essential in our education system.

However, for better or worse, the Committee has reported and 'the importance of knowledge about the Language' is now destined to become a central issue in future INSET programmes. I should be pleased, if only because I have tried to bring this about for a decade or more. But, in the event, I am very uneasy. The simple proposition that knowledge about the language and insights into how language works should be part of the English curriculum is perfectly acceptable. But what kind of knowledge? How will it be gained? To what extent should this one idea dominate the teaching programme? These are matters which must be debated even if it is too late to influence the assessment questions which are already being prepared and which will inevitably receive the emphasis in English teaching.

In the forthcoming debate it is to be hoped that some of the assumptions that underpin the Kingman Report will be questioned. For instance, any teacher of reading could testify to the fact that the transfer of knowledge about language into improved language performance is quite unpredictable. The most dramatic example of this is in the area of symbol-sound relationships where knowledgeable pupils sometimes fail and ignorant pupils sometimes succeed. There seems to be a great difference in effectiveness between implicit knowledge gained by language usage and knowledge made explicit by the teacher for pupil consumption. But this is not the whole story by any means. Then, there are studies about the process of understanding written and spoken language that stress the importance of attitude and purpose in comprehension. The phrase 'a readiness to reflect' comes readily to mind. There are countless classrooms where the need to reflect purposefully is a prerequisite for gaining knowl-

7 Reading re-vitalised: cognition, comprehension, culture and commonsense: developing a whole school language policy

Alexandra Dilks

This workshop report includes an excerpt from notes shared with participants in a morning of discussion at Meadow County Primary School, Leicester. After a tour of the school and viewing a videotape of the usual activity when the children are present, there was a delineation of changes in the approach to planning language work and the example of the 'Armada Project', which involved all the children aged 4 to 10 years. The school's involvement in school-focused INSET was described jointly by the LEA INSET Team representative, Bob Morley, and the Head Teacher, John Sutcliffe, and the workshop co-ordinating team of teachers. The notes have been deliberately left in note form, and offer an overview of the phases and stages which were experienced on the way to a clearer conceptualisation and sharing, throughout the school, of a sense of direction. The developments continue dynamically and links with the LEA Team and the University form an integral part of the dialectical development within the school. The INSET documents shared at the workshop are too extensive to be included here but may be requested from Bob Morley.

Outline of the approach

Structure of School:	Children on roll:	Headteacher
Group 6	320	(Appointed 1.8.86)
Reception Unit	*Infant Unit*	*Junior Unit*
2 Teachers	4 Teachers	6 Teachers
2 Nursery Nurses		

Phase 1: exploratory

The need: to formulate a policy to motivate and develop the strengths of the staff and promote whole-school cohesion.

Initial issues/questions
1 Where do we start?
2 What are our strengths?
3 What resources do we need to update?
4 How do we encourage working together and co-operation?
5 How do we actually learn to work together rather than independently?
6 What outside help can we draw on?
7 How will we know if we are really having an impact on the children's progress?
8 How do we inform parents and encourage home/school partnership?
9 How will we approach record keeping?

Phase 1: stages of approach

Starting points: Where we are now:
School holds a 'BOOK WEEK'

Stage 1: Curriculum review of language policy at fortnightly staff meeting Summer/Autumn Terms 1987:
• Aims and processes discussed
• Agendas circulated and relevant reading materials made available to staff
• Different aspects considered.

1 Reading (including video of story approach)
2 Reading for slower learners
3 Reading/language assessment
4 Writing – for different purposes
5 Handwriting
6 Spelling
7 Listening
8 Oracy
Language policy statement drawn up

Stage 2: New reading books, especially for infant aged pupils, identified as a priority area. Need for a cohesive whole-school policy (4 + to 10 +)

Stage 3: Staff visit outside agencies (schools and Literacy Support Centre) to view current reading materials. Books ordered.

Stage 4: Advisory teacher for school-focused INSET begins

working with nominated teacher in classroom on issues related to language development.

Stage 5: LEA supply team cover staff from 3 units to colour code and list new and existing books prior to implementation.

Stage 6: School uses INSET supply cover to release infant and junior staff for a morning to discuss reading issues on a departmental basis. This is linked with input of advice from advisory teacher on the observational possibilities that can be explored through 'paired' working in the classroom. (SF-INSET.)

Stage 7: Teachers transfer pupils to new reading books during January. Obsolete books removed. Letters explaining new reading programme sent to parents.

Stage 8: Two members of infant staff work with University Language Tutor and student teachers on language issues. IT-INSET – other staff released to observe.

Stage 9: Staff begin working together in pairs in classrooms on language issues of their own choice. Report back at staff meetings on SF and IT-INSET.

Stage 10: Staff meetings held to consider approaches to topic work during Spring term. Cross-curriculum policy adopted. Whole school theme for Summer term to be 400th centenary of 'Armada' – teachers select aspects of theme.

Phase 2: evaluation

What have we achieved?
Where do we go now?
What have been our successes?
What have been our difficulties?
How shall we approach curriculum review in Phase 2?

Model for curriculum review

The diagram on the next page is the LEA model for curriculum review (slightly adapted) as used by the school during 1987/88.

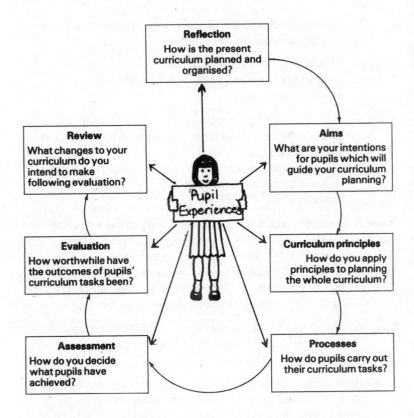

References

Leicestershire LEA (Draft 1987) *Handbook for Curriculum Review* p 83
Morley, B. Head Teacher, Merrydale County Primary School, Claydon Rd.
   Leicester
Sutcliffe, J. Head Teacher, Meadow County Primary School, Meadow
   Way, Wigston, Leicester.

Acknowledgements

Leicestershire Local Education Authority; University School of Education; Audio Visual Service; the children the staff of Meadow County Primary School particularly Janet Monday and Phillipa Norbury, Ruth Wallett (INSET Team) and Martin Cortazzi (University); Morag Hunter-Carsch for assistance in preparing the workshop and the report, and the UKRA for the encouragement to share the work.

8 A core of real books: a staff development programme for a 'real books' approach to reading

June Hall

This short report on an illustrated talk about 'Key Areas of Staff Development' includes an excerpt from the notes which were shared and discussed. The videotape illustrations aimed to share something of the atmosphere and kind of learning which took place in the schools working on the Core Books Project. These included Oakington Manor Primary School (where guidelines were drawn up) and Sudbury Infant and Junior and Barham J.M.I. Schools. The Core Working Party decided that they needed a framework within which to operate, to help them define aspects of reading and to monitor their provision of resources and reading experiences. Over a 16 month period, with the assistance of four Brent Learning Resources Service Staff, the four schools worked on the 14 key measures and areas of importance in relation to a 'real books approach to reading'. These are outlined below and may be of interest in sharing starting points with other teachers who are developing school policies. More detailed information is provided in the NFER National Teachers' Pack by Jill Bourne: Getting the Full Picture: Promoting Reading in Multilingual Brent Primary Schools (in press).

Key areas of development

The key areas of development identified by the Core Working Party were as follows:

1 Whole-school consensus
2 Designated key personnel
3 Specific criteria for selecting books
4 Whole-school book selection
5 Consultation with children, parents and teachers
6 Policy meeting with parents and governers
7 Weekly planning and evaluation for key staff
8 Regular meetings for all staff

9 Guidelines for classroom practice and evaluation

10 Recording and disseminating current practice

11 School-focused INSET

12 Development of language profile

13 Guidelines for new staff

14 Whole-school language policy

Guidelines for evaluating classroom provision

1 The book area

(It may be useful to include a map/diagram/photo of the class and book area)

These guidelines are intended to help staff and working groups evaluate provision in their classroom.

Is the area secluded/screened in some way?
Is it carpeted/comfortable/furnished?
Is it light and spacious?
Is there face-on display of books/adequate shelving/a convenient socket for tape-recorders?
Do you have a tape-recorder/book-making materials/ a typewriter/ computer printer/printing materials?
Are these readily available for children to use?
Do children have free access to the book area/free choice of reading material?
How are the materials arranged?
Is the book area used for other activities?

2 Book/story support

Do you have: a taperecorder/blank paper, story and multi-lingual tapes/headphones/slides/film strips/viewers/videos/puppets/dolls/ jigsaws/other visual language and learning equipment eg magnet boards?
Are these available for the teacher and children to use?

3 Book selection

What criteria do you use for selecting/keeping books in the classroom?
Is it an individual decision or based on a whole-school policy?
How are the children's views taken into account?
Who selected the books in your classroom? (Did you inherit the books? Were they chosen by someone else?)

What condition are the books in?
Does the book selection meet the needs of every child in the class?
Is there a good selection of hardbacks/paperbacks, fiction/non-fiction, poetry books, bilingual texts, books made by the children, story tapes, materials at different levels of complexity, etc?
What is the review procedure? Are the children involved?
How are they changed/rotated, and how regularly?

4 Time for reading

When do children read? What reading situations take place? (eg silent reading, shared/paired reading, class stories (read or told), talking about books, information-gathering, role-play, play-reading, story-telling and re-telling, book-making, sharing poetry, bilingual support for the above.)
Are thre visits to the school/local library?
Are children able to read when they choose?
What provision do you make for children experiencing difficulties with reading?

5 Reading across the curriculum

How are books, stories and other reading resources integrated with topic work?
How is reading related to current events?
How are the children helped to gain access to information for themselves?
How is topic work resourced?
Are there sufficient books (and books of sufficient quality) to resource the topic?
Are books made by the children and used as a resource?

6 Home/school liaison

What is the school policy on parental involvement with reading?
How is the home-school reading partnership introduced to parents? (Individually, by class or year, at a whole-school meeting?)
How is the scheme organised? (Book bags, home-reading books or cards, book stock, on a weekly basis?)
Do parents/teachers make comments regularly in each child's home-reading record book? If so, how often?
Are all parents involved? What is their response?
Are parents involved in the school? If so, how?

7 Monitoring and recording books

How do you record children's reading behaviour?
Is this related to school policy?
Is reading progress seen in relation to language and learning?
What is the recorded information based upon? (eg observation,
talking with the child and parents, informal assessments, tests,
miscues, . . .)
Is it accessible and meaningful to colleagues and parents?
Are examples of children's work included?
Are parents and children invited to contribute their perceptions?

8 Children's attitudes

What are the children's responses to books and reading?
How are these discovered? (eg observing, asking/listening)
Are children encouraged to bring in books from home or their
local library?

9 Published resources and promoting reading: libraries and literacy development

Keith Gaines, Bobbie Neate, Helen Pain-Lewins and Dina Thorpe

The following extracts are taken from several informative and detailed papers on reading as a recreational activity. Interested readers are invited to contact the contributors. The value of the librarian's work, especially in relation to the development of parent-teacher-librarian (and, of course pupil) exchanges is one of the messages which was repeatedly 'rediscovered' and reaffirmed throughout the conference. The fact that it started with a Publishers' Exhibition and the celebration not only of UKRA's 25th Conference, but the launch of a book, Dina Thorpe's Reading for Fun, characterises this spirit of recognition and respect for publishers and librarians as well as appreciation and enjoyment of books and the creativity of good writers.

Make time to read: reading and recreation with family reading groups

Dina Thorpe, writing on the above topic, notes the following answers to the question, 'Why do children read?'

Through reading we know that children have the possibility to re-create – to begin to make sense of the world around them by relating to it through assembling the facts and through reading fictional accounts of experiences which are not too dissimilar from their own. They read also to gain insights into ways of life and thoughts they may not yet have experienced but which they stand a better chance of recognising when they do, because they have read about them first. They read also to extend their imaginations and to escape.

She goes on to explore the ways in which Family Reading Groups appear to be an effective way of promoting reading and bringing about evident delight in just those benefits of reading. She sees libraries as being 'in the recreation business' and is enthusiastic about their potential for bringing real enjoyment and recreation through reading.

The nursery library project: reading as a recreation activity

Keith Gaines' project aimed to introduced home-based rather than school-based reading in ways that were designed to encourage nursery age children to acquire literacy skills. The use of audiotaped stories and book borrowing were explored and apart from measured results of the project, the children's delight in books was enthusiastically reported. Implications emerge for older children's library use and the increase in infant school libraries in the area speaks for itself.

Reading for pleasure and the school library

Helen Pain-Lewins challenged librarians and teacher-librarians to examine their priorities for the selection of books for school libraries. She expressed concern that if too much emphasis is put on the information role of the library there is a risk of relative neglect of the library's commitment 'to encourage reading and have concern for the enrichment of the individual's imaginative and creative life' (one of the aims set down in The Library Association's Guidelines). The inadequacy of some schools' libraries is evident or implied in some of the studies reported in her review of the literature. Other studies, however, include reference to a range of practical ways of promoting reading. These are helpfully described and useful references are included. It is encouraging to hear about the enactive links emanating from libraries, embracing poetry readings, mime and art exhibitions.

She concluded with a sobering thought and a warning:

> At a time when it is estimated that seven million of the United Kingdom's population are barely literate, and a large number of the young unemployed possess inadequate literacy skills, the need for the school and its library to develop and maintain reading skills is very urgent. It is hoped that when priorities are being determined for expenditure in education this will be remembered and resources will be forthcoming.

The diversity of registers found in primary children's information books

Bobbie Neate's concern is not so much for 'narrative texts', which she notes as the kind of texts on which children usually learn to read, but for 'information texts'. These, she pointed out, require very different reading strategies and ones which are seldom taught systematically. She concluded with a study of diversity in register of information texts suggesting that they may be 'regarded as the poor relation to narrative texts and it is perhaps time that the quality of texts from which we expect pupils to be able to learn is given as much attention as is given to narrative texts'.

10 Handwriting: the need for a whole-school policy

Peter Smith

A small group of teachers, writers and publishers met to discuss issues in the teaching of handwriting. Lively discussion ensued and ideas and perceptions were exchanged. Among the issues raised were: the need for a whole-school policy, handwriting instruction and developmental writing, the addition of ligatures (hooks) to lower-case print letters, when to join, which joined style to teach, standards and appropriateness of writing, individuality, handwriting and spelling, writing instruments and lined/unlined paper.

All members of the group contributed to the discussion with opinions freely expressed and practical ideas generously shared. Although total unanimity was rarely achieved, there was consensus on many aspects of handwriting and these are briefly reported below.

1 Whole-school policy

It was felt very strongly that there must be a policy, if possible from three to 13, so that teaching of letter forms and of cursive style is consistent. Within the agreed policy – which should be written down – there must always be room for individuals' preferences about precise teaching methods as well as flexibility within the school programme to meet the needs of individuals.

2 Handwriting instruction and developmental writing

The group applauded the move towards developmental writing and the use of invented spelling and felt that concern for 'perfect' handwriting should not be allowed to interfere with the fluency and purpose of meaningful writing. However, they were also concerned that children require the secretarial skill of handwriting and that, without help and guidance, children might develop bad habits that would impede their later progress. It was felt that teachers have to intervene sensitively to promote good practice eg by modelling correct formation when writing for an individual or group and by well-timed group lessons on formation. Such lessons are not boring for children but can be satisfying and even absorbing when such devices as *'Letter card'* are used to explain and illustrate. The correct process is far more important than uniform end products.

3 Addition of ligatures to lower-case print

The consensus of opinion was against this practice for the following reasons:

a) *in the early years exact correspondence between print in books and children's writing is helpful to the development of literacy.*
b) *many young children, when asked to add hooks to print letters over-exaggerate and therefore distort the letters.*
c) *a commonsense attitude would suggest that, since ligatures are for joining, there is no need to add hooks until the stage of joining is reached.*

4 When to join

The group agreed that, for most children, it is advisable to introduce and teach the joined style at about the age of seven or eight. It is important to start early enough in the junior/middle school to ensure a total commitment to joined writing before children move on to secondary school.

5 Appropriate style

While different styles are known to be supported, the most appropriate style is probably one which is largely cursive, which depends on simple rhythmical joins and does not require fundamental changes from lower-case print forms.

6 Standards and appropriateness

A school policy is not primarily designed to lead to aesthetic caligraphy by all. It should facilitate written communication by enabling all pupils to write quickly, legibly and pleasantly, in a variety of circumstances. At the same time, pride in well-presented work is also an aim of a good school policy so the chosen style should be one that is really pleasing when written carefully and more slowly ie when writing a piece to publish after drafting and editing.

7 Individuality

Individuality in handwriting is almost inevitable and the group decided that this individuality should be encouraged. However, it was felt necessary to stress that this development should not be fostered until the basis of a good, well-taught hand has been established. In other words, an individual style should grow out of well-learned, correct letter and join formation.

8 Handwriting and spelling

There is a strong link between orthographic patterns or letter-strings and consistent writing habits. It therefore seems that practice in good handwriting formation which also concentrates on words with common letter-strings must be advantageous.

9 Writing instruments

The need for flexibility and experiment was expressed. While many children at the beginning stage will happily write with special, thick pencils, others do better with normal, slim pencils. At all stages children are likely to write with coloured pencils, thin and thick crayons, felt pens, fibre-tipped pens, ball and roller points and Berol pens. They should be encouraged to experiment with the instruments to find the most satisfactory ones for them. Also, all children should experience the aesthetic pleasure gained from writing with a nibbed pen for presentation of published writing. This might be with a cartridge pen with a medium italic nib and should start by the time the children are in their third year at junior school.

10 Lined/unlined paper

This old chestnut was dragged out of the fire again. Once again the consensus was that, at the beginning stage, lines represent an additional hazard. Lines should be easily managed by most children of six and can be helpful at this stage. The point was also made that at the junior stage plain paper can facilitate aesthetic presentation, so plain paper and lined paper should both be available.

11 The National Writing Project: thoughts about the early years

Pam Czerniewska

The National writing Project (Sept '85 to Aug '89, England and Wales) aimed to encourage all writers – from beginning writers just starting school to more experienced writers entering the world of work – to become confident and competent. It is essentially a pedagogic project, involving thousands of teachers looking at their own practices, reflecting on the principles underlying such practices and developing more effective approaches.

Introduction

While there will be many differences between the practices, attitudes and expectations of teachers brought together by a project, it was quickly recognised that certain basic assumptions have unified Writing Project working groups. These assumptions about the child, the language and the learning task can be summarised as:

1 The child is actively involved in learning about the language system. Through a series of experiments, hypotheses and refinements children work out how adults use language.
2 Language is a complex set of social practices – having conversations, writing reports, reading instructions and so on – which cannot be reduced to a list of skills. Language work in school should arise within the context of use, with the child aware and in control of its purpose and audience.
3 Children learn language in interaction with others. They do not learn by working out bits of the language on their own but through participation in language events.

In the early years

With these assumptions in mind, nursery and infants' teachers began to look at the writing that young children were producing, both at home and at school, and at the contexts for writing that were being created within schools.

Perhaps the first observation has been that children already have extensive knowledge about writing some time before they come to school. Their early writing attempts may at first glance bear little meaning in adult terms, but closer inspection reveals a wealth of understanding.

Children's early scripts demonstrate their knowledge that, for example

- Marks on paper convey messages
- In English we write from left to right
- Different types of writing (eg lists, letter, forms) require different layouts
- A number of different symbols are combined in various ways to form texts.

Saiqa's text (Fig. 11.1) illustrates both her awareness of what texts look like and also her knowledge of how English and Urdu are written.

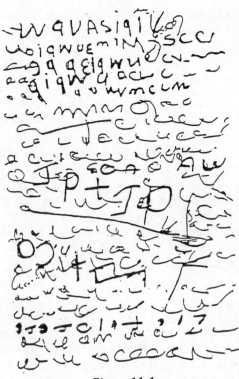

Figure 11.1

As their experience of language increases children will begin to experiment with writing. Through the mismatches between the adult and child's writing systems, we can observe the different yet clearly logical hypotheses children have generated about writing (Fig. 11.2)

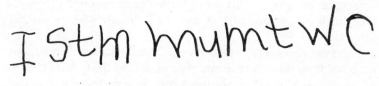

Figure 11.2

What is clear from the many examples collected is that children are highly committed to solving the problems posed by writing. These problems are not just about how the system works – its linguistic elements – but also how it is used and valued. Two examples neatly demonstrate this. The first (Fig. 11.3) comes from a nursery child who wrote from memory.

The strong, visual impact of the print around him is evident in Stuart's writing, so too is his recognition of the value placed by society on certain messages.

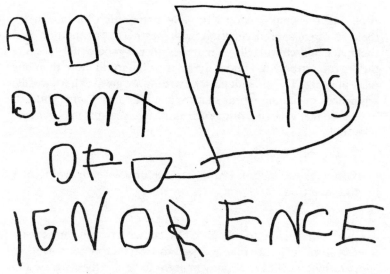

Figure 11.3

The second example comes from an ILEA classroom where the nursery teacher, Steve Cummins, put up some musical notation on the classroom walls as an experiment to see how the children would respond. Soon afterwards he received writing like that shown in Fig. 11.4, where the musical notes can be observed. Steve Cummins built on this interest by inviting a junior teacher to play the children's writing on her guitar. This led to further explorations by the children, such as a version of Jack and the Beanstalk with its musical script (Fig. 11.5).

These examples demonstrate how children construct their written language from their experiences of print around them. But children do more than this. They also construct how they should learn to write. For example, when young children are asked about writing – why they learn to write; what makes a good writer; what is easy/ difficult about writing – they demonstrate from a very young age how much they know about the learning process. Typically, children will give reasons for writing such as:

> *to get you ready for big school*
> *so you can write letters when you grow up*
> *because if you did not write there would be nothing to do in school all day*

Alongside this emphasis on writing as preparation for later work there is often a preoccupation with neatness, presentation and spelling. Children will tell you that they are not good writers because they're too scribbly, go under the lines or fail to fill more than one piece of paper. The difficult parts of writing are given as hard words, big pencils or finding words that rhyme. Of course, some children have a broader view of writing such as the five-year-old in Newcastle who said

> *Writing helps us learn. Learn to write for your own health, Mrs Adde and God.*

If we want children to become confident writers who can develop a sense of self as writer then we need to create the environments to support this aim. The environment needs to be able to recognise and value what the child already knows about language and her role in

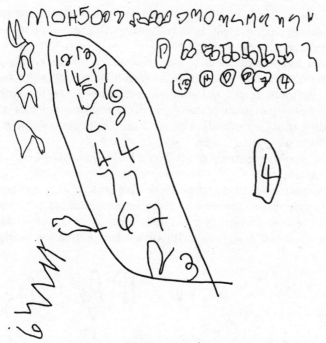

Figure 11.4

Figure 11.5

working out that knowledge. It also needs to recognise the forms and functions of writing, so that children can gain wide experience of the adult's language practices.

Such statements, as they were articulated by working groups around the country, resulted in a range of strategies which recognised the multiple uses and values of, and consequences for, writing. So, for example, many primary schools introduced, journals where children could try out ideas or jot down impressions without any emphasis on 'getting it right'.

Christopher's journal extract (Fig. 11.6) reflects his use of writing for thinking.

Alongside such personal and reflective writing were approaches which emphasised the need for purposes and audiences for writing: books written for younger children, instructions, school guides, letters . . . and much more. Important here is that the writing is

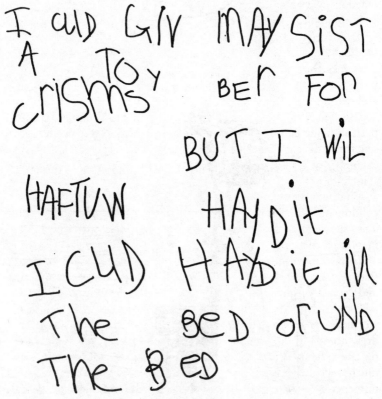

Figure 11.6

written for and read by specific audiences, and it is these readers who can judge its effectiveness. Even very young children can engage in such purposeful writing: a postbox in the nursery along with paper and envelopes can stimulate much letter writing, as can the cafe with its menus, order forms and bills or the office with its message pads, memos, forms and so on. Once children are given 'literacy events' (actual or in replica) they will usually respond with a wealth of writing.

The success of such classroom activities reinforced the belief that language learning was most effective when it had a recognisable context: letters were sent and replies received; stories were read and evaluated by their intended audience; school guides were actually clutched by the new entrants they were designed to help. But it was not simply that more ways had been developed for children to build up their repertoire of language uses. More than that, the approaches developed were ones in which the child's role in the construction of language was recognised.

The emphasis, to quote from Bruner (1986) was *'not only discovery and invention but the importance of negotiating and sharing'*. One example of this crucial point comes from some primary children in Lynne Clarré's class in Devon who were carrying out a project on mini-beasts. They were engaged in observing, discussing and reading about caterpillars and the like. One popular book, Eric Carle's *The Very Hungry Caterpillar* was read in detail and a comparison made between what the children observed and Carle's presentation of caterpillars. This then led to groups of children deciding to write to Eric Carle about certain mismatches (Fig. 11.7).

What is most significant in this example is the responsibility the children have taken for working out and questioning fact and fiction. They see themselves as part of the literacy culture, with a role to play in its construction.

Very young children, too, can demonstrate their ability to negotiate and share this culture. A powerful example comes from Fiona and Neil, two Shropshire five-year-olds who have become almost national celebrities through their dialogues about writing. They worked over a period of weeks on writing. Each child wrote and drew about a jointly-agreed topic, exchanged text and commented on the other's efforts. The following extracts demonstrate how much each child knows about the requirement of texts and the influence they can have on each other's development as critical readers and writers.

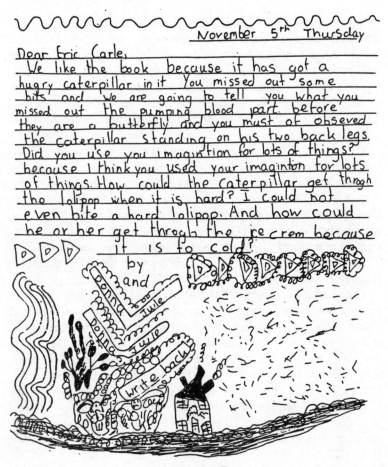

November 5th Thursday

Dear Eric Carle,
We like the book because it has got a
hugry caterpillar in it You missed out some
bits and we are going to tell you what you
missed out the pumping blood part. before
they are a butterfly and you must of obseved
the caterpillar standing on his two back legs.
Did you use you imaginstion for lots of things?
because I think you used your imaginton for lots
of things. How could the caterpillar get thrgh
the lolipop when it is hard? I could not
even bite a hard lolipop. And how could
he or her get throgh the ice crem because
it is to cold?
by
Donna and Julie

Figure 11.7

Week 1

Fiona wrote:	*I like black because I have a toy black dog and I have always wanted a real life black dog.*
Neil commented:	*She could have made it better if she'd put legs on the dog.*
Neil wrote:	*I like yellow wallpaper and I am going to ask my dad if I can have some.*
Fiona commented:	*He should have put 'wallpaper' at the end of the story.*

Week 2

Fiona wrote:	*Red makes my Mummy happy. She has a red Renault 5 car and there is a lot of room in the boot.*
Neil commented:	*She should have put spokes on the wheels and two lights front and back.*
Neil wrote:	*This is a red lorry and I like it.*
Fiona commented:	*He should have said where the lorry was going and why he likes it.*

Whereas Fiona was demonstrating considerable knowledge about what should happen in texts, Neil seemed to focus almost exclusively on the match between picture and reality. The teacher, a little discouraged, kept the activity going and by week 6 was rewarded by both the quality of the children's writing and the perceptions in their comments.

By week 6

Fiona wrote:	*The bear is trying to get some honey out of a tree. He looks very cuddly but really he is dangerous.*
Neil commented:	*Drawn a bigger tree. It is a good story.*
Neil wrote:	*My teddy bear is sitting by a tree thinking about doing something naughty.*
Fiona commented:	*Ears and paws on the bear. I would like to know what naughty thing this teddy was going to do.*

Two implications from all these examples are important to note here. The first is that with the focus on the actual uses of language, the literacy issue could not be seen as a strictly school one. The location of the problem shifted to involve home, local community and beyond. Teachers saw their responsibility within language learning as one that involved liaison with parents, local schools, senior citizens and much more. These contacts were not simply to tell people what was going on in school and to enlist their support, but also to involve them as co-writers, correspondents and informers. Parental involvement has been central and this has led to a whole range of initiatives, from home-school journals to community newspapers.

The second implication concerns assessment, a major issue as the government prepares attainment targets for a national curriculum.

Teachers in the National Writing Project have serious misgivings about the possibility (and desirability) of setting attainment targets for writing for specific ages. Whereas we know that children become more competent writers with experience, this does not imply that writing development can be marked off in a series of incremental stages . Our evidence suggests that language learning is recursive, children keep revisiting the same forms and functions of writing, each time building on their past achievements. The achievement of any one child at any particular time cannot be reduced to simple performance levels, it is far too complex and task-related for that. This is not to argue against careful monitoring of performance; teachers always have and always will monitor development and consider the types of opportunities that need to be provided to build on a child's strengths. Our argument is against a linear view of development which fails to take into account the crucial interaction of child, language and task.

From what has been said it will be clear that the teacher's role in the development of children's writing has changed considerably. The Manchester Writing Project categorised the teacher's roles as:

1 *Facilitator* – setting up a well-resourced environment which enables children to take responsibility, to experiment, to talk, to collaborate – in other words, to behave like writers;
2 *Model* – providing examples of writers' behaviour, from how to get ideas to how to evaluate the finished text;
3 *Adviser* – intervening at key points in a child's writing to support and further the process;
4 *Observer* – watching and monitoring development such that both teacher and child can have a sense of what has been achieved.

Above all, it is the teacher's role to respond to the knowledge that children bring to school and then to develop further their competence, pleasure and awareness of the nature and process of writing.

With acknowledgements to the many teachers, children and parents who have contributed to the development of NWP's thinking about writing in the early years.

References

Bruner, J. (1986) *Actual Minds, Possible Worlds* Harvard Educational Press.

12 Implications of the componential approach to learning to read

John R. Beech

The componential approach to reading considers the process of learning to read as involving the development of a complex collection of skills. If a child does not progress at the normal rate, this is considered to be due to a problem over the component or components which are necessary for the further normal development of that child. In his book (in press) The Acquisition and Performance of Cognitive Skills, John Beech reviews the approach at length and draws several conclusions which form the basis of an introducation to this chapter.

Introduction

The first aspect to note is that it would appear possible to select a set of children who are deficient in a particular skill, give them training in that skill and then find that their overall reading improves. By contrast, one might make a similar selection of children and give them the equivalent amount of attention in training on a skill unrelated to reading (Bradley and Bryant, 1983). Thus a 'spread of effect' has occurred whereby relatively minor training on a component skill has generalised to producing an overall improvement in reading. Training programmes potentially have a usefulness which goes beyond their area of training. However, there are possible areas of deficiency in children which are not causally related to reading and in which specific training will have little or no effect.

Another aspect of the componential approach which is noteworthy is the potential interaction with maturational development. One part of this is the idea of a 'sensitive period' in which a child is particularly open to training. If the specific training necessary to get the child over a hurdle occurs later in a maturing cognitive system, it may be more difficult, or at least take longer, for the training program to reach a satisfactory conclusion.

A third and final aspect of the componential approach to be considered in this introduction, and perhaps the aspect I am least happy with, is the assumption that there is a sequential element to skill development. The reason for caution here is that although there are several proponents of a stage approach to the development of reading (eg Marsh, Friedman, Welch and Desberg, 1981; Frith, 1985), there are cases of developmental dyslexia which have clearly not developed in a series of discrete stages. For instance, the case of R.E. (Campbell & Butterworth, 1985) is interesting in that she is an adult fluent reader who does not seem able to use a letter-to-sound route because of an inability to read non-words. This person learned to read without going through the sequence of stages proposed by Frith (1985). The resolution of this is to propose that there are several modules, or routes towards acquiring meaning from print, but within each module, development would be hindered by the absence of a component skill necessary to the development of that module. However, development of each of the modules can take place independently. I will now consider the various routes to reading and will then focus on the route involving translating letters to sounds as an example which has the previously described characteristics of the componential approach.

Modularity of skills

A module is an area of specialised activity which is relatively independent of other cognitive areas. It may need information from other areas and it will be impaired if there are heavy resource requirements in other regions. Modularity is a concept which is not without controversy. For instance, some theorists in the developing field of connectionism argue that there is little need for specialised processing areas, especially when the medium in which the activity is taking place (in other words, the neuronal circuits) has the same properties (eg Rumelhart and McClelland, 1986).

There are at least three ways in which meaning might be extracted from print. But, it is too early to draw boundaries around these routeways and call them modules. Nevertheless, I think the first of these, at least, letter-to-sound conversion, might well have modular characteristics. This route is often referred to as the grapheme-phoneme converter (or GPC) because, describing this back to front, the phoneme is represented either by a letter or a number of letters (eg **sh**). These letters, by definition, are known as graphemes. In order to have an adequately operating GPC the reader needs to develop several skills, such as a facility at handling phonemic information, which will be elaborated in the next major section. Another routeway is the lexical route.

The lexical route involves processing the letters and accessing the meaning of the word without the use of an intervening phonological code. This is a means to reading which seems to be relatively easy in the beginning and most children acquire at least a rudimentary sight vocabulary. An extreme example is Soderbergh's account (1971) of her three-year-old acquiring words very rapidly. At the moment I find that my own three-year-old daughter, Harriet, can acquire words relatively easily, and she could do so even at the age of two, but I am not testing this systematically. Frith (1985) calls this the logographic stage of development, which she sees as the beginning stage of learning to read. She proposes that the characteristics of this stage are that letter order is mainly ignored, that important features of the letters serve as cues to retrieval and that often, if the word is unknown, the child will refuse to name the word.

More analytically, a model which simulates this operation would store all the words within the visual lexicon. On presentation of the word, all the words in this lexicon are activated to varying degrees. The extent of this activation depends on the extent of the visual similarity between the presented word and the word in the lexicon. Paap, Newsome, McDonald & Schvaneldt (1982) describe how this mechanism might work for adult readers. Thus words visually similar to the presented word will be mistaken for ones in the lexicon. Seymour and Elder (1986) suggest a discrimination net process develops in order to distinguish words similar in appearance. As words are acquired in the lexicon, a basis for storage would be that they are distinguishable from others.

The third possible route involves reading by analogy. This is not a very well-defined route, but basically it involves processing the collection of letters constituting the word and searching the visual lexicon for orthographic patterns which give the greatest correspondence. This mode of processing is particularly prevalent in the case of presenting non-words to fluent readers, who will often produce pronunciations analogous to words they already know.

If one compares the efficiency of the three different strategies, defining efficiency in terms of the number of necessary units in operation, using the GPC is the most efficient as there are only about forty alternatives phonemes to choose for each grapheme (Beech, 1987). Next would come the analogical mode. In this case, storing orthographic chunks would involve operating with a much larger set of items. Finally, the least efficient method, in terms of involving and processing the greatest number of units simultaneously, would be the lexicon route. If one considers these contrasting strategies as

organised within modules, it is possible that more than one is simultaneously in operation. Normally the lexical route would obtain a
response for the adult reader, but the other routes may overtake if a
search for the appropriate response is exhausted. In the case of the
child, there is a very large disparity in the working units between the
lexical route and what is stored in the auditory lexicon. The likeli-
hood of encountering words not in the visual lexicon is much greater,
so the other systems or modules will play a more salient role, depending on their level of development. This is a contrasting view to one
which suggests that the reader progresses through fixed stages.

The Developing GPC

The development of the GPC or at least, that part of the GPC which
concerns development of the processing of phonemes is an aspect of
reading which has indirectly enjoyed a great deal of attention. The
link between phonemic processing and the GPC is that the reader, in
decoding words into their component sounds would be impaired in
the manipulation and retention of these sounds, for instance, while
blending them together to form a word. It is well-established that
poor readers tend to have problems in decoding words into their
component sounds and in such tasks as rhyming and alliteration.
Beech and Harding (1984) found the level of phonemic processing to
be significantly poorer in poor readers relative to normal readers of
the same age, whereas younger normal readers of the equivalent
reading age as the poor readers had developed to the same level of
phonemic processing as the older poor readers. It could be argued
that in order to develop a properly-functioning GPC, required for
the identification of words which are encountered which cannot be
initially decoded by the lexical route, the child needs to become
skilled in handling phonemic information. This level of phonemic
processing skill determines, or drives, the development of the GPC.
An adequately-operating GPC can assist the child in decoding text
which approaches the boundary of his decoding skill. This means in
turn that more words are being encountered and this can expand
and strengthen the information stored in the visual lexicon. This is a
long string of fanciful conditional statements. Furthermore, such
experimental evidence (as from the Beech and Harding study) is
insufficient to back this claim. A training, study, such as that carried
out by Bradley and Bryant (1983), provides much more convincing
evidence.

Bryant and Bradley selected a group of pre-readers who were behind in phonemic processing and divided them into four groups. Subsequent treatment of the groups varied, except that in each case their eventual reading performance was measured. One control group received no further treatment, another was given irrelevant semantic training and two other groups received training in phonemic processing calculated to eventually improve their reading. One of these phonemic training groups was also given plastic letters in order to teach the relationship between letters and sounds for those letters, while the other group was not. It was found that the plastic letter group significantly improved in reading relative to the semantic training group. But the group receiving phonemic training per se did not.

This finding strongly supports the concept of the development of the GPC being important for the subsequent development of reading. The componential approach would suggest that there is need to identify an impairment in a skill which may in the future hold up the subsequent development of a reading module. A spread of effect is also evident from this result. The plastic letters group were essentially being given training in the use of the GPC. Their subsequent reading performance was tested by means of a test involving the presentation of regular and irregular words. One interpretation of this is that an improvement of the GPC led to an increase in the units stored in the visual lexicon. In other words, there was a spread of effect of training from one module to another. Another view, perhaps not all that different from the first, in reality, is that an improved GPC enabled the child to assimilate more evidence when decoding an unfamiliar word. Once the child uses the GPC on a regular basis for decoding a word, even the irregular words might be decoded by an intervening mnemonic. For instance, when encountering 'quay', the child may assign a phonological code of 'kway' to this word. It may be common for such words to acquire a semantic context and an associated erroneous phonological code. The spoken version of the word may not be stored until much later. There may even be words in adulthood which have separate visual and verbal entries but no link between them has ever been forged. I chose the example of quay because in a recent experiment, (Beech, 1988), I found that when this word was presented in a mixed list of words and non-words undergraduates frequently produced the neologism 'kway'. It would seem that out of context this word still generates an erroneous code for many adults.

Practical implications

The componential approach does provide useful guidelines for the teaching of reading. However, it will be necessary to do a great deal of research in order to discover areas in which the approach might not be so successful. For instance, it seems that training in visual processing does not improve subsequent reading development, even though subsequent visual processing might be improved (eg Bieger, 1974). One might expect that, as the lexical route is generally the first one that children adopt in reading, difference in visual processing would have predicted subsequent performance in the acquisition of a visual lexicon. However, it is likely that such studies are not training the precise processes involved in the visual acquisition of reading vocabulary, such as the ability to make discriminations between visual features. Instead, they are training rather general visual skills.

One point that has emerged is that giving the beginning reader better facility at a skill could enable that reader to bring a larger quantity of evidence to bear on a word which is difficult to decode. This point is reinforced by a recent study by Reitsma (1988). Beginning readers were read a passage of text, in which were embedded 20 relatively difficult-to-read target words, each day, over a five-day period. A control group had a passage with no target words, and another group read the text while listening to the spoken version. Two other conditions involved either guided reading, in which the experimenter helped by providing cues to errors while the passage was being read, or independent reading in which the reader could select parts using a touch pad on a computer screen for speech feedback. These last two conditions were better than the first two in terms of rate and accuracy. Thus reading fluency can be improved in situations in which the child is given feedback, compared to when the child has a more passive role. It follows that if the child is given the tools for decoding words, such as by improving GPC skills, this enables the child to read more text when alone. This in turn will improve fluency, simply because more words are being encountered. The familiar ones are strengthened in terms of their retrieval times, and the less familiar are strengthened in terms of more evidence, such as graphemic and phonological information, being stored with their entries. Going round schools at the moment I gain the impression that such a view concerning reading is not a fashionable one. This is a great shame.

References

Beech, J.R. (1987) *Cognitive Approaches to Reading: Early Reading Development*, In Beech, J.R. and Colley, A.M. (Eds), Chichester: Wiley.

Beech, J.R. (in press) *The Acquisition and Performance of Cognitive Skills The Componential Approach To Learning Reading Skills*, In Colley, A.M. and Beech, J.R. (Eds), Chichester: Wiley

Beech, J.R. (1988) 'Comparing Three Routes to Reading Fluent Readers', *The Psychologist*, 1, A12

Beech, J.R. & Harding, L.M. (1984) 'Phonemic Processing and the Poor Reader from the Development Lag Point of View, *Reading Research Quarterly*, 19, 357–366.

Bieger, E. (1974) 'Effectiveness of Perceptual Training on Reading Skills, Non-Readers: An Experimental Study'. *Perceptual and Motor Skills*, 38 (3, Part 2), 1147–1153.

Bradley, L. & Bryant, P.E. (1983) 'Categorizing Sounds and Learning to Read: A Causal Connection' *Nature*, 301, 419–421.

Campbell, R. & Butterworth, B. (1985) 'Phonological Dyslexia and Dysgraphia in a Highly Literate Subject: A Developmental Case and Associated Deficits of Phonemic Awareness' *Quarterly Journal Of Experimental Psychology*, 37A, 435–475.

Frith, U. (1985) 'Beneath The Surface of Developmental Dyslexia.' In Patterson, K.E., Marshall, J.C. and Coltheart, M. (Eds). *Surface Dyslexia* London: Routledge & Kegan-Paul.

Marsh, G., Friedman, M., Welch, V. & Desberg, P. (1981) 'A Cognitive-Developmental Theory of Reading Acquisition.' In G.E. MacKinnon & T.G. Waller (Eds), *Reading Research: Advances in Theory & Practice*, 3. New York: Academic Press.

Paap, K.E., Newsome, S.L., MacDonald, J.E., & Schvaneldt, R.W. (1982) 'An Activation-Verification Model for Letter & Word Recognition: The Word Superiority Effect' *Psychological Review*, 89. 573–594.

Reitsma, P. (1988) 'Reading Practice for Beginners: Effects of Guided Reading, Reading-While-Listening, & Independent Reading, with Computer-Based Speech Feedback.' *Reading Research Quarterly*, 23, 219–235.

Rumelhart, D.E. & McClelland, J.L. (1986) *Parallel Distributed Processing Explorations in the Microstructure of Cognition*. Vol. 1. Foundations. Cambridge, MA: MIT Press.

Seymour, P.H.K. & Elder, L. (1986) 'Beginning Reading Without Phonology.' *Cognitive Neuropsychology*, 3. 1–16.

13 Text comprehension and study skills

Tony Martin and John Merritt

One of the most important aspects of teaching is helping children to organise facts and ideas so that they make sense. Most of the research in this area is so concerned with the underlying psychology of the learner that it fails to take sufficient account of the variety of challenges that the normal reader typically has to contend with. This has led to a continuing emphasis on the production of laboratory-like teaching materials – materials which teach children only that limited range of responses which are measured by so-called comprehension tests.

The authors of this paper have been working with top juniors (9–11 year-olds) and infants (5–7 year-olds) over the past year on strategies which take the challenges of everyday reading as their starting point. This, not surprisingly, involves a much greater reliance on the common sense of the teacher than on the input of an outside expert. It also involves a much greater emphasis on the common sense initiatives of children themselves than on the teaching of isolated skills.

An account is given here of three projects in which attempts were made, with varying degrees of success, to support the development of reading across the curriculum in the normal school setting. Paradoxically, perhaps, it is the account of work in the infant school that probably provides the best starting point for thinking about how best to prepare children for reading in adult life.

Introduction

The question of whether or not standards of reading have fallen tends to distract attention from the real issue, namely, the mismatch between the reading demands of the school and those of everyday life. Certainly, there is no substantial evidence to support the view that reading standards in our schools have declined. On the other hand, there is evidence from a variety of sources which shows that the quality of reading at adult level falls well short of what is needed to cope with the everyday world of print (see Merritt, 1986 and

Merritt, 1988). It is these broader needs that are the prime concern of the studies reported below.

Part of the present problem lies in our excessive dependence on a very limited range of research strategies – strategies which focus on the psychology of the reader. Most of the laboratory-type experiments conducted by cognitive psychologists have failed to take account of the *wide range of texts, the wide range of context* and the *wide range of purposes* that constitute everyday reading behaviour. The result has been a continued emphasis on laboratory-like teaching materials – materials which teach children only that limited range of responses to print which are measured by so-called comprehension tests.

For almost a century, research on 'transfer of learning' has shown the severe limitations of this kind of approach. The message has been clear and unambiguous: narrow, skill-based training will have little effect in situations which call for a much richer variety of responses than are actually provided in the learning situation. It is hardly surprising, therefore, that the most recent study of comprehension and reading performance (Moore and Kirby, 1988) confirms yet again that specific training in comprehension has very little impact on reading competence even within the relatively narrow range of contexts of a typical school curriculum. By the same token, we can hardly expect his narrow curriculum to provide competence in the wider range of activities that are involved in adult reading.

The issues

Clearly, the only realistic way to enable children to become proficient readers is to provide a range of relevant experiences. We must therefore think about enriching the curriculum in two ways:

First, we need to look at what an effective adult reader actually needs to do in order to get information from print in a form that enables him or her to *make effective decisions or take effective action*. This, quite obviously, is something very different from the 'tick, cross or underline' of the comprehension exercise – or the 'search and destroy' approach that children so often adopt when asked to summarise or paraphrase. Think, for example, of what you might do if you have to compare two insurance policies. The best approach might be to draw up a table of some kind to show what each policy covers – the sort of thing you might find in *Which* magazine. Or suppose that you want to sort out who did what, and when, from a rambling descriptive passage; in this case you might draw a flow diagram. Or if you need to get a clear picture of an organisation of some kind you might construct a tree diagram. This kind of response to print is therefore an essential ingredient in the curriculum if we want to improve reading competence.

These ideas were first introduced as a significant element in teaching reading in *The Open University* (1977) Course PE231 *Reading Development*. Here, however, there was an inadvertent emphasis on 'modelling' the information in a given text. In the present investigation we wanted to give much greater emphasis to the *need to decide on a suitable format or 'model' to match the reading purpose before trying to find the relevant information*.

Second, the curriculum must give rise to reading experiences that are more closely related to the circumstances in which we read in everyday life. That is to say we need to provide opportunities for children to generate their own *reading* purposes and priorities in a variety of contexts so that they are motivated to seek out the *variety of texts* that might provide what they want. And to have any chance of success, we must encourage children to bring into the classroom the questions, the motivation and initiative that they so often leave behind once they walk through the classroom door.

Naturally, the 'good' home provides many opportunities for 'real' reading and can therefore compensate for limitations in the curriculum. Unfortunately, many homes provide only a limited experience. The implications for what schools might need to do about this have been explored by Merritt (1986). In this investigation we were only in a position to sow a few seeds – or to nurture existing shoots!

In the event, we decided on two approaches – although it might be more accurate to say that two different approaches emerged, for there could be no sharp definition of what was to happen given the general principles we were supporting. In one approach, then, we decided to focus on ways of *organising information* in the curriculum that was already operating. In the other approach we set out, with the teacher, to modify the curriculum itself by emphasising the 'need-to-read'. What follows is an informal description of our experiences and our provisional conclusions.

Approach 1: Organising information

Two junior schools were involved in this part of the investigation. In one school we introduced five students and a tutor for one day a week for a term. This was part of the college IT-INSET programme and followed the general pattern described by Ashton et al (1983).

In the other school, both of the present writers worked for one afternoon per week for a term and then followed up over the next two terms.

In the IT-INSET school we decided to home in on the need to share information. We hoped that the idea of 'modelling' – organising information in different ways for different purposes – would be readily accepted as a natural extension of whatever was going on already. (See Figs. 13.1–13.7 for examples of the kinds of responses we were hoping to elicit.)

This worked well enough – as far as it went. For example, a start was eventually made on a data-base model for stock control, using the computer. This could have led to a regular flow of printed information from different classes for processing by the group who were running this particular operation. Another group made use of different formats or models in producing a guide to Barrow which was proudly displayed in the local Information Office.

Most of this work, however, was little more than an 'add-on': it had no real roots in what had gone before or what was to follow. Certainly, the children began to feel more at home with the different ways of organising information. Certainly, we all learned something about the problems of helping children to organise information.

A – *Sketching what people/things look like*

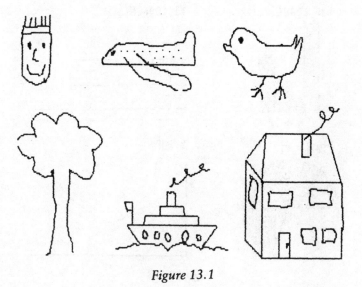

Figure 13.1

B – *Showing in what ways people/things are the same/different*

Same/Different Table

	Swims	Flies	Lays eggs	Suckles young	Nocturnal	etc.
Bat						
Owl						
Whale						
Shark						
Penguin						
Platypus						
Crocodile						
Snake						
etc.						

Figure 13.2

C – *Showing how many*

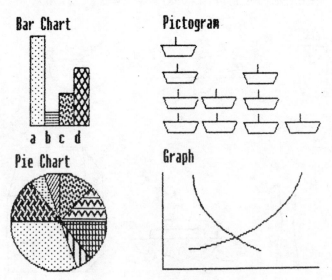

Bar Chart

a b c d

Pictogram

Pie Chart

Graph

Figure 13.3

D – *Showing how people/things can be classified or grouped*

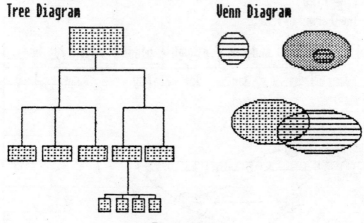

Figure 13.4

E – *Showing where things are/go*

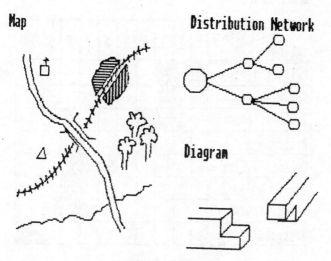

Figure 13.5

F – *Showing when things happened/happen/can happen*

Time Line
The Farmers Year:

Feed animals indoors	plough	plant	make hay; hoe

Jan	Feb	Mar	Apr	May	June	July

Flow Diagram

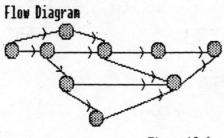

Figure 13.6

Gantt Chart

Action \ Week	1	2	3	4	5	6	7	8	9	10
Collect litter	▓	▓								
Assess waste		▓								
leaflets/posters		▓	▓							
Distribute				▓						
Collect litter						▓	▓			
Assess waste							▓			
leaflets/posters							▓	▓		
Distribute										▓

Figure 13.7

Certainly, we did have a good deal of consultation throughout the term because of the provision of supply cover for the teacher. But this kind of work can only be effective *if the teacher him/herself has had time to make a thorough review of the possibilities from his/her own point of view before ever agreeing to participate*. Everything that happens can then be integrated into the teacher's own thinking instead of being seen, to a large extent, as a contribution to the training of students.

In the second school, again a junior school, the effects of our intervention were very similar. The idea here was that we would begin with a demonstration of how the children could use one particular format for organising any information which they obtained from print, or elsewhere, in their work during the rest of the week. In the following sessions they would share and evaluate their work and review any new formats they had devised for themselves. We would then introduce another model to add to their repertoire if this proved necessary.

This class was taken by a 'teaching head'. The original intention was that the headteacher should be present at all the sessions taken by the experimenters so that he could develop his own ideas for what to follow up and in what way. Alas, the pressures of headship prevailed and, not unreasonably, competing demands for attention left little time to spend in a class when teaching cover was effectively available. Consequently, although much relevant work was already being done, eg the preparation of a wall newspaper based on a weekly review of the news, the full range of possibilities was never fully realised.

In the following two terms, administrative pressures again inhibited the more extensive development of the approach that we were hoping for. It is factors of this kind, rather than significant theoretical problems, that provide the greatest barrier to progress.

As in the first school there was certainly some gain in the ability of children to organise information in different ways for different purposes. In addition, the head felt that the work had been of value when used in other curriculum activities. A modest testing programme at the end of the year did not, however, support the hypothesis that any gains would transfer in measurable quantities.

Approach 2: The need to read

Once again, we were able to take advantage of the College's IT-INSET arrangements so, in addition to the teacher, three students were members of the team for a period of one term. We spent one morning per week in the classroom. Teaching cover then allowed us to spend the afternoon sharing and reflecting on our experiences.

We set off by trying to increase the children's interest in books and stories in the classroom. We were also concerned to use 'environmental print' in ways which reflected life outside and at home. It was not long, however, before we realised that our real starting point was considerably further back in the learning process.

We had paid a lot of attention to creating a 'comfy', attractive book corner, complete with colourful picture books and stories. As part of this we read a number of picture books with one group and explained that they were going to make puppets of the characters. We could then put on a puppet show for the rest of the class. Some tables had already been prepared for the work and a large box of 'junk' was available. In addition we provided some socks, suggesting they would make good puppets should anyone not want to use the junk.

The group set to work, each child working on his or her own puppet. Teaching time was largely taken up with keeping the activity running smoothly.

Two children could not think of what to make, and refused all of the group leader's suggestions. Eventually they got going but were never really involved. The others had plenty of ideas but they had some difficulty in cutting, glueing and painting (neither glue not paint wanted to adhere to plastic egg cartons!)

The group leader was constantly called on for help, dashing from one child to the next but, eventually, the puppets were ready to put on a shelf to dry. One child insisted early on that he was finished and inquired if he could go and play in the home corner.

At the afternoon team meeting, the student-teacher who had been observing noted that the children who had finished were seemingly satisfied with what they had produced first time. In addition she noted their desire to get us to help them – their 'dependence on the teacher', she called it. The class teacher commented on their age (just five years old) and suggested they were not mature enough to refine their work to any great degree. She recognised their need for teacher help, saying that this was what made teaching such young children so demanding. They were constantly in need of teacher attention and assistance. In fact, in my session they had behaved exactly as might have been expected.

A long and very profitable discussion then ensued concerning what five-year-old children are capable of and how we might improve on what had happened in the puppets lesson. Two major observations were made which seemed interesting enough to investigate during the following week.

First, there was the children's behaviour in the home corner, the sand tray and the sink and in their outdoor activities. This seemed to prove that they were not dependent: it amply demonstrated their ability to play together in pairs, and occasionally threes and fours. Two or more children could regularly be observed co-operating in a play activity, sharing apparatus and equipment and agreeing on the direction the play should take. Could they have co-operated in the same way on the puppets? Perhaps we could test this next week.

The second observation concerned the book corner and our attempts to encourage the children to use it. Having set it up we had been a bit surprised to notice that not many of the children were choosing to spend time browsing amongst the books. Two of us had therefore begun sitting in there every morning, reading books with obvious enjoyment. Immediately we had found ourselves joined by children – all extremely interested to see what we were reading and to share the books with us. The very fact of engaging in the activity ourselves had provided all the motivation that was needed. They wanted to join in. Could we take up a similar role in class activities? Would the puppets lesson have been more successful if we had made a puppet ourselves?

As a result of the afternoon's discussion we decided on a plan for the following week. With our 'Need-to-Read' project in mind we decided to organise a walk around Ambleside, focusing on the print around us in the streets and shops. Back in class we would suggest building a model of Ambleside – using cardboard boxes for buildings. The children would work in pairs, each pair making one building. In addition we teachers would form pairs and make buildings, thus contributing to the project. In this way we hoped to test both of the observations which had been discussed.

The walk proved to be extremely successful. Parents were invited to join us and four mothers did so – becoming fascinated by the comments of the children they took around. Some children knew a lot about the signs, names and shop window displays while others had obviously not had such print pointed out before. On the way back to school there was a great deal of excited discussion.

In the classroom we joined quite naturally in the talk – as excited as the children! We then gathered everyone together and explained that we had enjoyed the morning so much that we had wondered what else we could do connected with Ambleside. What about building our own model village of it? The children leapt at this idea.

Putting them into pairs proved no problem. Each pair was told to choose one of the buildings we had seen and the box of materials was pointed out. We explained that we too were going to work in pairs and therefore would not be able to help much. We were, however, sure that they could get on without us.

Each of the adult pairs sat down in different parts of the room and began to discuss (loud enough for the children to hear!) which building to choose. The children *all* sat and listened. Ignoring them, we began to collect boxes, other materials, paints, water and glue and to discuss how best to begin. Still the children sat and watched! Then, as we began to work, they started to talk – very serious discussions about which building to choose. Slowly decisions were taken and materials collected. Work began.

What happened now was fascinating. All but two of the pairs (who will be discussed below) organised themselves, deciding who should do what and when. There was a constant buzz of discussion and comment. One little girl approached the class teacher to ask something but was told she would have to sort it out with her partner because the teacher was too busy with her own model. The little girl looked somewhat perplexed and hung around for some moments before making her way back to her table. Sitting down she looked at her partner, words were exchanged and then they began to work again. Now the need to share resources became apparent – particular coloured paints were in short supply. We found ourselves being approached by children and asked if we had finished with them. The children began to pass materials around in a very mature way.

As children moved around the room in search of what they required, comments were heard on the quality of the work they were able to observe. One student was praised for the neatness of her painting of the roof! Other pairs were encouraged with 'That's good' and 'I like that'. The children began to ask real information-seeking questions (as they do at home!, cf Tizard and Hughes, 1984).

A lot of glueing was now taking place and we were learning about the problems of getting card to stay stuck. One of the team was forced to stand, gazing around, hands holding a chimney in place until the glue began to work. Children were most sympathetic! They obviously knew only too well what he was up against. 'It never sticks for hours' said one. The fact that a teacher was in this predicament seemed to encourage others so that soon there were a number of us waiting for the glue and carrying on a very natural conversation as we did so.

At this point it became apparent that the combined strategy of the children working in pairs and we teachers working as 'contributors' rather than 'controllers' was having a profound effect in three areas. First, these children (aged five), were going to work co-operatively in their pairs for a lot longer than we had anticipated. After an hour they showed no sign of wanting to be 'finished'. Each member of the pair wanted to ensure that their bit was good. Second, they really were working together: discussion of what they were producing was much better than in their previous efforts – and certainly an improvement on the episode with the puppets.

That afternoon in our discussion the students and myself were quite excited – but the class teacher was positively amazed. Her first comment was *'Were these the same children I taught yesterday?'*. She went on to comment on how they had worked together, taken decisions without reference to her, kept going for such a long time, shared materials, produced such lovely models. During similar lessons in the past she had been rushed off her feet, cajoling, helping, keeping things organised. She had felt that such young children would need a lot of adult help. They would depend on her.

As a group we explored how we had in fact provided just such help but in a more subtle and much more powerful way. *By acting as models for the children, demonstrating how we came to take our own decisions we had enabled the children to take decisions themselves.*

The exceptions to this had been the two pairs mentioned above who had found it difficult to agree on starting points. Each had decided eventually to split so that four children were working on their own making their own models. The contrast between these four and the others had been dramatic. They pronounced themselves 'finished' long before the first pair, happy to present their models for our approval (in their eyes that had been the aim of the exercise) and then to wander off to play in the sand. They had felt no ownership of the task. There did not appear to have been much excitement in their work.

The above account might imply that we have only to put young children into pairs and join in ourselves for the quality of the learning experience to be transformed. However, work over the next few weeks led us to a fuller recognition of the need for a third element. An art lesson the following week did not have the same dramatic results and only after discussion and further attempts in the classroom did we realise why. The model-building lesson had been introduced to the children following our walk and we had been so excited by what happened that we ourselves had thought it would be fun to make our own models. The children had simply been asked if they had wanted to make models as well. They had been involved in the decision to do so themselves.

There is a world of difference between the teacher announcing 'Today we are going to do . . .' (the sub-text of which is, 'because I say so – so you had just better do it well whether you want to or not') and the session which begins with a shared enthusiasm. In the former it is the teacher's lesson; she has ownership of it. In the latter the children feel that it is their lesson as much as the teacher's.

Our work in the infant school had begun as an investigation into developing the 'need-to-read' in the classroom. While this remained the major focus, it was the demonstration by the children of how they could work if we would only let them which excited us the most. They showed us that even at an early age they were capable of working co-operatively on shared projects. We had also learned that if we shared with them on equal terms we could provide both role-model and motivation – the seven-league boots of learning. The effect of this co-operation and sharing proved, in the event, to have a dramatic effect on the quality of any activity in which these considerations were uppermost.

A second feature of our project which also proved to be significant was the effort we had to make as teachers to work co-operatively ourselves. If we are to develop our ability to work with children we must first learn to work with each other. Children working together, co-operating to learn, should surely be a feature of classrooms – but all too often we teachers do not demonstrate the same willingness. Teaching can be a solitary activity. Talk about how to organise children to plan, work, reflect and evaluate takes on a new meaning coming from a group of teachers struggling to do so themselves. It is only by doing this that we keep in touch with the problems children are facing. In doing so we develop new insights into how best to enable them to help themselves.

Conclusions

Straightforward prose is not always the most convenient way of presenting – or representing – information. This we would regard as self-evident. Consequently, children need to learn to select and use whatever form, format or 'model' is most appropriate for their imme-diate purpose. If we encourage children to adopt whatever approach to handling information is most appropriate, and if they then fail to show significant improvement on comprehension tests, this leaves us with two possibilities: (i) the test is of limited validity, and/or (ii) the curriculum-in-action is not sufficiently well-conceived.

In our first approach to this problem we were, for the most part, simply teaching children the tricks of organising information in different ways. Typically, therefore, they merely learned the rules of this particular game. This is not the same as teaching them to use this knowledge when a genuine need arises. It is little better, in fact, than teaching mechanical arithmetic and expecting children to use this ability in solving problems.

To be effective, the curriculum must enable children to exercise that amazing potential which they so clearly demonstrate in their lives outside school. It must provide opportunities for children to define their own needs and priorities, to plan their achievement, to manage their own implementation and to evaluate both process and outcome. To be realistic, it must also relate to the real problems of life in the community – and as actor, rather than as mere observer.

Such a curriculum can only be achieved if teachers participate whole-heartedly in a continuous process of curriculum evaluation and development – co-operating with each other in solving their own problems – just like the children. This, arguably, is the most important element in school-based INSET. One way of bringing this about is to relate in-service work of this kind to a system for gaining modular credits. Such an approach is now part of College planning for future INSET activities.

If the foregoing analysis is correct then those who limit their attention to the teaching of 'comprehension skills' – or any other set of skills – are like the musicians on the Titanic. Gallant, undoubtedly. But, Great Education Reform Bill notwithstanding, is it not time we embarked on a more sea-worthy vessel?

References

Ashton, P., Henderson, E., Merritt, J. and Mortimer, D. (1983) *Teacher Education in the Classroom: Initial and In-Service* London: Croom Helm.

Merritt, J. (1986) 'What's Wrong with Teaching Reading?' In Cashdan, A (Ed). *Literacy: Teaching & Learning Language Skills* Oxford: Blackwell.

Merritt, J. (1987) 'Parents & Teachers in Reading Education: Let's Get Our Act Together!' in Smith, Peter (Ed). *Parents And Teachers Together* London: United Kingdom Reading Association/Macmillan Education.

PART 3

Communication and the Classroom

14 Movement and dance, a major contribution to literacy, language and communication

Vi Bruce

Conscious of the aims of the conference and of its content, this short chapter has an accent upon those aspects of the art of dance which are linked most clearly and immediately with language, as stimulus and as consequence, in talking, in writing, in art and in music.

Dance embraces many styles and techniques. We are concerned that dance in education is for *all* children, whatever their body build or shape, whatever their background, temperament or ability. Always there must be concern for movement which is as mobile and complete in quality as is possible, consistent with bodily growth and development. All children can dance, but a teacher does need to have a deepening knowledge of human movement and to foster it intelligently in the service of the art of dance itself and of other learning which is so readily involved.

The work was designed to illustrate the way in which movement and dance involve the use of language in communication, in teaching, in sharing ideas, in the practical expression of dance form and in discussion and writing about work in progress or completed.

Movement is for children a natural, growing ability which is of their very being so that movement experience is clear, vivid and meaningful. Many children who are not successful in other activities move well and can express themselves clearly this way. So it is that words are involved, meanings clarified, and language becomes part of a child's ready communication.

Drama and dance are very close together as art forms. Indeed, sometimes there can be no definite division as some children dance and some act in response to an idea. Dramatic material is often more easily expressed as spoken drama or mime, but sometimes dance offers greater scope. So one uses story taking the underlying theme or idea, rather than the progressive narrative, although there is no rigid ruling. When using the creation myth from the Gilbertese Islands, for instance, the creation of the sun, moon and stars became dance, whilst the action of the characters remained essentially drama. The magic of the island in *The Tempest* easily becomes dance as does the drama of a windy day. There is a wealth of stimuli for dance. The stimulus may of course be movement itself, its energy, its rhythm, the beauty of gesture, the excitement of leaping. It may be sound or music which inspires and gives shape to the dance. It may be costume or design.

The workshops concentrated on language: written and spoken; as stimulus and as consequence; in discussion; in the written word, sentence, paragraph or article; in poetry and story.

There is always the need to educate the body. This instrument must be the most fluent for each child. Yet, even as one is concerned with joints, muscles, movement quality, spatial issues and with rhythm, shape and form, already words are in abundance. Often a teacher will accent her words as she describes gesture or steps: 'With strength', 'Hastily, you have no time', 'Smoothly, do not make jerks'. Words initiate action, 'Jump', 'Whirl', 'Falling, then quite still'. Concepts are important, 'Under and then through', 'Around and about', 'Gather together'.

Poetry and dance have much in common in their mode of expression: one often finds a poetic stimulus for dance and children writing poetry as a consequence of dance experience.

JUMPING
> Twisting and twirling,
> Romping and whirling,
> Up in the air, down to the floor,
> Legs up, hands high,
> Straddling and sprawling,
> Shooting into space,
> Light as a feather,
> Up went I – Down to the earth,
> From the sky.   (Kevin)

We must be aware of the many ways in which children learn to use and to love language. The arts communicate so readily and teaching goes on all the time with skill and artistry so that children's needs are met.

References

V R Bruce (1988) *Movement and Dance in the Primary School – into the nineties* (Open University Press).

15 Developing and assessing oracy across the curriculum

Maureen Hardy and Ann Glenton

This paper is based on three workshops carried out at Conference. They involved reporting on classroom research and discussion of the following issues: the state of 'oracy' in schools; the nature and development of discussion as an avenue for learning and practical ways of both teaching and evaluating oracy (including MODIC) in primary, secondary or special classrooms.

What is 'Oracy'?

'Oracy tends to be regarded as a new concept connected with GCSE, Curriculum documents from the DES, and the Kingman Report. In fact, Wilkinson defined the term in 1965, indicating that it combined 'deliberate adequate verbal expression' with 'adequate listening skills'. Since Socrates, discussion has been an acknowledged tool of learning. In recent times, successive Government Reports have recommended that more attention should be given to the development of oral/aural abilities, eg Bullock (DES 1975) and Cockcroft (1982). Many educationalists have echoed the theme, eg Barnes (1975), Tough (1977) and Wells (1981). The impact of these initiatives is now becoming visible in schools.

Traditionally, teachers seek to promote language development and use discussion as a tool of teaching. However, as Widdowson (1978) indicates, it is assumed that 'speaking and hearing' alone constitute a meaningful discourse. To be effective it is necessary to refine these raw abilities into 'talking', 'listening' and 'saying'. Here *talking* implies intentionally participating in a purposeful dialogue. *Listening* involves interpreting, intelligently, what is heard in order to make a meaningful response and contribution to the discussion. *Saying* refers to significant utterances which lead the discussion forward or open up new avenues of enquiry. Such 'communicative abilities' are fostered in situations where teachers and pupils form learning partnerships and use dialogue as a significant part of the teaching/learning process.

Wells (1981) indicates that learning through interaction involves the negotiation of shared meanings. Tizard and Hughes (1984) and Wells (1985) demonstrate that, contrary to popular notions, most young children receive such help from their parents. When a mother and child talk together about a simple observation, say 'a bird', they form part of a communication triangle, in which both are growing in understanding. and at the same time enlarging their concept of the topic. This process involves the framing of messages and the creation of images, which are interpreted and re-created by the other participant(s) and are eventually enlarged into a better understanding of self, others and the surrounding world. Oracy is part of the process even when the word-store is sparse and the topics simple, but it opens up channels which lead to clearer thinking and effective communication. Unfortunately, as Willes (1983) has indicated, even in the reception class, it is difficult to replicate this process, because of factors such as the ratio of adults to children; the need to keep order; also the tradition that teachers ask questions to which children respond. However, it is not impossible to translate a little of the ideal into classroom practice (for an example of such an attempt see Hardy, 1985 and 1987).

The ideal is not easy to attain, but it is worth the effort, for as Wilkinson (1985) indicates – the communication triangle is in itself a creative agent, overtly as dialogue and sometimes covertly as in a silent dialogue with a lecturer, actor or writer. He states – *'I communicate – therefore I am; I communicate – therefore you are; I communicate – therefore it is'*. Teachers and pupils alike benefit from engaging in such a process, but, as yet, it is a rare event in many schools.

The state of oracy in schools today

There is evidence to suggest that a mis-match exists between intention and practice in relation to language development in schools, probably arising from a lack of clarity on the part of teachers, as to an explicit and shared definition of oracy. The APU Report *Speaking and Listening – Assessment at Age 11* (1986) lists the following abilities as employed by 11 year-olds – 'narrating, describing, giving instructions and conveying information acquired through listening'. It notes, however, that these are evident when tasks are presented in a form that is clear and carefully structured. Unfortunately, life seldom provides situations with as much explicit structure as may be required. The report also indicates useful strategies which are rarely present at 11 years. They include evaluating evidence, speculating about possible alternatives, hypothesising and justifying an argument or point of view. Teachers in tertiary education, and employers, may reflect that such abilities often remain under-developed at 18 plus. Clearly schools should seek to improve this situation.

Leicester University's ORACLE survey (Galton et al 1980) commented that few children returned from school having had sustained work-orientated discussions with either teachers or peers. Talk is a feature of modern school life, but it is not always recognised that differences exist between social chatter, instructional conversations and learning discussions. All aspects of talk help to build learning partnerships, but only the highest level provokes thoughtful learning. Frequently, class discussions involve only a few of those present and it cannot be assumed that the rest are listening or understanding. Also, as Barnes (1975) indicated, they tend to consist mainly of 'filling in predictable slots' by the process of guessing what is in the teacher's mind, rather than engagement and comprehension of the issues.

To illustrate the above point, it is possible to conceive that many pupils could answer correctly 'Who? – What? – Where?' questions applied to the following nonsense statement – 'Tha Thunkans art gabberly danking bie Tackly Tam'. Lack of comprehension can only be revealed by questions probing 'Why? or How?', efforts to predict consequences, or attempts to assess the feelings or intentions of the participants. The easier questions (Who? What? Where?) tend to predominate because they can be answered speedily and thus aid teacher-control. Pupils prefer such surface questions, because their lack of full understanding is less likely to be exposed. However, to formulate relevant questions and carry out meaningful investigations, they require feedback which alerts them to identify what they do not yet know.

The ORACLE study indicated that the most effective teachers are those who organise to provide scope for interaction. They know when best to intervene and are constantly challenging their pupils intellectually, while subtly assisting them to make investigations. The fact that this study revealed that some teachers do have such skills and demonstrated that they were able to overcome the problems of space, time and resources, provides hope that others may be helped to achieve similar goals. At a UKRA workshop in the London Day Conference on 'Communicating Kingman' (June, 1988) it was suggested that teachers should set targets for themselves as well as their pupils, since there is a direct relationship between the quality of teacher-input and the quality of pupil-outcomes which becomes possible no matter what the classroom situation initially involves.

The movement towards improved practice in developing oracy is escalating. The issue is actually less complex than might originally be supposed. Despite the fact that some teachers assert that they need special resources and such resources are desirable, they are not essential. As Wilkinson (1982) indicates, pupils may be offered the 'verbalisation of experience' together with 'the experience of verbalisation' within the realistic context of every lesson in the school curriculum. Organisational skills to facilitate such practice exist, eg part of a class may be gainfully occupied with activities requiring minimum supervision, while the teacher engages the others in intensive discussion. Groups of children may be encouraged to collaborate on a project, which must later be clearly explained to others. Any available adults eg ancillaries, parents, students, may be persuaded to assist from time to time. All that is required is commitment to the cause and the will to find ways of putting it into operation. Once it is seen as viable, then desirable extra resources may be forthcoming and their value properly acknowledged.

Teacher initiatives in relation to developing and assessing oracy

Example 1: Primary

As 'Teacher in charge of Language Development' in a multiethnic school, Hardy used audiotaping of discussion to explore the monitoring of oral/aural development as a part of the class teachers's normal work. She advocated use of group discussion and set out to demonstrate that it could be achieved within the normal routine. The children involved in the research had no idea that their efforts were being specially studied as group discussion had become a regular activity in school. They thought that they were making tapes in the same way as they made up plays in drama sessions. They listened to their tapes with satisfaction and began to suggest ways of improving them, eg 'not talking on top of each other'. The topics they discussed were not separate from their work but always related to current learning or interests being developed in routine classwork.

'MODIC' – a practical method of 'Monitoring Oral Development In the Classroom' was gradually developed (Hardy, 1985).

This approach uses audio-tapes, but records results on a grid, thus avoiding time-consuming transcripts. An observational chart is available for assessment between recorded samples of discussion. This method was used to trace the oral/aural development of groups (10/12 children) and individuals, highlighting strengths and weaknesses for enrichment or remediation. Progress was far from linear, but in a relatively short period, many children seemed to have improved their facility in this direction. Such improvement was often reflected in other areas of school work, self-confidence and willingness to collaborate. 'MODIC' has been tested in a variety of ways both to scrutinize the apparent results and to ensure that other teachers can use the approach effectively.

The approach provides a means by which teachers can monitor and improve their own oracy. For this purpose some of J. Tough's *Teacher Dialogue Strategies* (1977) have been combined with others found useful, eg arbitrating in large group situations (teachers learned much from examining their own discussion techniques). It was found that in discussion, for example, messages and meanings could be rendered more explicit by combining everyday terms with specialised subject-specific terminology. Also that one could not assume that the pupil's interpretation of an explanation matched that of the teachers. It was discovered that questions could be orientated in a manner which assisted the children to find the solutions or to ask other relevant questions. It was further discovered that there existed non-threatening ways of reflecting back children's comments and thus helping them to clarify their initial ideas and ask divergent questions without embarrassment. The results of the study are being disseminated. The intention is partly to provide reassurance to teachers that their communication abilities and those of their pupils may be fostered within the scope of everyday classroom experience. Although developed in a primary school, MODIC is an open approach suitable for use with any age group and within any school context.

Example 2: Secondary

In another initiative, the oracy component of GCSE assessment encouraged Glenton and colleagues in a family of secondary schools to use INSET provision to examine the ways in which oracy was being fostered and could be further developed in school, and how oracy could be assessed at different stages of its development. Teacher attitudes and situational difficulties were taken into consideration.

The group found that already they were opening up some worth-while opportunities for fostering oracy, but that much more could be done in this direction. In particular, they wished to make it clear that oracy could and should be developed in the context of each subject area, rather than solely in *'fabricated situations in the English Departments'*. As Barnes (1987) states, there is *'little value in development of oracy skills out of context'*. It was considered, however, that the discussion of literature and literary skills were particularly appropriate in English work.

It was recognised that, despite timetable constraints, if a whole-school approach were to be fostered, it would be necessary for greater collaboration and flexibility and for all staff to become aware of the total curriculum offered to the pupils. The Assessment of Performance Unit (APU) report *Speaking and Listening – Assess-ment at Age 16* (1986), like that for age 11, raises many of the relevant issues.

In examining videotapes of pupils' formal presentations prepared specifically for assessment purposes the teachers concluded that the more interesting work probably takes place in the preparation period (prior to the video making) when the pupils are selecting aspects of the topic and finding and sequencing relevant informa-tion. It was therefore concluded that the process itself should be considered as a part of the assessment, in addition to the final product.

These videos were presented to groups of pupils who were asked to draw up their own criteria for assessment. It was interesting to note the sensible suggestions which arose, eg that pupils should 'behave in a mature manner' and 'get messages across clearly and confidently'. The initial list of criteria led to reconsideration and introduction of procedures similar to those used in the OCEA Proj-ect (The Oxford Certificate of Educational Achievement). By involving pupils in developing their own assessment techniques, the importance of oracy was being reinforced and at the same time pupils had the opportunity to use oracy as a means of resolving practical problems. They were learning 'to understand and influence the world through speech' (Barnes, 1987).

These endeavours to foster oracy by the primary school and clus-ter of secondary schools demonstrate that problems may be over-come once the nature of oracy is recognised and it is seen to be a priority area. In this cause, teachers should endeavour to convince pupils, parents, headteachers and governors of the importance of talk in schools, the quality of talk required and the facilities which would aid its development. The recommendations of The Kingman Committee and also the requirements of the GCSE lend weight to this argument. Since there is no other aspect of education which is assessed without years of formal preparation, it becomes evident that education in oracy is essential. Such preparation need not constitute a new communication subject area, but is one which can be used in every aspect of the curriculum to raise the level of awareness and sharpen perceptions in relation to 'reading' the myriad symbols surrounding us, not only in print, but represented through art, music, dance and drama, the humanities and also in mathematics, science and the products of technology. To increase understanding through all these modes of communication, we are required to co-operate, collaborate, question, investigate, create and recreate images and negotiate shared meanings – all of which involve oracy.

References

APU (1986) *Practical Assessment in Oracy at Age 11* DES
Barnes, D. (1975) *From Communication To Curriculum* Penguin.
Barnes, D. (1987) *English Magazine* Vol. 19. Autumn.
Brooks, G. (1986) 'Speaking and Listening–Assessment at Age 16' APU Report. NFER – Nelson.
Cockcroft, W. (1982) *Mathematics Counts* Report of the Committee of Inquiry appointed by the Secretary of State for Education and Science. HMSO.
DES (1975) *A Language for Life* Report of the Committee of Inquiry appointed by the Secretary of State for Education and Science. The Bullock Report: HMSO.
DES (1988) *Report of the Committee of Inquiry into the Teaching of English Language* (The Kingman Report) HMSO.
Galton, M. et al (1980) *Inside The Primary Classroom* ORACLE Survey. Routledge and Kegan Paul.
Galton, M. and Simon, B. (1980) *Progress and Performance in the Primary Classroom* ORACLE Survey. Routledge and Kegan Paul.
Hardy, M.A.A. (1985) 'Developing Oracy As An Aid To Learning (MODIC)' Unpublished M.Ed. thesis, University of Leicester.
Hardy, M.A.A. (1985) 'Developing Discussion Skills in the Classroom' *Spoken English* Vol. 18, No, 1. English Speaking Board.
Hardy, M.A.A. (1987) 'I, You and it – together we learn' in *Forum* Vol. 30. No. 1
McLure, M and Hargreaves, M. (1986) 'Speaking and Listening – Assessment at Age 11' NFER – Nelson.
Tough, J. (1977) *Talking And Learning* Ward Lock.
Tizard, B. and Hughes, M. (1984) *Young Children Learning* Fontana.
Wells, G. (ed) (1981) *Learning Through Interaction* Cambridge University Press.

Wells, G. (1985) *Language Development in the Pre-School Years* Cambridge University Press.
Widdowson, H.G. (1978) *Teaching Language as Communication* Oxford University Press.
Wilkinson, A. (1982) 'The Implications or Oracy' in Wade B. (ed.) *Language Perspectives* Heinemann.
Wilkinson, A. (1985) *Educational Review* Vol. 37, No. 1.

16 Re-creation through writing

Richard Binns

Re-creation through writing allows the writer opportunities of time and space to explore experience in a way that is not possible in speaking. The possibility of returning to the text to explore experience permits the writer to adopt a more reflective stance in evaluating what to say, before deciding how to express thoughts and feelings. Persuading pupils, especially those aged ten to fourteen, of the value of taking time to re-read what they have written and reflect on what to say depends, in my experience as a secondary teacher, on offering them some means whereby they can continue to develop more complex ideas in increasingly fluent writing, and at the same time begin to cope with the creative difficulty of pausing in written, as distinct from spoken language, without an audience to act as a guide.

The important place of reading in the writing process

Observation of the important place of reading in the process of writing is often made in the classroom, when pupils pause in the process of writing, look back over their work and look up, with a puzzled and reflective expression. The following example of 'free' personal writing from the work of a boy aged 8.6 in a primary 4/5 composite class in a rural school (Fig 16.1) reveals a tremedous struggle to re-read and pause to gain a 'sense of audience'.

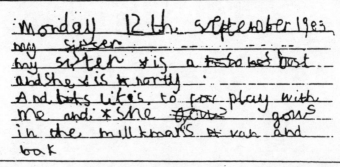

Figure 16.1 Difficulty in pausing to re-read and gain a 'sense of audience'.

At the time, the class were about to be encouraged to spend more time working on what to say and less on revising persistent 'mistakes', with the aid of the editorial procedure of drafting and re-drafting. To prepare the class to write in a more adult way, like professional writers, they had been asked not to rub out. This was also expected to afford a truer impression of difficulty in developing written language. Impressive signs of attempts to pause to gain a 'sense of audience' in the above pupil's 'free' writing are evident in the following line-by-line analysis (Fig 16.2) which shows hesitant *'crossings outs'* and tentative re-ordering of the relationship between words.

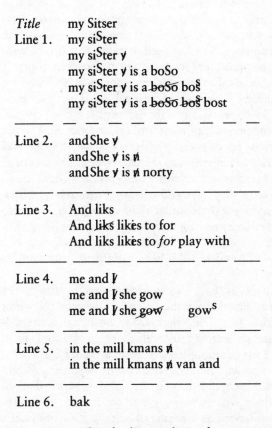

Title	my Sitser
Line 1.	my si^{S}ter
	my si^{S}ter y
	my si^{S}ter y is a boSo
	my si^{S}ter y is a ~~boSo~~ bo^S
	my si^{S}ter y is a ~~boSo~~ ~~bo^S~~ bost
Line 2.	and She y
	and She y is n
	and She y is n norty
Line 3.	And liks
	And ~~liks~~ likes to for
	And liks likes to *for* play with
Line 4.	me and V
	me and V she gow
	me and V she ~~gow~~ gow^S
Line 5.	in the mill kmans n
	in the mill kmans n van and
Line 6.	bak

Figure 16.2   A line-by-line analysis of pauses to re-read (scan back) in the ordinary process of writing.

The dependence of the process of writing on the variable of reading emerged from this analysis of error. Errors took the form of slips, 'false starts', redundancy and omission, even 'gaps' in the flow of words and ideas. What became clear was the importance to the pupil as a writer of being able to deal with these in the ordinary process of writing through the independent variable of reading and of pausing for reflection. The value of pausing lay in adjusting the text to meet the demands of the creative element of rehearsal in the relationship between thought and language.

Treating the beginning writer like the professional writer or adults, means, in the classroom, encouraging pausing to re-read, as a distancing device. Professional writers and adults understand the value of distancing themselves from the text between drafts to take the pressure off having to continue to write, when they are not sure what to say. Pupils are often relieved to hear about any need to pause to work out how to spell eg *'develop'* (Should it be spelt like envelope?). They can appreciate the need to pause and also be willing to take greater responsibility for their writing between drafts. It is said of Yeats that he used to re-draft some poems up to 34 times: whereas Orwell rehearsed what to say during discussion, as a means of getting the text down practically right first time for *The Tribune*. Businessmen ease the pressure of transcription by dictating a rough draft to a secretary direct or on a cassette. They use drafting and re-drafting as a device to help them to sketch out ideas like an artist; between drafts they read (scan) at leisure the typed-up original as an initial spectator to see if they have said what they meant to say; then they proceed either to get the content right during revision or to prepare the final version by editing, proof-reading and revising with an eventual reader in mind. A similar technique for drafting and re-drafting (Binns 1978 and 1980) is briefly outlined at the conclusion of this chapter.

The aim of this paper is to give more adequate recognition to the formidable task of composition at the *'intermediate steps'* (Newbolt Report, 1921, Section 78.). The object is to reconsider the nature of difficulty and progress in learning to develop written as distinct from spoken language. Two questions need to be answered. First, why is it hard to begin to cope with the creative difficulty of pausing to gain a 'sense of audience'? Second, how may the visual arts contribute to progress in developing written language? In conclusion, formative evaluation is recommended as a means of helping pupils to gain a 'sense of audience', as they learn to rely less on an 'ear' for language and more on an evaluative eye (Smith, 1982, p. 129).

The need to pause to gain a 'Sense of audience'?

Treating beginning writers as if they are professional writers means expecting them to experience the strain in gaining a 'sense of audience' or making a critical judgement. This may lead to psychological or procedural 'blocks' (Smith, 1982 pp. 129–137).

Furthermore, as adults we may not remember the frustration of learning to write. The frustrating experience of writing about different kinds of subject matter of an increasingly complex nature was reported by Britton et al (1975, pp. 35). They experimented in writing with 'worn-out ball-point pens' (without any ink). they observed in pausing to re-read ('scanning back') to gain a 'sense of audience', that the more complex the subject matter the greater the probability of pausing too long and losing the thread of meaning.

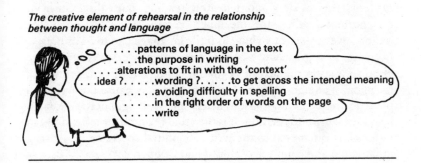

The creative element of rehearsal in the relationship between thought and language

. . . .patterns of language in the text
. . . .the purpose in writing
. . . .alterations to fit in with the 'context'
. . .idea ?. . . . .wording ?. . . . .to get across the intended meaning
. . . . .avoiding difficulty in spelling
. . . . .in the right order of words on the page
. . . . .write

Figure 16.3   Trying to gain a 'sense of audience'.

Re-focusing

Re-focusing is, from these brief observations, the source of difficulty in pausing to develop written language. Difficulty in re-focusing is ascribed here to two aspects of the intervening variable of reading in the writing process: i) difficulty in relying on long-term memory and ii) lack of linguistic awareness. This is especially the case when *'the intention fades'* (Donaldson, 1978, pp. 74–75).

We ordinarily speak within the flow of a meaningful context which as it were, supports – or at least does not conflict with our language because we fit our utterance to its contours.

When short-term memory (working memory) becomes over-loaded, awareness of 'context' as a determinant of meaning is vital in re-reading the patterns of language in the text as a whole, as a guide to gaining a 'sense of audience'.

An inferior strategy for developing written language is one in which the beginning writer may be observed to stick at the point when he or she is invited to go beyond rehearsing the relations between words in the context of a sentence as a unit of meaning.

The evolution of a superior strategy for developing written language permits the beginning writer to adopt very gradually a more reflective stance, by pausing to differentiate experience on re-reading the original text and building up a picture of an effect in long-term memory *(See below Fig 16.4 Learning to re-focus: conducting 'an internal debate' about what to say through scanning between drafts.).*

Revising in its proper place has much to recommend it, as proof-reading 'requires slow and deliberate reading, quite different from our normal reading for meaning' (Perera, 1984, p. 210). Yet treating every piece of writing as if the language had to be as precise in its use as a great work of literature often overlooks invaluable opportunities in the text of beginning writers' drafts for growth of meaning. The imprecision of a draft text may cause the writer to pause for reflection, not just to detect mis-spelling, but to seek fresh inspiration prior to revision. It is then that the time for re-reading, to re-focus, is often vital to the writer, as initial spectator, in gaining momentum and continuity (Hourd and Cooper, 1959, p. 130).

Falling back on proof-reading and revising to deal with persistent 'mistakes' may aggravate difficulty in developing written language in two main ways. First, producing a 'fair copy' runs the risk of becoming a mindless chore; errors may be overlooked if there is no real purpose in re-writing. Second, beginning writers' preoccupation with 'mistakes' may cause them to gain a 'sense of audience', by making only a word-by-word check, as at the stage of 'mechanics'. To get as it were 'lift-off', the beginning writer has to cease sticking at anything beyond checking handwriting, spacing between words, spelling and full-stops to mark the end of a sentence (Fig. 16.4).

Proceeding too fast to revision may be equally dangerous (Rosen and Rosen, 1973, p. 123).

the temptations are alluring, for here there seems to be the promise of 'structure' and 'sequence'. The price of succumbing to the temptation is usually a premature restriction on the choices open to children.

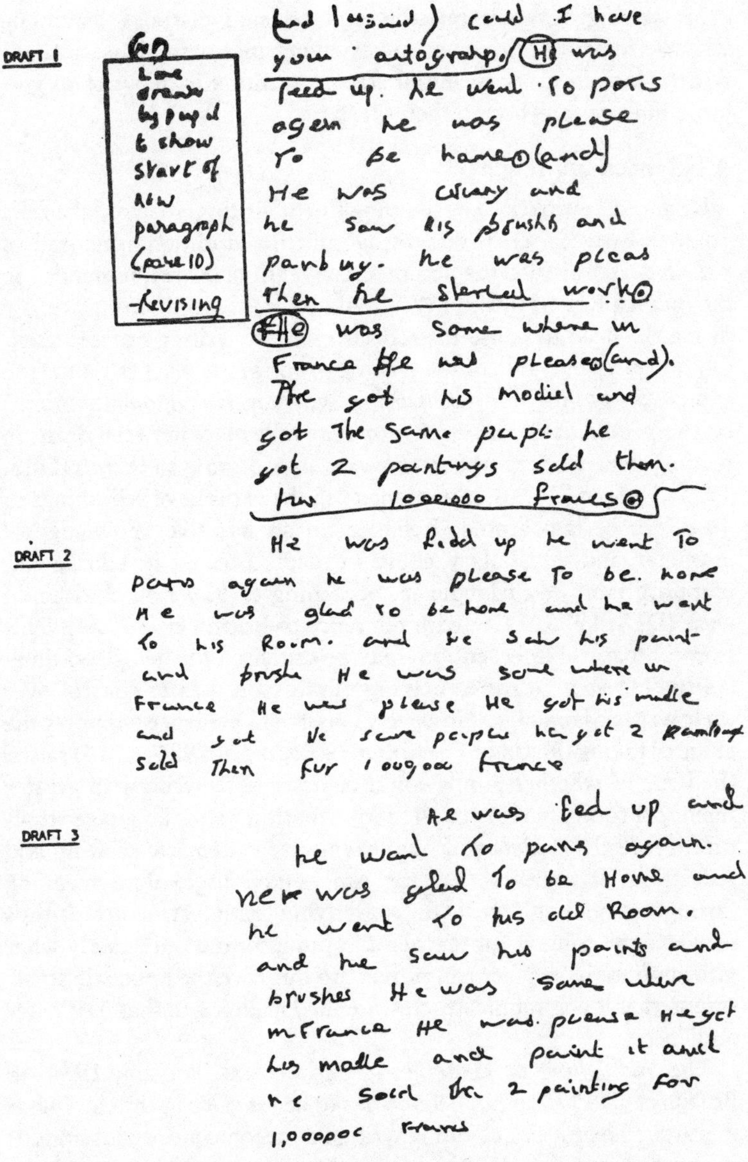
DRAFT 1

(10)
Line drawn by pupil to show start of new paragraph (para 10)
Revising

(and I asked) could I have your autograph. He was feed up. he went to paris agen he was please to be home (and) He was crazy and he saw his brushs and painting. he was pleas Then he started work. He was some where in France He was pleased (and). The got his modiel and got the same peple he got 2 paintings sold them. fur 1000,000 frances

DRAFT 2

He was fedd up he went To paris again he was please To be. home He was glad to be home and he went to his Room. and he saw his paint- and brushe He was some where in France He was please He got his modle and got the same people he got 2 painting sold Then fur 1,00,000 france

DRAFT 3

He was fed up and he went to paris again. He was glad To be Home and he went to his old Room. and he saw his paints and brushes He was some where in France He was please He got his modle and paint it and he sold the 2 painting for 1,000,000 frances

Figure 16.4 Learning to re-focus: conducting an 'internal debate' about what to say through scanning between drafts (Binns, 1978, p. 34).

FOOTNOTE: These three drafts of the ninth/tenth paragraph of a story about *'An Artist'* were written by a second year secondary pupil, asked to re-draft to complete a composition to hand in for assessment. Originally, these three drafts were laid out side by side in the classroom. Here the three drafts are shown one above the other for convenience.

See-sawing between revision and revising distracts beginning writers from the enjoyment of reviewing their experience in their written language, as an initial step to wanting to re-write to give more fluent expression to their ideas.

A balanced approach

A balanced approach to developing fluent writing, to avoid the false polarity between 'creative writing' and the traditional method of revising according to the accepted conventions, is recommended in the *Bullock Report* (DES, 1975). Balance is achieved through recognising the need to pause for reflection in the **writing process** itself. On the *'receptive'* side of the writing process, the teacher's aim is to extend *'the pupil's power as a writer'* working *'first upon intentions'*; on the *'productive'* side, discussion may take place between drafts in reading over work of the *'techniques appropriate to them'*. (DES, 1975, 11.5 and 11.10). Spontaneity in the expressive beginnings of an utterance is accepted. Reliance on an intuitive knowledge of grammar and vocabulary could be demonstrated in editing out inappropriate use of language, according to *'function'* and *'audience'* (DES, 1975, 11.6; with reference to Britton et al 1974). This form of 'natural intervention' may be criticised for being too time-consuming as a means in helping pupils gain greater control over their written language. However, classroom evidence supports the value of taking this time. The *Kingman Report* of 1986 (p. 14) raised the issue of whether pupils could be assisted to write with greater fluency through making explicit information about language structure. From the evidence of pupils who use systematic drafting and redrafting, it appears that the time taken to explore meaning through re-reading reveals the underlying textual structure. It thus provides the context for teacher and pupil to find out exactly what information the teacher can provide to improve the linguistic structure so that it communicates the intended meaning to that particular audience.

The *'indwelling of reader in writer'* is vital (Polyani, 1964, in Britton et al, 1974, p. 21). Time has to be set aside in the classroom it is argued here, for beginning writers to become more conscious of the real place of reading in the writing process. This can only be done through leading pupils to switch their behaviour in gaining a 'sense of audience' from reliance on the 'ear' for language, to an evaluative 'eye'. At the outset, beginning writers may not realise, in re-reading to review a passage, the risk in relying on an 'ear' for language or referring only to the 'context' of a possible world outside the text (Olson and Hildyard, 1983, pp. 52–53). Re-reading on the 'receptive side' of the process supports pupils, who may also be 'poor readers', in obtaining feedback; if necessary, from identifying unsure memories for words and patterns of language (Clay, 1980, p. 32).

Slowing down the writing process

Delay on the 'receptive' side of the writing process allows time for re-reading (scanning) to take place; first to retrieve meaning from the original text; second, to generate content from a fresh sense of purpose. Beard (1983, p. 91) distinguishes between *'horizontal'* scanning to gain a sense of the *'meaning of words in their setting'* and *'vertical'* scanning to get at the rhythm, symbolism and setting of words, as they combine to give a feel of unity. The issue in facilitating development of written language is how to lead beginning writers to scan flexibility between drafts; 'as artists react to their paintings or sculptures, as something **accomplished**, separate from ourselves, stepping stones to new creations.' (Smith, 1982, p. 129).

How may the visual arts contribute to progress in developing written language?

> The *'discovery in respect of writing'*, as *'in the visual arts'* *'that children could express their individual responses to experience without first acquiring techniques by deliberate practice'* is very important (DES, 1975, 11.3).

The importance of this discovery is commonly referred to in comparing the exploratory thrill of manipulating language to playing with paint to see the effect of combining colours.

During the transition to the later stage of learning to write, the importance of the contribution of the visual arts is rarely stated. The writer, like the painter, has to learn to read (scan) the trial of an effect. Pausing to gain a 'sense of audience' in painting involves the technique of scanning to and fro over a picture to get the feel of the whole effect (see below, Fig 16.5).

Teaching and learning the development of written language depends likewise on slowing down the pace of writing between drafts to allow beginner writers time to realise for themselves the value of standing back, as it were, with the purpose of re-reading – of pausing for reflection and re-focusing their impression of what to say. For example, the re-visualisation of an effect may be aided in both painting and writing. In Fig 16.5 the artist is shown working from a 'squared-off sketch'; similarly in Fig 16.4 on page 105 the writer relies on the adaptation of symbols from a Printers' and Authors' proof-reading guide to 'block-off' part of the original draft, as a guide to the text in his mind's eye.

Formative evaluation

Teacher appraisal is dependent on **close** reading to keep track of the relation and the integration of ideas in a series of drafts. For example, the three drafts in Fig 16.4 show the **flexibility** of scanning:

Draft 1 *'weary'*; Draft 2 *'he was please to be home'*; Draft 3 *'He was glad to be home and he went to his old Room'*. Persistent **mistakes** are progressively eliminated at the same time as growth takes place in meaning.

Pausing to stand back from painting to scan the trial of an effect.

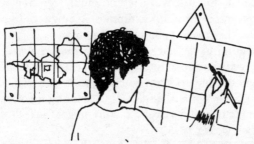

Working from a rough sketch, 'squared off' for painting a composition.

Figure 16.5   Gaining a 'sense of audience' in painting, by scanning an effect.

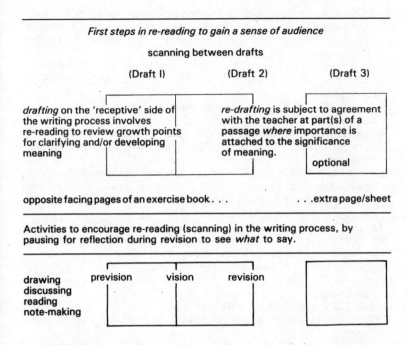

First steps in re-reading to gain a sense of audience

scanning between drafts

(Draft I)   (Draft 2)   (Draft 3)

drafting on the 'receptive' side of the writing process involves re-reading to review growth points for clarifying and/or developing meaning

re-drafting is subject to agreement with the teacher at part(s) of a passage *where* importance is attached to the significance of meaning.

optional

opposite facing pages of an exercise book. . .   . . .extra page/sheet

Activities to encourage re-reading (scanning) in the writing process, by pausing for reflection during revision to see *what* to say.

drawing discussing reading note-making

prevision   vision   revision

Reflection during revision may be helped through reading back the draft and agreement to postpone editing, proofreading and revising.

Figure 16.6   Outline of a technique for developing written language.

Contrastive evaluation between drafts follows up re-creation through writing. Difficulty / progress in developing written language may be observed in the extent to which beginning writers are able to make greater use of opportunities to return to the text and become increasingly self-reliant in reviewing their work, prior to re-writing. (Fig 16.4)

References

Beard, R. (1984) *Children's Writing in the Primary School* Hodder and Stoughton.
Binns, R. (1978) *From Speech to Writing* Centre for Information for the Teaching of English / Scottish Curriculum Development Service, Moray House College of Education, Edingburgh Centre.

Binns, R. (1980) 'A Technique for Developing Written Language' in Clark, M.M. and Glynn, T. (eds), *Reading & Writing for the Child With Difficulties* Education Review, Occasional Publication No. 8., Faculty of Education, The University of Birmingham.

Binns, R. assisted by Liddle, I. (1984) 'Some Issues in the Teaching of Spelling' in Dennis, E. (ed) *Reading: Meeting Children's Special Needs* Heinemann.

Britton, J. et al. (1975) *The Development of Writing Abilities 11-18* Macmillan.

Chapman, J. (1983) *Reading Development and Cohesion* Heinemann.

Clay, M.M. (1979) *What Did I Write? Beginning Writing Behaviour* Heinemann.

Clay, M.M. (1980) 'Early Writing and Reading: Reciprocal Gains.' in Clark, M.M. and Glynn, T. (eds), *Reading & Writing for the Child with Difficulties* Education Review, Occasional Publication No. 8., Faculty of Education, The University of Birmingham.

DES, (1975) *A Language for Life* (The Bullock Report) HMSO.

DES, (1988) *The Report of the Committee of Inquiry into the Teaching of English Language* (The Kingman Report) HMSO.

Donaldson, M. (1978) *Children's Minds* Fontana.

Graves, D.H. (1983) *Writing – Teachers and Children at Work* Heinemann.

Greber, J.W.P. (1972) *Lost for Words* Penguin.

HMSO, (1921) *The Teaching of English in England* (The Newbolt Report.).

Hourd, M.L. & Cooper G. (1959) *Coming into their Own* Heinemann.

Hunter, C.M. (1984) 'Meeting Teachers' Special Needs Through Collaboration Research in Dennis, D. (ed) *Reading: Meeting Special Needs*.

Murray, D.M. (1978) 'Internal Revision' in Cooper, C.R. & Odell, L. (eds) *Research on Composing – Points of Departure* NCTE.

Olson, D. & Hildyard, A. (1983) 'Writing and Literal Meaning.' in Martlew, M. (ed) *The Psychology of Written Language – Developmental Educational Perspectives*, Wiley.

Perera, K. (1984) *Children's Writing and Reading: Analysing Classroom Language* Blackwell in association with Deutsch.

Peters, M. (1975) *Diagnostic and Remedial Spelling Manual* Macmillan.

Smith, R. (1982) *Writing and the Writer* Heinemann.

Welch, J. Ashton, A., Thornton, G., (1978) *Helping Pupils to Write Better* ILEA Learning Materials Service.

Acknowledgements

For their helpful discussion: Dr L.J. Chapman (Open University); Dr. A. Davies (Edinburgh University); Mrs. M. Hunter-Carsch (University of Leicester); Ms. M. Miles (Henley County Primary School, Suffolk); Ms. B. Smith (Steward's Comprehensive School, Harlow, Essex).

17 'The quest for Dr. Violet Krystle': from adventure game to writing adventure

Vivienne Cato and John Trushell

In 1982, the Assessment of Performance Unit (APU) Primary Survey contrasted pupils' passive role in a conventional teacher-directed situation with their active role when participating in discussion and collaboration. The APU, citing Barnes (1976), noted that discussion and collaboration by small groups of pupils could:

> elicit from pupils a higher-order level of hypothesizing and critical reasoning than they typically display in more standard teacher-to-class lessons.
>
> (APU Primary Survey, 1982)

Barnes (op cit), although not recommending group work per se, emphasised that unsupervised small group activities provide a forum for speaking, contending that:

> The more a learner controls his own language strategies, and the more he is enabled to think aloud, the more he can take responsibility for formulating explanatory hypotheses and evaluating them.
>
> (Barnes, op cit)

However, Barnes (op cit) conceded that 'it is not easy to make this possible in a typical lesson': the conventional teacher-directed classroom may not lend itself to small group activities involving discussion and collaboration, and may constrain pupils' development in speaking, reading and writing. The review of APU Language Monitoring 1970–83 reported that pupils performed less well when required to extract relevant information from read texts and express this information in different written forms: however, the APU pointed out that pupils were 'rarely set the task of developing and practising these skills on their own initiative or in collaboration with others.' (APU, 1988).

Introduction

Advocates of microcomputer adventure games, or micro-quests, claim that these programs provide opportunities for unsupervised small group activities, involving discussion and collaboration. Chandler (1984) stated that such programs have 'potential to focus discussion on a shared experience without intervening and controlling the shape of the discussion as teachers almost invariably do' Harrison (1987) observed that these programs 'required a great deal of discussion, hypothesis generating and hypothesis testing'.

A Micro-Quest with word processing facilities

The study reported here concerns a micro-quest with word-processing facilities conducted by 33 12-year-old pupils, arranged in collaborative groups of three, who then composed an account of that quest.

Organisation

The study was conducted as a co-operative venture between the researchers and the teacher of a middle school in Slough. The teacher and the pupils participating in the study had only limited experience of questing and word processing. The school acquired the adventure game *Dinosaur Discovery* (4Mation, 1986) and the NFER provided a word processing program, *Wordwise Plus* (Computer Concepts, 1984).

During Autumn Term 1986, the participating fourth year pupils were released in collaborative groups of three, selected by their class teachers. Seven collaborative groups (21 pupils: 12 boys and nine girls) were selected for particular observation.

The project consisted of two phases: a quest phase and a composition phase. During the quest phase, pupils completed the adventure game in four to five sessions. Further sessions were timetabled for complementary classwork, one for reading preparatory to the quest and others for recording the quest in a journal. Copies were taken of every pupil's journal. During the composition phase pupils word processed an account of their quest over four sessions. Print-outs of each draft were retained by pupils, teachers and researchers.

The two phases are described in detail below.

Quest phase

Previous observations of microcomputer activities in primary schools (Potter and Walker, 1984; Johnson, 1984) have recommended groups of four pupils as the optimum size for microcomputer activities. However, in this study each group comprised only three pupils, in order to:

- facilitate equable access to the microcomputer keyboard for each pupil;
- prevent the groups splitting into equal factions;
- conform to the size of each group for word processing (Broderick and Trushell, 1984; Trushell, 1986).

The goal of *Dinosaur Discovery* is to locate and incubate a brontosaurus egg. The quest is in three stages (see Fig 17.1) which provide passages to be read for information.

Stage One consists of a short booklet, 'A diary of my exploration of the mines of the Stegosaurus Straits Region'. This is a facsimile of a legibly 'hand-written' journal containing first-person narrative entries, a 'Tide Table for Stegosaurus Straits' and a sketch diagram. From reading the booklet, pupils may infer the goal of the quest and deduce the locations of certain 'articles' and information by which the quest may be resolved.

Stage Two, the first sequence of the program, requires pupils to investigate the coastal region of 'Stegosaurus Straits', a circuit of locations and obstacles to which pupils may gain access:

- by utilising the appropriate given article, eg a torch for a subterranean location or obstacle; and
- by navigating a route, eg a path through a maze, *or*
- by completing a code, eg an alphabetical sequence.

Each location provides *found articles* or specific information to be collected for the third stage of the quest. Such articles may be either necessary or merely helpful for the successful competition of the quest.

Stage Three, the second sequence of the program, requires pupils to have selected the particular *given* and *found articles* and the specific information necessary to:

- navigate across the final obstacle, 'Stegosaurus Straits';
- complete a code for access to the final location, the laboratory;
- program the incubator to hatch a brontosaurus.

Stage One

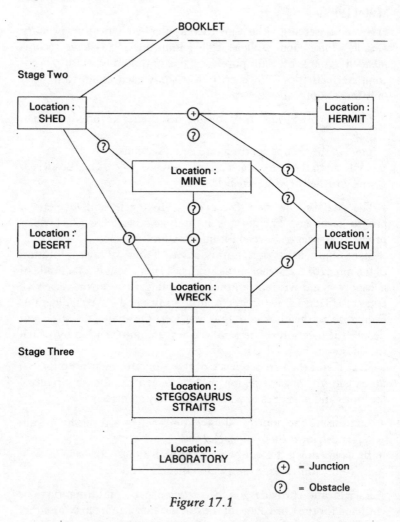

Figure 17.1

The caption in Excerpt 1 features the utilitarian language for which 'interactive' microcomputer programs, such as adventure games, have been criticised.

Excerpt 1

> *You are outside the shed.*
> *Which way do you want to go?*
> *East, South, West, into the shed.*
> *Which?*

The function of the captions as cues for specific actions or locations places language under constraints. However, within the screen-windows displayed at location, language is not so restricted: As Harrison remarks, the 'reward for reaching certain locations . . . is a lengthy purple patch worthy of a travel agent's brochure' (op cit).

Dinosaur Discovery features several locations which display screen-windows of text for pupils to read. The Museum, for example, features a catalogue (see Fig 17.2) from which readers may select six titles.

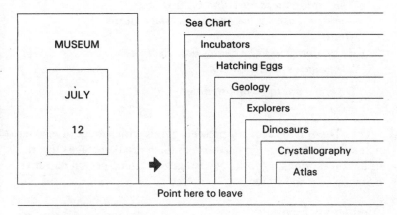

In the museum there is a library.

The Librarian shows you a catalogue of useful books.

Use the grey arrow to choose a book to read, or to leave the museum.

Figure 17.2

Each title calls up a short expository passage which must be read for information germane to the quest, eg 'Incubators' (see Excerpt 2).

Excerpt 2

> *The hatching of ancient eggs needs a special machine to check on the temperature and conditions for hatching the young.*
> *Brontosaurus eggs need to be kept at 28 degrees Celsius.*
> *They also need violet crystals to ensure incubation.*
> *Press Space Bar to continue.*

By contrast, the screen-window at the 'Hermit' location displays a third-person narrative in instalments. Captions cue or curtail the instalments, permitting only limited 'interaction' with the text (see Excerpt 3).

Excerpt 3

<u>You are talking to the Hermit.</u>

The hermit says he used to know an old explorer.
The explorer was hurt after his boat was wrecked, crossing the dangerous 'Stegosaurus Straits'.
The hermit thinks he knows how to cross 'Stegosaurus Straits' safely.

Do you want to go on listening?
Yes or no. Which?

Thus 'Dinosaur Discovery' presents pupils with a range of reading materials: the first-person narrative of the journal in Stage One; the utilitarian captions, expository passages and third-person narrative in Stages Two and Three.

Conducting the quest

Dinosaur Discovery also presents pupils with problems which may be resolved by utilising their 'action knowledge' and / or their 'school knowledge' (Barnes, op cit). 'Action knowledge', for example, would enable pupils to select the appropriate *article* to negotiate obstacles; such as choosing a torch, not a compass, to traverse a tunnel or explore a mine. 'School knowledge', arguably, would allow pupils to manipulate language and number: such as re-ordering words alphabetically (to descend or ascend a cliff) or deci-phering alpha-numeric codes (to cross a forest). The solution of these problems would also involve pupils being or becoming familiar with the conventions of adventure programs: in fact, acquiring a certain *genre knowledge*.

Genre knowledge requires that pupils, while conducting the quest, suspend disbelief at the improbability which is the common factor of adventure programs: for example, a rescue from quicksand that requires the solution of a Hangman problem. Accomplished questors are accustomed to the 'Alice in Wonderland' logic that pervades adventure programs: a logic which requires that questors retain *given* and *found articles* irrespective of their apparent use-lessness and that they discern the informational value of apparent whimsy embedded in nonsense.

The explorer's journal provides material from which pupils may infer the goal of the quest. Observations revealed that two of the eleven groups failed to infer that goal: instead, these groups attempted to accumulate *found articles*, eggs and crystals. Doing so incurred penalties: accumulating eggs caused breakages while accumulating different types of crystals caused an explosion, as stated in the journal.

Only three of the seven observed groups inferred the goal of the quest and deduced a route for Stage Two, via the Tunnel and past the Mine, to the Museum. These pupils selected from the Museum catalogue those titles which were obviously relevant to the goal inferred from the journal, such as 'Crystallography' and Hatching Eggs'. These groups also selected titles seemingly less relevant to the quest: in particular 'Incubator' which provides information on crystals and eggs, or 'Sea Charts', which provides information vital for crossing 'Stegosaurus Straits' in Stage Three.

Groups which had not selected 'Incubator' from the catalogue at the Museum collected the wrong colour crystal from the Mine. Groups which had not read the journal carefully and/or not selected 'Sea Charts' could not appreciate the hazards in setting sail against the tide across 'Stegosaurus Straits': five of the seven observed groups attempted the voyage and were penalised by shipwreck (see Journal Extract 1).

The high proportion of observed groups incurring such penalties, particularly shipwreck, would indicate that pupils had failed to infer these hazards from their reading of the explorer's journal and/or the selection of titles from the catalogue at the Museum. However, the conduct of the quests became less haphazard throughout Stage Two: groups returned to locations to collect the complement of articles and information (see Journal Extract 2).

Journal Extract 1

> . . . *we decided to go to Dinosaur Island. We chose a time to leave, that was when the computer told us that unless we left at high tide we would run into strong currents and hidden rocks. We set off hoping we'd picked the right time. But as soon as we set off we crashed into a rock. Next time we will find out what time high tide is.*

Journal Extract 2

We went to the museum, it said the yellow egg had to be heated at 30 degrees. The date was the 23rd July, the high tide was at 9.52 and 10.17 . . . We went to the mine . . . We took the torch and got a green crystal.

The effect of each inferred or incurred penalty upon the pupils of the observed groups had been to focus discussion and stimulate collaboration (see Journal Extract 3).

Journal Extract 3

Inside the museum we read the book about Sea Charts. It said we should leave one hour before high tide. We also checked the date to see exactly when to leave, we weren't taking any chances after what happened last time.

We went back to the swamp and I led the way through quite successfully. We went back to the wreck, checked all our information thoroughly and prepared to set off for the island.

Michael our sea captain led us through the rocks and tides to safety. Having left at 6.03am it was a perfect voyage.

Approaches employed by pupils involved in small group work have been defined by Barnes (op. cit) as 'closed' or 'open': 'closed' approaches were 'confined to labelling processes' by assertion while 'open' approaches involved analysing processes by collaborative discussion. Pupils participating in this study were deterred from 'closed' approaches by penalties incurred while collecting and selecting *found articles* and information during Stage Two: for example, the hazardous accumulation of *found articles* occurred when the quest was being directed by the assertions of individuals rather than the collaboration of pupils. The increased incidence of collaborative discussion prevented pupils incorrectly selecting *found articles* for Stage Three, when the insertion of a wrong crystal into the incubator would have caused an explosion and the incubation of the wrong egg would have hatched a parrot. The success of the observed groups in completing the quest without incurring these penalties was determined by the pupil development of 'open' approaches involving discussion. Pupils' reading strategies were also affected by their development of 'open' approaches: pupils collaborating openly tended to read aloud to facilitate the selection and organisation of relevant information.

Pupils co-operated in the conduct of the quest: within each group the tasks of keyboarding and note-taking spontaneously devolved to two pupils while the third normally initiated the community.

Composition phase

In plenary session, pupils were set an assignment to word process an account of their quest which would accompany a display of thematically related classwork. They were able to anticipate a familiar or known audience in the parents and younger pupils who were to view the display.

Pupils were discouraged from word-processing 'fair copies' of their journals, which often reported the group's route and listed information and articles, *given* and *found*. 'Fair copy' of such material would have produced the *documentary* writing which Eyre and Marlowe (1984) noted that adventure games elicit. Only one group composed a *documentary* account: it is effectively a recollection of entries from their journals (see Assignment Extract 1).

Assignment Extract 1

We then went to the tunnel and bumped 39 times and it took us 142 seconds. Then we went to the mine and we found an egg and crystal, then we went to the snakes, the answers were 'eggs', 'shaft' and 'crystals'. Then we went to the museum.

Stripped of metaphor, this text gives equal weight to each event, whether central or incidental to the main purpose of the quest (eg 'We . . . bumped 39 times'). The syntax of listing by simple conjunctions (ie 'Then . . . then . . .') reinforces this tendency. These *documentary* writers failed to complete a procedure of the writing process: to select events perceived as significant and then to organise them into a coherent account.

Researchers had inferred, from comments during the plenary discussion, that certain events which occurred in the program were inconsistent with pupils' expectations of the real world. For example, hostile adders would not normally demand the solution of anagrams. A few pupils omitted any reference to such inconsistencies, but most slelected such events for organisation within their accounts. Some pupils did not attempt to reduce the obtrusiveness of these inconsistencies within a realistic account – thus, 'I . . . came to some snakes, to get past them I had to solve three anagrams, and they were, down, torch and crystal' – but others attempted to reduce obtrusion by devising a *deus ex machina* character (see Assignment Extracts 2 and 3).

Assignment Extract 2

Suddenly, out of nowhere three snakes appeared. We tried to get past them, but an old hag appeared and said, 'Ye, children 'ave to solve these 3 anagrams, before thou can get past' then she cackled and disappeared. We soon solved the anagrams and found ourselves outside a museum.

Assignment Extract 3

I wanted to explore this strange land so I decided to go west of the shed. Then I came to a crossroads. I wanted to go west again so I did. Unluckily I began to sink in some quicksand. A little man came up to me and said 'If you can answer this word puzzle I will rescue you.' I answered the word puzzle and got out of the quicksand. I decided to go back to the crossroads.

The little man may derive from the screen-window graphic which depicts a pin-person – intended to represent the questor – who sinks by degrees into the quicksand. By constrast, the hag indeed appears from nowhere, having no relation to the program beyond, perhaps, a family connection with the Hermit.

The introduction of *deus ex machina* characters provided literary contexts which could accommodate inconsistencies. One group provided a sustained literary context: their account retained the format of the diary of the explorer, personified as 'Dr Violet Krystle', and alluded to 'her' quest (see Assignment Extracts 4). These literary devices supplemented the chronological organisation of the pupils' accounts.

Assignment Extract 4

October 20th
We'd just moved into an old house miles away from anywhere, apart from an abandoned railway track. We started to explore our new garden, and we found an old-looking shed. Wandering inside, we found an old dusty book, which, on the cover read, 'Mines in the "Stegosaurus Straits" Region.'

> *It was about a famous explorer named, 'Dr Violet Krystle' and on the first page it talked about a shed, in the garden of a house, named, 'Bayhouse.' Then we realised that it was our house!*

The events selected and organised within pupils' accounts were generally appropriate content for an anticipated audience with no prior knowledge of *Dinosaur Discovery*. The appropriate tone in which accounts of the quests should be written also had been discussed in plenary. Critical of the utilitarian tone of episodes in the program and of reports in their journals (see Journal Extracts 1, 2 and 3), pupils had intended that the accounts of their quests should be dramatic narratives (see Assignment Extracts 5 & 6).

Assignment Extract 5

> *We entered the musty, smelling wreck and using the keys we opened the chest revealing a sea chart. We took the chart and left the wreck heading for the straits. We arrived at a small bay in which a boat was tied up. We rested in the boat until 6.03pm, for this was the time we had to leave for the Island. Michael was our navigator and led us through the rocks and currents safely.*

Assignment Extract 6

> *We set off on the quest which the other scientist failed to do. So we ventured out into the wilderness. First we went east towards the desert, so Sunita and Kelly ran towards the mountains while Matthew was daydreaming back at the shed.*
>
> *He dawdled westward and met the hermit who had not had a bath since 2000 BC, He talked about the scientist he once worked with.*
>
> *Meanwhile Sunita and Kelly were trying to climb a mountain. We came to a steep ledge and Kelly tried to. act so great by climbing it, but she slipped 20 feet down and broke her arm. Sunita climbed back down and ran to find Matthew. Matthew soon came back with Sunita and made a sling out of his scarf. So we carried on with the journey, towards the eastern side of the desert.*

Pupils' accounts of their quests were collaboratively composed directly at the keyboard. Although pupils were provided with print-outs of each draft of their accounts, revision between drafts was minimal. The low incidence of revision may be attributable to the planning required prior to each session to ensure that the pupils completed their accounts for the scheduled display.

Summary

Current quest programs can elicit open-learning strategies. Indeed, the success of pupils in this study, conducting the quest in groups without intervention by teacher or researcher, was determined by the development of such 'open' strategies, involving collaborative discussion and reading. However, the substance of current quests seems to be flawed by the conventions of the genre. Future quests could be enhanced by author/programmers operating not an 'Alice in Wonderland' but a 'real world' logic, where tasks are accomplished by the utilisation of appropriate skills.

The pupils' word processed accounts of their quests, with one *documentary* exception, were chronological narratives which incorporated literary devices to reconcile inconsistencies in material. The low incidence of documentary may be attributable to pupils composing accounts appropriate to a real purpose – to accompany a display – and for a real audience.

References

Barnes, D. (1976) *From Communication to Curriculum* Penguin.
Broderick, C. & Trushell, J. (1985) 'Word Processing In The Primary School' in Reading and the new Technologies J. Ewing (ed) Heinemann.
Eyre, R. & Marlow S. (1984) 'Crystal' in *Micro-explorations 1* Potter, F & Wray, D. (ed), UKRA.
Gorman, T., White, J., Brooks, G., Maclure, M. & Kispal, A. (1979–83) Language Performance in Schools: Review of APU Language Monitoring HMSO.
Gorman, T., White J., Hargreaves, M., Maclure, M. & Tate, A. (1982) Language Performance in Schools: 1982 Primary Survey Report HMSO.
Harrison, C. (1987) 'Reading And The Microcomputer: More Answers Than Questions' in *Micro-Explorations 3*. Smith, B. (ed) UKRA.
Johnson, B. (1984) 'Spacex: Using The Adventure Game In the Secondary Classroom' in *Micro-Explorations 1*. Potter, F. & Wray, D. (eds), UKRA.
Potter, F. & Walker, S. (1984) 'Using Language Programs With Groups' in *Micro-Explorations 1*. Potter, F. & Wray, D. (eds), UKRA.

Trushell, J. (in preparation) 'Llanfairpwyllgwyngyllgogerychwywndrob-wllllantsilogoch Re-Drafted' in *The Moving Cursor: A Word Processor in the Language Classroom* Trushell, J. (ed).

Acknowledgements

The authors wish to express their gratitude to the teachers and pupils of St. Ethelbert's Middle School, Slough, and to their 'questing' colleagues at the Centre for Research in Language and Communication (CRLC) at the NFER.

18 Learning to read: A study undertaken by the Leicestershire Literacy Support Service 1986–7

Muriel Bridge

How DO children become readers? Are there optimum conditions for learning to read? Why do some children turn into competent, life-long readers while others do not?

These key questions have long vexed educators. Between 1985 and 1988 the Leicestershire Literacy Support Service (LLSS) undertook a Literacy Initiative. As part of the initiative (known locally as 'LITINIT') an evaluation project was planned. It was hoped that observations of developing reading behaviours in two populations of five-year-old pupils would make a small contribution towards answering the opening questions.

Introduction

It was decided that one population of five-year-olds would be taught to read using a *Traditional* method (ie employing reading schemes, flash cards and phonic skills). The other population would experience a *Story Approach* (ie using unstructured 'real' books chosen by the pupils in 'whole-language,' shared reading situations). Parental understanding and co-operation would be an important feature.

The evaluation project – *Learning to read* – followed county-wide dissemination and discussion of current literacy theory and practice, viewed on a world scale.

The formulation of Story Approach by the LLSS was a combination of a base of many years experience with older, failing readers ('remedial') plus an 'acid' awareness of new internationally-canvassed rationales. Writers such as the Goodmans, Frank Smith, Marie Clay, Dorothy Butler, Don Holdaway and Margaret Meek inter alia, stimulated questioning reactions. In the case of the LLSS, the catalyst for action was the changed brief of the Service from 'remedial' to 'literacy support' – a broader role. Since Story Approach had proved successful with hard-core, learning-resistant older pupils, might it not be appropriate for five-year-olds? Might it perhaps pre-empt some of the effects of failure associated with the small but inevitable number of problem readers?

Following a series of seminars attended by 93 per cent of the LEA's primary school Headteachers, 56 schools volunteered to take part in the evaluation project. From that number, 12 pilot and 12 control schools were randomly selected.

During the academic year 1986–7, all project schools received equal support from an LLSS Area Head, each supervising three pilot and three control schools. They documented their visits in 'log' form. The team of 12 LLSS teachers was trained in strictly impartial assessment procedures, each being responsible for one pilot and one control school. 14 pupils were randomly selected from each school (336 pupils).

During the year it became apparent that some schools were deviating from their briefs. In the case of controls, some were actively exploring and even adopting elements of Story Approach. Some acquired Story Approach books, which was hardly surprising given the pressure from publishers caught up in a national Story Approach 'snowball'. Some encouraged parental support along Story Approach lines or asked for information or INSET. In the case of pilots, some schools did not implement the approach in full. One school lost its inducted reception teacher soon after the start of the project and her several replacements had had no previous knowledge of Story Approach. Consequently, for the project to retain integrity it was regretfully decided that the sample would need to consist of 'Pure' schools only. Data from all schools is retained at Collegiate House, Leicester, but only seven schools, with 87 pupils, met the stringent purity demands.

Results

Results from this population were obtained from three sources:

1 Area Heads' logs of their school visits.
2 Class teacher interviews based on a questionnaire.
3 Pupils' assessment interviews.

Two book-focused sessions were recorded with each pupil in September 1986 and May 1987. Attitude, book awareness and reading behaviours were assessed and a standardised Reading Test was administered.

- Attitude was assessed by 'like / don't like' responses to pictures of 'funny faces' questions and general impressions throughout

| | PILOT SCHOOLS | | | | | CONTROL SCHOOLS | | | | | |
| | PRE-TEST | | POST-TEST | | GAIN | PRE-TEST | | POST-TEST | | GAIN | Significance |
	Mean	S.D.	Mean	S.D.	Mean	Mean	S.D.	Mean	S.D.	Mean	
Attitude	4.92	1.09	5.31	1.01	0.39	4.31	1.31	4.58	1.13	0.27	none
Book handling	5.41	1.15	5.92	0.39	0.51	5.17	1.30	5.89	0.46	0.72	"
Basic terms	8.47	3.74	13.98	5.01	5.51	6.69	3.16	12.75	4.27	6.06	"
Voice-print	1.02	0.62	1.63	0.60	0.61	0.72	0.57	1.64	0.68	0.92	"
Shared book A	3.45	2.03	3.94	2.09	0.49	1.94	1.55	3.22	1.62	1.28	"
Shared book B	13.73	4.75	9.84	6.55	-3.89	12.11	3.88	6.78	4.59	-5.33	"
Shared book C	30.02	21.57	38.88	27.02	8.86	25.67	12.46	33.89	19.99	8.22	"
Shared book TOTAL	47.20	26.33	52.49	33.66	5.29	39.72	15.70	43.89	23.50	4.17	"
Reading behaviour	66.98	29.80	78.82	38.42	11.84	56.61	18.10	68.75	27.75	12.14	"
BURT n/o words	2.98	6.30	13.00	14.27	10.02	0.72	1.88	12.36	9.34	11.64	"
BURT: R.A. (mths)	61.71	5.77	70.88	13.03	9.17	59.67	1.69	70.50	8.54	10.83	"

Figure 18.1

eight days of observation.

- Book-Awareness (book handling skills and knowledge of basic terms) was assessed using a nursery rhyme book and a 'reading' book.
- Reading Behaviours were assessed by sharing a story book, noted: response to 'story' through priming discussion of title, cover and internal pictures; response to pauses in teacher-read text (cue-sampling); independent reading of final 38 words.

No significant differences between the two groups were apparent for reading age gains measured on the Burt G. W. R. Test (1972 norms) or for reading behaviour gains when assessed quantitatively, as the table shows (Fig 18.1).

However, a number of important differences in the quality of pupils' learning were observed, as follows:

Control schools

- The continuation of existing reading methods ensured stability and teacher equanimity.
- Pupils' progress satisfied normal expectations.
- The degree of home-school liaison was similar to that of previous years.
- Pupils' attitudes to learning to read were usually positive, but those pupils who made the least gains lost their positive attitude to reading and their confidence in themselves as readers at an early age.
- *Traditional* methods seemed to offer a more limited range of pupil-teacher interactions than did a *Story Approach*.
- *Traditional* methods demanded less exploration by the teacher of the reading process than did a *Story Approach*.
- Pupils' progress was generally fairly even and steady throughout the year.
- Parents had confidence in a familiar, school-based method where progress was measurable by clearly-labelled graded books.

However,

- Some parents were using a *Story Approach* at home.
- Some schools showed an increasing interest in and practice of *Story Approach* elements.

Pilot schools

- *Story Approach* engendered teacher innovation and development of insight into the reading process.
- Pupils chose to read and re-read more books, more often, with a greater depth of involvement in the story.
- *Story Approach* fostered an improvement in both the quantity and quality of home-school liaison.
- All pupils, including the weakest, evinced enthusiasm for learning to read and for books and stories.
- Pupils gained an earlier understanding of the purposes of reading and a broader understanding of the processes involved.
- All pupils showed confidence in themselves as readers, even the 'slow starters'.
- Pupils showed increasing critical awareness of books, authors and illustrators.
- Story Approach appeared to encourage generalised progress across a broad front including: language use (especially the oracy of pupils from deprived backgrounds); social aspects (more frequent and more positive book-mediated contacts were made between pupils and their teachers and between pupils and their parents); reading aloud (which tended to be expressive from the beginning); curriculum participation. (Pupils tended to take a fuller and more confident part in other areas of the curriculum; in particular, the content of spoken and written language was enhanced by an awareness of a range of linguistic registers and styles, together with sharpened observation skills.)

However,

- Teachers experienced the stresses entailed in piloting a different approach (extra record-keeping, pupils' demands to share books, their own uncertainties, and those of some parents, in the early stages).
- Pupils were slower to establish a sight vocabulary, often seeming to be at a standstill until a sudden 'breakthrough' point was reached, after which progress accelerated.

Discussion

The findings of the study suggest that the main difference in learning to read between pupils using a traditional method and a story approach is one of quality and variety of experience and expectation. Both seem to be equally fast – or slow – in the early stages, but story approach learning appears to be more broadly based.

To return to the opening questions – most children would appear to learn to read whether the method of teaching is traditional or by a story approach. However, are optimum conditions for creating life-long readers more likely to be those where pupils begin by under-standing the purposes and pleasures of reading, and where pupils voluntarily initiate many interactions with texts at many levels of meaning and in a variety of social contexts? Clearly, further studies and longer observations are needed for any definitive answers. But this present study would seem to hint at such possibilities.

Notes

1 Of the two populations, the Pilots felt disadvantaged by uncertainties. All those involved – the LLSS, class teachers and parents – were in a learning situation. All were refining their understanding and practice week by week and none were free from doubts. Such stress may be said to have more than counterbalanced the expected Hawthorn effect of teacher enthusiasm.

2 It should also be observed that the study was a model of inexpensive co-operative research. Advice on the research model was freely given by Glenys Jones and Mike Burton of Nottingham University. Richard Laycock, a computer specialist and husband of an LLSS teacher, wrote the computer program. Students of the Wyggeston Collegiate 6th Form College made a statistical analysis of the data as part of their A-level studies under the supervision of Gwen Royle.

3 'ONCE UPON A TIME'. . . A Story Approach to Learning to Read – a 60-page handbook for parents and teachers written by Muriel Bridge for 'LITINIT' – became so popular that three reprints were needed. LLSS were surprised and gratified by unsolicited requests for almost 1000 copies from many parts of the country and abroad, demonstrating the effectiveness of a 'teachers' grapevine'!

The results of the second year of the study, which involved the use of refined techniques for assessment, further endorse the findings of the first part of the study.

References

Arnold, H. (1982) *Listening to Children Reading* Hodder & Stoughton.

Bennett, J. (1985) *Learning to Read With Picture Books* Thimble Press.

Bettelheim, B & Zelan, K. (1982) *On Learning to Read: The Child's Fasci-nation With Meaning* Thames & Hudson.

Butler, D. (1987) *Cushla and Her Books* Penguin.

Butler, D. (1980) *Babies Need Books* Penguin.

Butler, D. (1986) *Five to Eight* Bodley Head.
Clark, M. (1976) *Young Fluent Readers* Heinemann.
Clay, M. (1979) *Reading: The Patterning of Complex Behaviour* (2nd ed) Heinemann.
Davies, P. & Williams, P. (1974) *Aspects of Early Reading Growth A Longitudinal Study*. Blackwell.
Donaldson, M. (1978) *Children's Minds* Fontana.
Francis, H. (1977) *Language in Teaching and Learning* Unwin.
Gollasch, F. (Ed.) (1982) *Language & Literacy: The Collected Writings of Kenneth S. Goodman*. Vol. 1,2. Routledge and Kegan Paul.
Goodman, K. (1967) 'Reading: A Psycholinguistic Guessing Game' in *Journal of the Reading Specialist*.
Goodman, K. (1987) *What's Whole in Whole Language* Scholastic.
Heeks, P. (1982) *Ways of Knowing* Thimble Press.
Holdaway, D. (1979) *The Foundations of Literacy* Scholastic.
Kennedy, A. (1984) *The Psychology of Reading* Methuen.
McKenzie, M. (1979) *Learning to Read and Reading* ILEA.
Meek, M. (1982) *Learning to Read* Bodley Head.
Meek, M. (1988) *How Texts Teach What Readers Learn* Thimble Press.
Smith, F. (1985) *Reading* (2nd ed) Cambridge University Press.
Smith, F. (1982) *Understanding Reading* (3rd ed) Holt, Rinehart & Winston.
Southgate, V. et al. (1981) *Extending Beginning Reading* Heinemann.
Tizard, B. & Hughes, M. (1982) *Young Children Learning* Fontana.
Wade, B. (1984) *Story at Home and School* University of Birmingham.
Wade, B. (1987) *Talking to Some Purpose* University of Birmingham.
Waterland, L. (1985) *Read With Me* Thimble Press.
Wells, G. (1981) *Learning Through Interaction* Cambridge University Press.
Wells, G. (1987) *The Meaning Makers* Hodder & Stoughton.
Warlow, A. & Meek, M. (Eds.) *The Cool Web* Bodley Head.

19 Factors affecting reading comprehension in primary pupils

Morag MacMartin

Teachers frequently complain that children who appear to read competently, often do not seem to have understood what they have been reading about. This has important implications for learning from text in secondary school and later.

When investigating this in the course of my work as a Learning Support Teacher, I found that misunderstandings were much more widely spread than realised, and that they cross age and ability groups. They are not, in general, caused by difficulty with vocabulary or textual structure, and often fail to appear in classwork because pupils develop strategies of surface reading by which they can often locate the required answer to a question in an exercise.

Relevant literature

In reading round the subject, I found, amongst others, these reports of research. They are especially relevant to the problem described above.

Adele Abrahamson (1975) in research with undergraduates in California, suggests that subjects

> *pick a very few salient elements and use whatever language is handy to express them, with little concern for what else is dragged in or excluded by the choice.*

Stein and Glenn, discussing comprehension in elementary school children in 1979, write that

> *Substitution of more probable events may help the processor to maintain the structure and semantic cohesiveness of the story.*

Sanford and Garrod (1981) discussing Bartlett's research, noted that

> *systematic distortions crept in which fitted the story, the subjects sometimes invented plausible stories around details, and there was adherence to stereotyped situations.*

Diane Schallert (1982) writing about Craik and Lockhart's Depth of Processing Theory, says

> *the model predicts that subjects' performance on memory tasks will preserve real-world information at the expense of linguistic information.*

In a study of fifth and seventh graders, Brown and Day (1983) describe a 'copy-delete' strategy employed in summarization tasks. Pupils

i)   read text sequentially,
ii) decide on inclusion or deletion,
iii) copy the sentence more or less verbatim.

Marjorie Siegal of the University of Utah (1983) in research in a fourth grade classroom over a period of seven months, writes

> *Asking students to draw their interpretations of stories and arti-cles, admitted the possibility that some meanings would be com-municated, that would not be made public if language were the sole sign system used. In order to draw what they thought the article was trying to teach them, students had to reflect on what they had read and draw what the experience brought to mind. Recall and summarisation tasks, on the other hand, direct the reader to record the way the discourse has been represented in memory. Findings suggested that the children's interpretations were influenced by their embedded theories of the social situa-tion, their skill as artists, and the nature of the activity of sketching as 'work'. 'Work', was something assigned and graded by the teacher.*

Research studies

In early education children often draw pictures and the teachers write the children's story captions until they can do it for themselves. The words follow the picture which has been generated by the pupil. Beyond the infant class, illustrations related to text tend to dis-appear except in unit studies of novels or project work, when the situations are usually thoroughly discussed before the drawings are produced.

In pilot studies and the main study for this research, I collected material from about 250 pupils aged 8–11 years, in both rural and urban schools. The texts used were extracts from children's literature and the recall tasks were half pictorial and half written. I reversed the infant school practice of 'draw and write', to 'read and write or draw' to show what the text is about. That choice was made by me and not by the pupils.

Results

From the 1000 or so protocols, certain types of error began to appear. Casting the net wide, I listed ten categories and distributed definitions of these, together with lists of the errors found, to primary and secondary teachers to assess the extent of their agreement over classification of errors into categories.

From this first validation trial, it appeared that errors fell into child-generated and text-generated types. Although some categories tended to overlap and others were so wide as to merit sub-division, the overall level of agreement suggested that some categories could be identified. The agreement level was higher for text-generated errors.

As it had become obvious that similar misunderstandings occurred whether the text was retained or not, the main study involved both situations. Protocols from 80 children aged 8-11, were set aside for later study. The pupils who produced them were slightly above or slightly below average in reading ability as tested by the Primary Reading Test. A new set of categories, modified in the light of the first trial, was prepared together with a new set of 'errors', collected from the non-target pupils in the classes used. All pupils in the selected classes took part in the study so that pupils could not know whose work would be used.

The new material and definitions were distributed to the teachers in a wider geographical area, for validation. Over four broad categories the level of agreement between teachers reached 71.6 per cent and agreement with my classification was 65.3 per cent. The category system will next be used to classify the errors which arise in the protocols of the target group.

The hypothesis

The hypothesis is that readers in the eight – 11-year-old group display certain categories of error in their comprehension of text and that such categories are affected by age and ability of the subjects, by textual factors, and by mode of presentation eg writing or drawing of the subject summaries.

Discussion

From observation of results so far, it appears that errors are not generally random, but have a basis which seems logical to the reader. They tend to arise when there is conflict between the information in the text and the reader's personal knowledge and experience which frequently suppress the message intended by the author. Discrepancies show up mostly in illustrated recall and are frequently missed in general class assignments.

Unlike Marjorie Siegel, I did not get the impression that the pupils treated the drawing sessions less seriously than the writing ones and although their opinions of themselves as artists may have influenced what they drew, I still found ample evidence of misunderstanding in the illustrations. Children's opinions of themselves as authors can also influence what they write and spell.

To see if similar errors appear when pupils' attention is focused on sections of the text, I tried presenting an interpretation exercise with questions and answers to be followed by drawings of the text. This showed that a pupil who could score quite highly on the written work, could read and write about a golden dragon lying asleep and draw a bright green one walking about.

Category system

Child-centred errors

1 *Extraneous items* Extras which do not contribute to the meaning of the text. Although not in the text, and possibly out of place in the given context, they fit in with the reader's picture of the scene. (See Figure 19.1 Viking feast complete with disco party.)
2 *Influence of previous knowledge* Facts which are wrong in the given context but arise from knowledge previously acquired by the reader. They do contribute to the reader's visualisation of the scene. (See Figure 19.1 Viking feast complete with disco party.)
3 *Predominance of stereotypes* Overruling of given information because of a fixed idea that '*things are so*'. (See Figure 19.2 The text referred to *people* looking out from a train and *watching animals in a jungle*. The child illustrated monkeys, not people, behind bars.

Figure 19.1 Influence of previous knowledge

Figure 19.2 Predominance of stereotype

Text-centred errors

4 *Disregard of explicitly-stated facts* Contradiction of facts clearly expressed in the passage due to focus on individual key words or fragments.

5 *Confusion of word-meanings* Misunderstanding arising from selection of word-meaning which does not fit in the context.
6 *Discrimination error* Misunderstanding arising from visual mis-reading of words, supported by the reader's assumptions.

Effort after meaning

7 *Justifications* Wrong explanations offered to reconcile apparently discrepant facts due to misunderstanding of the given text. (Figure 19.3).
8 *Transpositions* Descriptive words and phrases transferred from their place in the text, to another reference.

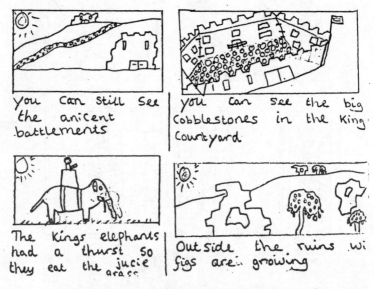

you can still see the anicent battlements

you can see the big cobblestones in the king courtyard

The kings elephants had a thurst so they eat the jucie grass

Outside the ruins wi figs are growing

Figure 19.3 Justifications The passage read 'a great roofless palace crowned the hill and the cobblestones in the courtyard where the King's elephants used to live, had been thrust up and apart by grasses and young trees'.

Surface reading

9 *Literal information* Surface reading of text, displaying failure to understand underlying metaphorical ideas. (Figure 19.4).
10 *Reproduction* Verbatim presentation of given words and phrases, showing that they have not been absorbed and understood. (Figure 19.5).

..the long house rang with their
laughter and song...

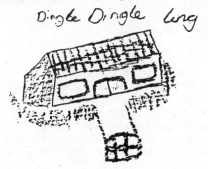

Figure 19.4   Literal information

Figure 19.5   Reproduction

Future action

The next step is to classify the errors made by the target group,
according to the category system.

Finally, I hope that, on the basis of the results and from the lessons learned in the course of the study, some teaching material to promote comprehension skills in the primary classroom, might be developed.

References

Abrahamson, A. (1975) 'Experimental Analysis of the Semantics of Movement' (pp 247–276) in Norman, D.A. and Rumelhart, D.E., *Exploration in Cognition* W.H. Freeman and Co. San Francisco.

Bartlett, F.C. (1932) *Remembering: A Study in Experimental and Social Psychology* Cambridge University Press, Edition 1954.

Brown, A, L & Day, J.D. (1983) 'Macro: Rules for Summarizing Texts – The Development of Expertise' *Journal of Verbal Learning and Verbal Behavior*, No. 22 pp. 1–14.

Craik, F.I.M. & Lockhart, R.S. (1972) 'Levels of Processing – A Framework for Memory Research' *Journal of Verbal Learning and Verbal Behavior*, Vol. 11 pp. 671–684.

France, M. (1979) *Primary Reading Test – Level 2* Thomas Nelson & Sons Ltd, Surrey.

Stein, N.L. & Glenn, C.G. 'An Analysis of Story Comprehension In Elementary School Children' pp. 53–120 in Freedle, R.D. (ed), in *New Directions in Discourse Processing*, Ablex, New Jersey.

Sanford, A.J. & Garrod, S.C. (1981) '*Understanding Written Language – Expositions in Comprehension Beyond the Sentence* John Wiley and Sons, New York.

Schallert, D.L. (1982) 'The Significance of Knowledge, – A Synthesis of Research Related to Schema Theory, pp. 13–48 in Otto, W. & White, S. (eds), *Reading Expository Material – Educational Psychology Series*, Academic Press.

Siegal, M. (1983) *Toward An Understanding of Reading as Signification* Education Resources Information Center, Washington D.C.

PART 4

International sharing: Linguistics and learning

20 Historical dimensions: The International Reading Association, The European Committee and the United Kingdom Reading Association

Marian J. Tonjes, Alastair Hendry and Douglas Dennis

The three contributors consider, from their own perspectives, the origin and development of the International Reading Association (IRA), the European Committee, and the UK Reading Association (UKRA), and the current concerns of the Associations.

The International Reading Association (Marian J. Tonjes)

Knowledge of our beginnings can be important in helping us shape the nature and direction of development. We need to both understand and appreciate our shortcomings as well as our accomplishments.

If we follow the above advice from Albert J. Harris while we look briefly at the origins and intertwining of the International Reading Association, the European Council and UKRA, I believe we might gain a better perspective a sense of identity if you will – from knowledge of our roots. It is my task to cover broadly the IRA dimension. Figure 20.1 is a timeline of IRA's development.

Beginnings

It was a hot summer afternoon in 1947 in Philadelphia, Pennsylvania, USA. Six people gathered informally at Temple University to plan for an organisation on reading instruction. As Bob Jerrolds reports in *Reading Reflections: The History Of The International Reading Instruction* Emmett Betts paid 36 cents for six bottles of Coca-Cola for the little group. Twenty-four years later he (Betts) was presented with the IRA Citation of Merit and an extraordinary

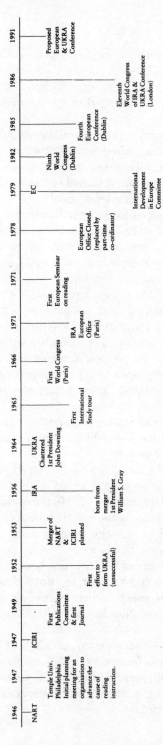

Figure 20.1

desk set consisting of a pen, six coke bottle caps and 36 cents in coins minted on or before 1947.

In the autumn of that year 34 people gathered to form a reading organisation and the next month they reconvened and adopted a constitution.

It was assumed at first that this organisation would be concerned solely with reading in the United States. However, two Canadians had asked to become members. Because they would have had difficulty then in sending dues out of Canada to an American organisation, the group decided to 'go international'.

With no undue modesty they agreed to name themselves the International Council for the Improvement of Reading Instruction (ICIRI), or 'I CRY'. As one wag pointed out, this pronunciation violated several phonic generalisations and two syllabication principles – not to mention violating the whole spirit of the organisation.

The next year (1948) the group, astonishingly enough, was talking about holding international conferences, establishing local councils and publishing a sophisticated journal.

An interesting early decision as to membership was made then, and this has been one of the greatest strengths of IRA. Membership was – and still is – wide open to all interested teachers, parents, administrators, authors and researchers, not only to reading 'specialists'.

In 1949 the 'I CRY' publications committee was formed and the first journal, *The Bulletin* was published. It eventually changed its name to *The Reading Teacher*.

The next year saw the formation of the first local council, not in the United States but in Toronto, Canada. The second council was also from Canada. That same year (1950) the leaders felt they were 'too local' to continue running the rapidly broadening organisation. However, they agreed to continue to serve until, by action of the board, replacements could be found.

To show the informality of the time, one board member wrote to Albert J. Harris and Gerald Yoakum to inform them that although they were not members, much to their astonishment, they had been elected Vice-President and President of ICIRI. Good naturedly, they then agreed to serve.

Membership of the Association rose steadily. In 1948 there were only 234 members but in four years (1952) membership had grown to approximately 1400, representing the US, Canada, Hawaii and Puerto Rico. Efforts at that time to set up councils in England and Ireland were unsuccessful.

Even with such growth the organisation (ICIRI) was financially unstable. In 1953 they had to wait for new subscriptions to pay the bills. Alarmed at this situation the leaders established life memberships of $50.00, and enough people took advantage of this offer to save the organisation from possible dissolution.

At a casual picnic in the summer of 1953 discussion started as to the possible merger of two organisations – ICIRI and NART (The National Association of Remedial Reading Teachers). In 1955 the ICIRI held its final General Assembly where it was proposed that the merger be called the International Reading Association. IRA then was officially born on January 1st, 1956, just 32 years ago, and held its first convention in Chicago that same year. The first President was William S. Gray.

Here are a few fact and figures about the IRA today.

1 Currently there are 75,000 members.
2 There are 12,000 councils and national affiliates.
3 Four professional journals are published:
   a) *The Reading Teacher*, 42,000 circulation
   b) *Journal of Reading*, 18,000 circulation
   c) *Reading Research Quarterly* 10,000 circulation
   d) *Lectra y vida*, 1,000 (Spanish speaking) circulation plus the Newsletter – *Reading Today*.
4 There are 200 Publications (books, monographs,) in the catalogues.
5 Volunteer national committees (14 of these are award committees) explore specific subjects in depth, they include adult literacy, computers, early childhood, adolescent literature, teacher effectiveness . . .
6 The Budget for 1986–87 is approximately $4 million.
7 At the 1988 Conference in Toronto, on *Reaching New Heights*, attendance reached over 16,000 and there were over 1000 presentations.
8 There is a 12-person board of directors and an executive director, Ron Mitchell.

The stated aims are very straightforward: IRA is working towards a literate society by:

• *improving* reading instruction through study and research dissemination;
• *promoting* life-time reading habits through increasing awareness of the impact of reading;
• *developing* everyone's proficiency to the highest possible level.

If we look at the themes of conventions over the years we can get a flavour from key terms in the title. These include the following:

Better readers
Reading in action
Reading for effective living
Reading in a changing society
Reading: new frontiers
Reading: challenge and experiment
Reading: intellectual activity
Reading: progress and promise
Reading: a basic human right.

Current concerns, as noted by resolutions passed this year at the delegates' assembly involved the following 12 items.

1 Increase book funding
Increase funds for books by three-fold for ease of access for all levels of students.

2 Unabridged texts
Recommend publishers select and present complete, unattended texts, not censored or abridged, – or clearly state in the text the nature, extent and reasons for changes.

3 Sustained funding for 'At Risk' readers
Provide sustained funding for those termed 'at risk' in reading.

4 Standards for training voluntary tutors
Develop and promote standards for volunteer tutoring programs and training literacy volunteer tutors.

5 Reading and writing across the curriculum
Encourage emphasis on reading and writing across the curriculum at all levels.

6 Qualifications
Urge that all personnel responsible for teaching reading and language arts be appropriately prepared, qualified and 'certified' (that means licensed!) using IRA guidelines.

7 Censors
Commend all those who support teachers' professional judgement in book selection when attacked by censors, and condemn narrow interest censors.

8 Ethnic minority teaching materials
Urge publishers to portray a broad perception of human history including an accurate account of radical and ethnic minority groups and their contributions.

9 Corporal punishment
Condemn cruel, degrading, humiliating treatment of students and call for an end to physical abuse and corporal punishment.

10 Curriculum development and teachers
Affirm that teachers are best able to make qualified decisions on what constitutes informed practice and curriculum content in their field.

11 Parents' support in language development
Affirm the importance of maximising language development in early years and provide parents further information as to their role.

12 Assessment
Affirm that reading assessment should reflect recent advances in understanding the reading process, discouraging the definition of reading as a sequence of discrete skills, and opposing comparisons of scores between schools, districts, states or provinces.

(Further details can be found in IRA's *Reading Today* Vol. 5–6. June/July 1988).

Conclusion

In completing this section of the report, I would like to make a few observations.

1 From my own perspective the IRA does have some short-comings. It seems too political (but perhaps such a vast organisation would be unwieldy otherwise). For example, candidates for offices and board members must actively campaign at length if they want to be assured of having a chance of winning. Second, I have found that convention presentations lean overwhelmingly towards the class-room reading teacher, with less choice available for the lecturer/ researcher. Lastly, international conventions are now so huge (16,000) that it is necessary to make appointments ahead of time in order to be sure of seeing colleagues.

2 IRA, however, has played a vital role in developing a better understanding of reading, and in promoting higher levels of literacy, especially on the American continent. It has also been very influential in researching, reporting and disseminating information on reading.

The International Reading Association and Europe (Alastair Hendry)

The planned involvement of the International Reading Association in Europe during its early days was directed from headquarters in the United States. From 1971, this process was supported by a field consultant working from her office in Paris. Indeed, she was a very welcome visitor to the UKRA Conferences during the 70s. UKRA members also helped in various ways, eg in planning for World Congresses. Among them were Joyce Morris, Vera Southgate-Booth, John Merritt and Elizabeth Hunter-Grundin.

The Paris office was closed in 1978, and shortly afterwards the consultant's duties were taken over by a part-time co-ordinator. It was her function to continue to support, to stimulate and to co-ordinate all the various activities aimed at promoting the growth of IRA membership in Europe. Her work was to be done in co-operation with the different national organisations affiliated to IRA. Living in Paris, working for the European Parliament (and therefore travelling widely within Europe on business) and speaking fluently at least six major European languages, the co-ordinator was perhaps uniquely placed for this work. The future looked promising!

Furthermore, in 1979, in the United States, an International Development Committee was formed to promote and oversee all such activities throughout the world. It had several sub-committees with a geographical focus. One sub-committee was concerned with Europe and it later attained full status as the International Development in Europe Committee. The person who chaired the first sub-committee was Mrs Gwen Bray, President of UKRA 1978–79.

International Development in Europe Committee Membership (1988)

The Committee consists of representatives of the national affiliates of International Reading Association as follows:

Austrian Society for the Promotion of and Research in Reading
Belgian Reading Association (Flemish Speaking Section)
Association Belge Pour La Lecture
Danish National Association of Reading Teachers
Finnish Reading Assocation

Association Française Pour La Lecture
Deutsche Gesellschaft Für Lesen und Schreiben
Reading Association of Ireland
Association Luxembourgeoise Pour La Lecture
Swedish Council of IRA
United Kingdom Reading Association.

In addition, it is hoped that representatives of the following countries will be able to attend as observers during 1988–89:

Hungary	Italy
Spain	Switzerland
East Germany	Czechoslovakia

Charges (remit)

The Board of Directors of IRA each year charges the Committee:

1 To develop specific proposals to help IRA serve Europe and pro-mote co-operation among the affiliates in Europe
2 To develop activities to increase international awareness, involvement and participation in Europe
3 To work to increase IRA membership and local councils in Europe
4 To work co-operatively with other committees on International Development.

Fulfilling the remit (1979–88)

The Committee has sought to fulfil this remit in a variety of ways at different levels, by:

- arranging exhibitions and sales of IRA publications at congresses and conferences
- encouraging the translation of articles from journals etc (eg the brochure for parents was translated into French and sold over 15,000 copies in its first year)
- involving headquarters personnel in meetings and visits.
- publicising IRA and European affiliates' activities, eg conferences and publications through the *News Bulletin*. This is produced three times a year for IRA members in Europe, reprinted and included in some associations' publications (eg Germany, Finland) or relevant contents are extracted and included in an association's own Newsletter (eg UKRA)
- by organising symposia and panels of speakers for IRA World

Congresses, eg at Dublin (1982), and London (1986)

- by arranging for individuals to participate in Conferences of allied organisations. Dr John Chapman chaired a symposium on Linguistics and Reading Comprehension at the World Congress of the International Association of applied Linguistics in Brussels (1984). Dr Frank Potter and Pauline Bleech attended the seminar on the Application of New Technologies organised by the European Commission at University of Ghent in Belgium, one outcome of which has been a research project on Word Processing and Literacy Skills
- by arranging that as far as possible each meeting of the Committee coincides with a seminar or Conference of a national organisation. In this way the Committee members can provide support by participating in the programme in the local language, eg

1982 Chartres, France: Second Language Learning
1983 West Berlin: Training Teachers of Reading
1984 Reutlingen: Microcomputers and Reading
1985 Vienna: Children's Interests and Reading Habits

- finally, the greatest amount of effort is expended in planning and running the biennial European Conferences on Reading. In accordance with our policy, these are truly international, both in terms of speakers and delegates, and are held in different parts of Europe to help strengthen an existing organisation or assist in the process of forming one. The locations have been

Paris, 1979	and at the planning stage
Joenssu, Finland, 1981	Salamanca, Spain, 1987
Vienna, 1983	Berlin, 1989
Dublin, 1985	United Kingdom (?) 1991

In the main, the themes of these Conferences are sufficiently broad to encourage the participation and sharing of experiences by the greatest number of teachers and researchers. As an example of this, the Sixth Conference in Berlin at the beginning of August, 1989 has as its theme *Reading at the Crossroads* (Hat Lesen Zukunft?) which will include the topics:

Reading, Language and Culture
Reading in a Multimedia Context
Reading and Metacognition

In summary, then, it should be evident that although the Committee has met ONCE (occasionally TWICE) A YEAR a very great deal has been achieved.

Above all, the levels of co-operation, enthusiasm and working relationships within this group and the organisations it represents have never been better.

Problems (1979–88): Communication

In a group which uses four or five major European languages communication with understanding can at times be difficult to achieve.

Different cultural and political backgrounds (past as well as current) have very significant implications with regard to views and behaviour.

The period in question has been marked by a general decline in membership in the various national organisations, coupled with rising costs in administration and services provided – such as publications.

The International Reading Association itself has had its own financial problems. The early 1980s were marked by a number of cut-backs. The concessions to non-American members with regard to subscriptions were removed. Unfortunately, this change came abruptly and without warning to the European member. The rise in the exchange value of the dollar at the same time meant that for most Europeans the cost of IRA membership was trebled, without any improvement in services. This led immediately to serious questioning of the value of these services. To the non-American, IRA seemed totally insensitive both to needs and protests.

Downing (1984) reported to the IRA Board of Directors:

> *Something has gone very badly wrong in IRA's relations with our European affiliates. I believe that IRA has suffered its greatest setback in International development in two decades.*

Sadly, but understandably, that report (Downing, 1984) was negative, pessimistic and seriously flawed because of its limitations. On his visits to the different associations, Downing did not indicate that he was preparing a formal report on IRA status in Europe. Understandably he only got answers to the questions he asked, and he appears to have been unaware, for instance, of the work of the European Committee. In July 1985, the European Co-ordinator, who had played a major role in the work of the European Committee was dismissed without warning and without any consultation with the Committee. At this point several of the national associations discussed revoking their affiliations with IRA.

The way ahead: International sharing

At present, feelings have calmed somewhat, but the problems have still to be solved. To help solve them through informed discussion, IRA have funded a Project which will provide basic information on the current situation of the different affiliates in Europe, together with their recommendations as to how co-operation between IRA and the European organisations can be made more effective. The Project Report will be finalised in October 1988, and immediately thereafter will be available to the IRA Board of Directors.

It remains to be seen, therefore as the communication and relationships amongst the European Associations continue to grow and strengthen over the next few years, whether it will be possible to re-create that true spirit of internationalism which has been the driving force of many of the great past leaders of the International Reading Association.

The United Kingdom Reading Association 1963–88 (Doug Dennis)

From its initial conference in 1964, the UKRA has adopted an internationalist approach which belies its name but clearly acknowledges its origins in the International Reading Association. Not surprisingly the earliest overseas speakers were Americans, Helen M Robinson and Nila Banton Smith contributing to the 1964 Symposium, and Ralph C Staiger and Edward Fry, amongst others, to the 1965 Symposium, where European contributors also appeared from Finland and France. The pattern set by the first President, the late John Downing, has been maintained to the present day.

Over the past 25 years, conference papers have been presented by colleagues from Australia, Austria, Canada, Finland, France, Ireland, Jamaica, Japan, the Netherlands, New Zealand, Nigeria, Sweden and the USA. There has always been an American presence at our conferences, with a number of colleagues holding dual membership and contributing on a regular basis. During the last decade this has been increasingly true also of colleagues from Australia. This international perspective is an important and valuable feature of our Conferences. A large-scale recent event, typifying this co-operation, came in 1986 with the Eleventh World Congress held in London. Here was the IRA organisation (co-ordinated in London by Joyce Morris), the UKRA strand (organised by President, Peter Smith), and a strong European input to the Congress. It is hoped that the next stage in international co-operation will be a joint European and UKRA. Conference in the UK in 1991.

The introduction to the First International Reading Symposium (Downing, 1966) included some comments on the formation of UKRA and listed its eight aims, which parallel those of the International Reading Association of which UKRA is a national affiliate. These aims were, and are:

1 To encourage the study of reading problems at all educational levels
2 To stimulate and promote research in reading
3 To study the various factors that influence progress in reading
4 To publish the results of pertinent and significant practices
5 To assist in the development of teacher training programmes
6 To act as a clearing-house for information relating to reading
7 To disseminate knowledge helpful to the solution of problems relating to reading
8 To sponsor conferences and meetings planned to implement the purposes of the Association

These aims will form the focus of my comments on the progress of the first 25 years.

The same introduction also included the following passage, referring to the papers in the proceedings, which:

> represent the growing realisation that the teaching of reading is not something which is confined to the first two or three years of school . . . Reading needs to be treated as a developmental process and one which is subject to improvement throughout life. Also, teachers of reading have to be concerned with more than the mere mechanical decoding of the printed or written symbols into the sounds, words and sentences of speech.
>
> (page ix)

One of the more surprising aspects of the teaching of reading is that this comment would not be out of place in any of the 23 subsequent collections of proceedings. It is as timeless as Huey's (1908) statement that:

> attention to reading as an exercise in speaking . . . has been heavily at the expense of reading as the art of thought-getting and thought manipulating.
>
> (page 359)

the truth of which was rediscovered during the *Extending Beginning Reading Project* (Southgate et al 1981).

The focus of UKRA activity in the early years was upon aims seven and eight – the dissemination of knowledge and the sponsoring of conferences. This 25th conference demonstrates that this was a sound strategy, for on many occasions the two have combined so that the annual conference has provided the platform for the dissemination of some major research or inquiry. Early examples are: *Standards and Progress in Reading* (1966); the many and various ita experiments and evaluations; *The Primary School in Scotland* (1965); *The Plowden Report* (1967); and more recently *The Bullock Report* (1975); *The Bradford Book Flood Project* (1981); *Extending Beginning Reading* (1981) *Reading for Learning* (1984); the *Foundation of Writing* Project (1987) and, of course the *Kingman Report* (1988). In this respect UKRA can look back on a proud record and a valuable service performed.

Through the annual volume of proceedings the Association also achieves its fourth aim – publishing – and to this list can be added an important series of monographs on significant topics within the language arts field; some occasional publications – such as *The First R* (Morris 1972) a collection of seminal papers from proceedings of the '60s, a second volume – *Reading Concerns* – drawn from proceedings of the '70s (Raban 1989). There are three slim volumes from the Research Committee of UKRA called *Micro-explorations*, two series of flyers on topics of the moment, and, of course, the journals: *Reading* – now in its twenty-second volume, and *Research in Reading* – currently in volume eleven.

The concerns of the UKRA

A review of the past 25 years seemed at first to pose an impossible task. However, this is not an attempt at a history, which task was undertaken to celebrate the 21st anniversary, and a perusal of the the 24 published volumes of proceedings was reassuring as a relatively small number of recurring themes could be identified. There are, of course, two ways of looking at this situation – as with the half-glass of water which according to one's point of view is half-full or half-empty. Either UKRA has made no discernible progress in 25 years, or it is operating a spiral curriculum.

A comparison of the concerns of UKRA, as represented by its conference proceedings, with those of the International Reading Association, as represented by the resolutions passed by the Delegate Conference in Toronto earlier this year shows a substantial difference of emphasis. The resolutions of the Delegate Conference focused on general issues which add up to a kind of policy statement on topics like accreditation, book supply, censorship (see the section by M. Tonjes). UKRA conferences have, in general tended to focus on more specific matters, particularly following the leadership and expressed interests of the Presidents.

Phonics versus Whole-word/Real books debate

What then are some of the common themes? Probably the hardiest annual of all is the *Phonics verses Whole-word/Real books debate*. This featured in the first (1964) conference and was still going strong in 1987. Closely associated with this methodological argument has been a series of discussions about the medium, with the use of colour, code modification (as in ita and diacritical marks), a variety of programmed approaches, television and, in the last four or five years, computers, all coming under repeated scrutiny. Despite the obvious truth, and apparently wide acceptance, of this much-quoted statement from the *Bullock Report*, 1975:

> . . . *There is no one method, medium , approach, device, or philosophy that holds the key to the process of learning to read. We believe that the knowledge does exist to improve the teaching of reading but it does not lie in the discovery or rediscovery, of a particular formula. Simple endorsements of one or another nostrum are of no service to the teaching of reading. A glance at the past reveals the truth of this. The main arguments about how reading should be taught have been repeated over and over again as the decades pass but the problems remain. (Para. 6.1)*

the search for the panacea continues unabated. (Despite the good humour and gamesmanship might it appear as if we are reluctant to let anything so ephemeral as evidence influence our thinking, attitudes and practice?) Flesch, in 1981, described the International Reading Association as the '*look-and-say defence league*', and UKRA has been criticised recently for not throwing its weight behind a particular approach to reading. To accept either of these criticisms would be to retreat from the '*open forum philosophy*' and from reliance on properly accredited evidence which is the only acceptable route for a professional association to take.

Reading 'failure' and assessment

The second most popular topic is reading failure in all its various forms and with all its various euphemisms. A closely associated area is assessment and the relationships between tests and reading, testing and standards. One aspect which has caused concern from time to time, particularly to politicians , is the fact that norm-referenced testing continually shows that half the children are performing below average. Judging by the number of teachers still aiming to have all their children with reading ages at or above their chronological ages, our spiral curriculum is not proving very effective. The notion of reading failure also has about it the suggestion that the fault lies in the child, or in the materials being used. The school system, teacher expertise and the interrelationships of possible causal factors are less frequently questioned. This approach leads to two games: one is to invent a name for the problem as an alternative to solving it; the other is to keep searching for material to resolve the problem for us. Both games and indeed other false polarisations offer 'no win' situations for teachers and pupils alike.

Teacher education

The third topic which has stood the test of time at UKRA conference is teacher education. From the outset, there has been quite severe criticism of teacher education courses, in terms of the time devoted to *'reading'* and also of the content of the courses offered. I would not wish to attempt a whitewash, but I do suspect an element of scapegoating here, with teachers, adminstrators and politicians all joining in the condemnation of the quality of training; a training which, incidentially, is more closely controlled from the centre than any other educational courses at any level, and has recently been changed to the detriment of literacy courses in England.

This has arisen as a result of many language and literacy courses being shortened and re-orientated selectively towards curricular specialisations in order to conform to the regulations set by the Committee for Accreditation of Teacher Education (CATE).

Whereas this may have raised the number of stated hours of subject training in some courses it has unquestionably reduced others and changed the nature of the courses. In so doing it also neglects to take into account the loss of study and practice of actual relationships between professional skills and learning within and across subject specific frames of reference. The kinds of professional skills which are pertinent include understanding of learning as well as showing facility in communicating with learners and a practical grasp of the way in which accessing and classification of information has been organised in the past and is currently effected, particularly through technology. Communication, including oracy, numeracy and literacy in this sense must surely assume greater cross-curricular as well as subject-specific emphasis.

Of particular gravity is the anti-intellectual attitude which our training seems to engender – the *'I'm a practical person, I don't have time for theory'* viewpoint which is so commonly expressed. A harsh interpretation of this would be: *'don't expect me to think about what I'm doing'*. If UKRA is to make real progress in developing member-ship and effectiveness, it must tackle this issue squarely and demon-strate clearly to teachers the inter-dependence of theory and practice in producing the best and most coherent literacy education for children, and in rendering account for the decisions taken and the standard achieved. I am, as you have realised, in the 'born-again teacher' business. A major problem is the persistent amateurism of the British – more specifically the English – tradition, with its very grudging and belated acceptance of the need for a proper professional training for all teachers, a recognition already being undermined by the proposals for 'licençed' teachers at present under consideration.

The development of teacher-training programmes

The fifth aim of UKRA is 'to assist in the development of teacher training programmes'. It might be suggested that UKRA contributes to in-service education of teachers through its national conferences, local and regional meetings and publications as well as on-going work of the Research and Teacher Education Committees. Its influ-ence at pre-service level may appear to be limited, as yet, despite the fact that an analysis of members' views (1982–84) carried out by M. Hunter-Carsch on behalf of the Teacher-Education Committee sug-gested that there is a need for support for beginning teachers and did list suggested topics, techniques and texts which might be used in pre-service courses. It is to be hoped that the recent appointment of offi-cial observers from both the Scottish Education Department and the Department of Education and Science may make it possible for UKRA to share its recommendations beyond its immediate members.

An opportunity to make progress did occur after the *Bullock Report* (1975) but little was achieved, partly because there was no political will to implement the expensive recommendations – as with the *Newbold Report* (1921). The *Kingman Report* offers another such opportunity and the Association must not miss this one. I would like to see UKRA involved at national level in the accreditation of both initial and in-service courses in the language arts, and membership of the Association become a professional requirement for all specialist reading teachers and post-holders. It is only through the establishment of this type of professional critical community that: standards of teaching in reading can be maintained and improved; a proper recognition of the need for reading development to continue throughout life be achieved, and an antidote provided for suggestions of a restrictive nature with reference to procedures for evaluation. Behaving professionally must be the first step towards recognition as a profession.

A problem identified 20 years ago was the resistance in educational circles to the notion that 'reading' was a topic which merited the attention of specialists, academics and researchers, and that reading teachers needed particular and focused training. Despite the sterling work of the Open University in raising consciousness in this area through its course development, and the emergence of Diplomas and Masters programmes at a wide variety of institutions, it has to said that reading is still a 'non-subject' in the eyes of the education establishment. The Reading Development Institute proposed by UKRA President Joyce Morris in 1966, and identified by John Daniels (1967 President) as something to be achieved in the next 20 years, is still not even at the blue-print stage despite the emergence of a number of 'Reading Centres' under both Higher Education and Education Authority auspices. Perhaps this idea should be reconsidered in the light of the Kingman recommendations.

Much has been achieved, much remains for us to do, and the challenges increase daily. There is a strong tide in the affairs of education at the present, which (if we show professional strength, conviction and mutual support) the Association can take at the flood and move on to increased power and influence in improving the quality of the learning experiences we offer to children. Only involvement in change provides the opportunity to influence its direction – UKRA must be involved.

References

Board of Education (1921) *The Teaching of English in England* (Newbold) HMSO.
Daniels, J.C. (1970) *Reading; Problems and Perspective* UKRA.
DES (1967) *Children in Their Primary Schools* (Plowden Report) HMSO.
DES (1975) *A Language For Life* (Bullock Report) HMSO.
DES (1988) *Report of the Committees of Inquiry Into the Teaching of English Language* (Kingman Report) HMSO.
Downing, J. (1966) *The First International Reading Symposium* Cassell.

Huey, E.B. (1908/68) *The Psychology and Pedagogy of Reading* MIT Press.
Ingham, J. (1981) *Books and Reading Development* (The Bradford Book Flood Experiment) Heinemann.
Jackson, W.J. & Michael, B. (1986) *Foundations of Writing* SCDS.
Lunzer, E. & Gardner, K. (1979) *The Effective Use Of Reading* Heinemann.
Lunzer, E. & Gardner, K. (1984) *Learning From the Written Word* (The Reading for Learning Project) Oliver & Boyd.
Morris, J.M. (1966) *Standards and Progress in Reading* NFER.
Morris, J.M. Ed. (1972) *The First R, Yesterday, Today and Tomorrow* Ward Lock.
Raban, B. (Ed.) (in press) *Reading Concerns* Ward Lock.
SED (1965) *The Primary School In Scotland* HMSO.
Southgate, V., Arnold, H. & Johnson, S. (1981) *Extending Beginning Reading* Heinemann.
Microexplorations, and Flyer Series obtainable from UKRA Administrative Office.

Appendix: A few of UKRA's publications

Conference proceedings
1 *Reading : Meeting Children's Special Needs* (1983) editor Doug Dennis
2 *Reading and the New Technologies* (1984) editor Jim Ewing
3 *Resources for Reading : Does Quality Count?* (1985) editor Betty Root, Macmillan
4 *Parents and Teachers Together* (1986) editor Peter Smith, Macmillan
5 *Reading: The abc and Beyond* (1987) editor Christine Anderson, Macmillan

UKRA monographs
1 *Listening to Children Reading* (1983) Helen Arnold, Hodder & Stoughton
2 *Teaching Information Skills Through Project Work* (1985) David Wray, Hodder & Stoughton
3 *Children's Writing in the Primary School* (1984) Rodger Beard, Hodder & Stoughton
4 *Partnership with Parents in Reading* (1987) Wendy Bloom, Hodder & Stoughton
5 *The Emergence of Literacy* (1987) Nigel Hall, Hodder & Stoughton

UKRA occasional publications
1 *How to run Family Reading Group*, Cecilia Obrist
2 *Investigating Reading in the Classroom*, Sue Beverton and Frank Potter
3 *Studies in the History of Reading*, editors Greg Brooks and A.K. Pugh
4 *Micro-Explorations* (1), (2) and (3), editors Frank Potter and David Wray

21 Linguistics in a lifetime of learning about language and literacy

Joyce M. Morris

Many academic disciplines contribute to our knowledge about language and literacy, none more so than linguistics. Nevertheless, in some educational circles, there is still a very strong resistance even to the notion of, for example, 'linguistics in teacher education'.

With regard to the teaching of English, it is hoped that the authoritative Kingman Report will weaken this resistance, and especially help to heal the breach between linguistics and literature. Meanwhile appropriately, the theme chosen for this article is 'linguistics and learning'.

As indicated by its alliterative title, this invited paper is a personal statement by a researcher with a penchant for mnemonical tongue-twisters. It tells the story of past efforts to use relevant knowledge from linguistics to improve the teaching and learning of English and, notably includes a tribute to the work of UKRA's first President, the late Professor John Downing. Finally, it attempts to answer the question, 'Where do we go from here?'

Childhood experience

Looking back I realise that, once upon a time, I was a pre-school child destined by inclination and lucky circumstance to spend a lifetime learning about language and literacy. As I vividly recall, my interest in alphabet letters began with the gift of a ragbook *ABC* from my teacher-godmother. I disliked its indestructible texture and crude taste, and was about to toss it out of my pram when, in a shaft of bright sunlight, I noticed that the thick black 'squiggles' on one side of a rag page did not match those on the other.

I understand that my persistent curiosity about those black squiggles so delighted my godmother and parents that, henceforth, I was provided with every opportunity in my home environment to become a reader and writer. This was along the lines nowadays recommended by the movement towards parent-teacher co-operation in children's literacy.

Additionally, I was fortunate in three educationally significant respects. First, my father, who was a 'reading addict' partly because of rest-requiring war injuries, encouraged me to share his love of the English language, especially its etymology and the delights of word play. Second, my paternal grandmother in the USA kept up a regular correspondence with me which began, on my part (at the age of four) with simple thank-you notes for gifts received, and subsequently developed my interest in the differences between American and British English. Third, my wise and ever-loving mother ensured that I had plenty of other enriching childhood experiences. These included learning to play the piano informally with her and then, from the age of seven, formally but still happily when we both received lessons from the same professional pianist. In this way, she was responsible for enlarging my early linguistic repertoire with the language of music.

Undoubtedly, my early childhood experience with language and literacy gave me a headstart with my formal education. For instance, I started school in a top infants class and proceeded to an upper junior class at the age of seven. Moreover, in terms of examination results, this advantage was evidently consolidated at secondary and further education level with the help of a succession of excellent teachers of English, French, Latin, Music and other subjects.

Teaching experience

Paradoxically, when I became a qualified teacher my previous linguistic experience proved at first to be a shocking handicap. Because of it and inadequacies in my pre-service course, I had neither insight into the special needs of my 'remedial' class of 40 illiterate pupils aged seven to ten, nor professional knowledge of how to meet them. In other words, I was distressingly ill-prepared for an unexpectedly traumatic situation, and all I could do was try to find solutions to the children's difficulties through trial and error and further private study, there being no appropriate in-service courses available in wartime London.

During that frightful period when my colleagues and I evacuated children to safer areas, or waited with our remaining pupils for the 'All clear' in school air-raid shelters, I secretly vowed that if my life was spared, I would devote it to a good cause. And what better than the cause of literacy for which I already had a sense of vocation? Meanwhile, after analysing my childhood experiences to discover what seemed to be the main ingredients for success in learning to read and write, I applied some of the findings in classroom practice. For example, remembering how I was provided with a 'rich' reading environment, I built up, from personal gifts, a class library collection of story books for me to read to the children and for them to borrow which, according to a visiting HMI, was the first of its kind he had seen in those days of scarce school resources. As my father had taught me, so I taught my pupils to use verbal mnemonics and, especially, to appreciate alliteration, onomatopoeia, rhyme and rhythm. I also used my secondary role as a 'specialist' music teacher to give them additional multi-sensory training through choral reading, song and country dance.

Learning to do all those things effectively contributed greatly to my ability to teach literacy for seven years in a primary school and three in a secondary school. The experience was unforgettable, and laid the foundation for my subsequent work as a professional researcher in the reading field. Not surprisingly, it also caused me always to question the theories of academics who have never been class teachers responsible for ensuring that children make a good start on the long road to literacy.

Early research experience

In 1953, when I was appointed reading research officer at the NFER, most of my colleagues were, like me, graduates in psychology with additional relevant qualifications. This was partly because, at that time, psychology was considered the most appropriate basic discipline for educational research. Moreover, in the key area of 'language and literacy development' academic knowledge had, by then, been contributed mainly by psychologists.

As a professional researcher, I was fortunate in having as my first 'guide and mentor', the late Dr A F Watts, whose essay in educational psychology *The Language and Mental Development of Children* (Watts, 1944) is a landmark classic in the field. However, although we often discussed the nature of English, he never suggested that I might improve my knowledge through the study of linguistics. Neither did Professor W S Gray, IRA's first President, when he visited the National Foundation for Educational Research in 1954 and invited me to collaborate in the international survey of *The Teaching of Reading and Writing* (Gray, 1956) which he conducted for UNESCO. Furthermore, to my knowledge, none of the other distinguished visitors from overseas with whom I was privileged to discuss language and literacy, came from university departments of linguistics.

By chance, while conducting the primary phase of the Kent Reading Inquiries, I heard about the 1954 'Inglis Lecture' given at Harvard University by Henry Lee Smith and entitled Linguistic Science and the Teaching of English (Smith, 1956). I obtained a published copy and discovered a new world of enlightenment. For instance, the author stresses the importance of understanding that 'referential' meaning is what educational psychologists and teachers mean when they define reading as 'getting meaning from the printed page'. He then contrasts it with 'differential' meaning, ie the kind of meaning employed by linguists in the analysis and description of all linguistic systems. The example given is the two responses one is likely to get if one asks someone whether 'pin' is the same as 'bin'. The answer in terms of 'referential' meaning might be; 'Pin' is something you use to stick things together, and 'bin' is a place where you store coal or grain'. In terms of 'differential' meaning the answer might be, 'One begins with 'p' and the other with 'b'.

Henry Lee Smith goes on to say,

> The linguist is appalled by the educator's lack of even the most basic facts about language in general or the English language in particular. The educator is chilled by the mechanical and lifeless approach the linguist seems to bring to reading which his experience has shown him to be an educational process of primary importance in the child's development rather than simply a mere skill or tool. The reactions of each are understandable, but in the light of the knowledge we now possess, the failure to work together can no longer be condoned.

Thirty years later, with notable exceptions such as members of the 'language awareness' movement (NCLE, 1984), linguists and educators still fail to work together, there is much muddled thinking about the concept of 'meaning', and general confusion about the relationship between spoken and written language to which Henry Lee Smith also drew attention. Furthermore, to this day, relatively few teacher-trainers would agree with his observation that 'the teacher of reading has to be aware of the complete sound system of the language and know first systematically the consistencies that are present in the writing system as well as the inconsistencies'.

Be that as it may, by 1959 when my report Reading in the Primary School was published (Morris, 1959), I was convinced from my research in 60 schools and my own teaching experience that, to be effective, teachers of literacy need far more explicit linguistic knowledge than had hitherto been officially acknowledged. I was also convinced that they must not only motivate children to read and write but, within a framework of clear objectives, provide systematic instruction of which phonic training is an essential ingredient because of the alphabetic nature of the English writing system. Here, of course, the knowledge that some children may need less instruction than others does that not alter the fact that it should be available to all.

Orthographic innovations

My research report (Morris, 1959) included results of the first-ever survey of the reading standards of seven-year-olds. These were interpreted by some researchers, though not by me, as providing a rationale for experiments with what might be called 'orthographic innovations' as they were designed to remove, or at least mitigate, the learning/teaching difficulties caused by the irregularities of traditional orthography. Most publicised of these were the initial teaching alphabet experiments conducted by the late Professor John Downing, then a psychologist with ten years' teaching experience.

As I have written elsewhere (Morris, 1987), John was a remarkable man in many ways. We especially remember him at this Silver Jubilee Conference as a co-founder and first President of UKRA. But we should never forget his other great contributions as a scholar of international repute. Particularly relevant to the theme of 'Linguistics and learning' are his varied contributions to knowledge about children's language awareness and literacy development. It is also indicative of his scholarship and pragmatism that, right from the start of ita experimentation in 1959, he acknowledged the importance of linguistics and appointed the British linguist, John Mountford, to be a key member of the Reading Research Unit at London University of which he was director.

I was the reading researcher on the University's Steering Committee for the ita experiments and John and I became close colleagues. I was also fortunate in finding in another member of that Committee, the mentor I needed to help me through the period of orthographic innovations when I was convinced that there was a better solution to the problem of traditional orthography. He was the late Professor Dennis Fry, Head of the Department of Phonetics and Linguistics at University College, London.

We privately discussed the solutions offered by ita and, for example, by *Regularized English* (Wijk, 1959) and *Words in Colour* (Gattegno, 1962). He agreed with me that what was really needed was a reform of teacher-training. This would put language and literacy at its very heart, and ensure that, amongst other things, all teachers have explicit knowledge of the sound system of English and its orthography as the linguist Henry Lee Smith had previously advocated.

Linguistic approaches to literacy

In 1960, there was little prospect of such a reform and so, guided by Professor Fry, I began detailed study of his publications, and those of other linguistic scientists, which have something important to say to teachers of literacy. With his encouragement, I also decided to try and provide a more informed base for the phonic ingredient in initial literacy provision. Eventually, my researches led to the development of the linguistics-informed system now known as *Phonics 44* (Morris, 1984), to its incorporation in 1965 in the pioneering television series *Look and Read* and subsequently to *Language in Action* (Morris et al 1974–83) whose story titles are mnemonics for the basic spelling patterns and main sound-symbol correspondences of English.

During this 15-year period before publication of the *Bullock Report* (DES, 1975), there were a number of other examples of what might be called '*linguistic approaches to literacy*'. Unfortunately, those provided by linguistic scientists themselves are typical of what Henry Lee Smith has described as a '*mechanical and lifeless approach*'. For example, *Let's Read* (Bloomfield and Barnhart, 1961) developed by Bloomfield, one of America's greatest linguists, produced as Lesson 1:

> *Nan can fan Dan.*
> *Can Dan fan Nan?*
> *Dan can fan Nan.*
> *Nan, fan Dan. Dan fan Nan.*

In contrast, Professor Halliday, then a junior colleague of Professor Fry at University College, London, decided wisely to appoint three experienced school teachers to carry out that part of the *Schools Council's Programme in Linguistics and English Teaching* which led to *Breakthrough to Literacy* (Mackay et al, 1970). Consequently, although not exempt from criticism as a 'highly-contrived' language experience approach, its component materials and suggestions for classroom use have been widely accepted by teachers of initial literacy.

Linguistics and UKRA

Nowadays, there are comparatively few classroom resources which, like *Breakthrough to Literacy* and *Language in Action* are linguistics-informed. This is largely because, in some education circles, there is still a very strong resistance to, for example, 'linguistics in teacher education'. Accordingly, as long as that continues, educational publishers will not go out of their way to produce 'linguistics-informed' materials, the significance of which is not generally understood.

The *Kingman Report* (DES, 1988) may change all that as unusually generous financial resources have been allocated to implementing its recommendations. Meanwhile, it is worth remembering that, from the very start of UKRA, there has been concern among its members that there should be a multi-disciplinary approach to literacy, in which linguistics has an important role. For instance, as President, John Downing invited the distinguished American linguist Charles Fries to take part in UKRA's first Conference at Oxford University in July, 1964. Sadly, his plenary paper on *Linguistics and the Teaching of Reading* was generally misunderstood as, amongst other things, it seemed to be recommending a return to 19th century phonics. Afterwards, Professor Fries discussed with me the adverse reactions to his contribution and, unfortunately, he decided that there was no point in having it published in the Conference Proceedings. Instead, he suggested that, in any follow-up discussion, reference might be made to his then most recent article with the same title in *The Reading Teacher* (Fries, 1964).

To this day, that short article remains an excellent introduction to what linguistics has to offer the reading teacher. Moreover, in the following statement, it allays fears about the linguist's attitude to meaning.

> *Linguistics does not ignore meaning of any kind. It insists that statements about the signals of meaning, to be scientific, must be made in physical terms, but it does not deny that practical language deals with a complex range of various kinds of meanings*

which must be understood. In the teaching of reading, even from the very beginning, there must be complete meaning responses, not only to words but to those words in full sentences, and to those sentences in sequences of sentences.

At the second UKRA Conference held in London (in July 1965) John Mountford provided a comprehensive survey of the literature from the science of linguistics as it relates to the study of reading and writing (Mountford, 1967). After that, successive conference proceedings bear witness to the fact that the contribution of linguistics has not been neglected in our deliberations.

It is also interesting to note that David Crystal was among the distinguished conference contributors, and he supplied the article on *Linguistic Perspectives* (Crystal, 1975) in the special issue of *Reading* on the *Bullock Report* (DES, 1975). In this, he stressed that teachers need an explicit understanding of the nature of spoken and written language and the fundamental differences that exist between them. He also stresses that this understanding, and the skills to put it into practice, requires '*a rigorous and systematic component*' in teacher-training. A year later, he wrote another reminder of the same requirement and stated,

> For the mother tongue teacher, the question that should be being asked is not, 'How little linguistics can we get away with?', but, How much linguistics do we need?
>
> (Crystal, 1976)

Linguistics in teacher education

Like Professor Crystal, other linguists, and fellow UKRA members, I have tried very hard to influence the continuing debate about teacher-training for literacy so that it includes knowledge from linguistics. Evidence for this is to be found in many publications including, for example, my evidence 18 years ago before a House of Commons Select Committee on *Teacher Training: Teaching of Reading* (Morris, 1970), and in my UKRA Conference paper, '*You can't teach what you don't know*'. (Morris, 1973).

However, by 1983, I was distressed by the general lack of progress in this direction, and by appeals from teachers to put on even 'private' courses to help them understand especially the nature of English orthography, and how best to help slow learners acquire initial literacy skills. I decided then to try to discover to what extent student teachers had acquired basic linguistic knowledge before their pre-service course began and, hence, how much linguistics they would need during their training.

The generally poor results for 275 undergraduates caused mixed reactions when first reported at the 21st UKRA Conference in Dundee (Morris, 1985). Some delegates said the evidence confirmed what they already knew or suspected. A few suggested that a good deal of the ignorance apparently revealed by my *'Linguistics in Teacher Education Questionnaire'*, (LITE Quiz) was the result of students having 'fun' at the researcher's expense. However, subsequent studies using the same questionnaire, such as those analysed here at Leicester University by Dr George Young and Mrs Hislam (Hunter-Carsch, 1987) confirm that unless most testees set out to ridicule research, the linguistic knowledge of today's pre-service and in-service teachers leaves much to be desired. Moreover, as reported by Dr. Mary Joyce Lynn at the 11th World Congress on Reading and at this Conference, the same might be said of teachers in the USA.

One consequence of such revelations has been the formation, in 1985, of the UKRA Special Interest Group on Linguistics in Teacher Education. There are now over 50 members, and from the enthusiasm expressed by some of them, orally and in writing, there is a good prospect that, together, we shall be able to make a substantial contribution to the LITE debate. Meanwhile, as the representative of UKRA on the Committee for Linguistics in Education, I am able to keep members in touch with mainstream developments in this field.

The next 25 years

At present the British education system is in a state of flux, and is likely to remain so for some time. Consequently, nobody can predict the outcome of current efforts to heal the breach between linguistics and literature which, if anything, has grown wider since 1977 when I drew attention to its dangers at the First European Conference on Reading which was held in France (Morris, 1977). Personally, I cannot understand why otherwise sensible people with children's interests at heart, take up extremist positions. In my lifetime, 'structure' with appropriate instruction to meet individual needs, **and** 'motivation' with 'real' books, have always been essential elements in effective literacy teaching, and I suspect they will be during the next 25 years.

Reflecting on the disastrous effects of 'swings of the pendulum' in the past, I suggest that what is needed for 'real' progress towards universal literacy is for teachers to make a habit of asking, '*Where is the "real" research to support proposals for curriculum change and practice?*' More publicity should also be given to research findings which run contrary to popular beliefs. For example, in recent years, much publicity has been given to the psycholinguistic view of reading when, in fact, there are several conflicting views. The research-based view of Charles Perfetti, Professor of Psychology and Linguistics at Pittsburgh University, is a case in point – in that it is quite different from the widely publicised view of Professor Kenneth Goodman (Goodman, 1967). Perfetti states (1985) that,

> *For the skilled reader, reading is psycholinguistic but is no guessing game.*

He also agrees that reading ability involves multiple linguistic processes, – syntactic and semantic as well as phonographic, but he disagrees about the role of decoding skill and the contribution of phonic instruction. In short, Perfetti regards accurate efficient word recognition, knowledge of orthographic structure and decoding skill as fundamental to skilled reading. What is more, so do I, and many other researchers and teachers around the world.

Finally, as this is a requested personal statement about linguistics and learning, I should like to stress that I do not believe that linguistics or any other academic discipline alone holds the key to improving provision for literacy. A multi-disciplinary approach is essential. Moreover, it is as well to remember that teaching is an art, and no amount of academic knowledge will make up for a lack of rapport with pupils and enthusiasm for the task in hand. At the same time, without the requisite knowledge, rapport and enthusiasm will not suffice.

Once upon a time, I was an enthusiastic young teacher of co-operative pupils, but without the requisite linguistic knowledge to meet their special needs despite, and because of, my favourable background. Now that I have acquired more knowledge, it is far too late to help them, but I can meet requests to help other children and teachers. This is what I will continue trying to do as long as I have health and strength. I will also continue trying to give the kind of support to other less experienced researchers which I was fortunate to receive from psychologists like Dr Watts and linguists like Professor Fry. In short, I will continue trying to be helpful while learning as much as I can about language and literacy, which is what fellow members of UKRA have done over the past 25 years, and doubtless will continue to do in the post-Kingman era.

References

Bloomfield, L. & Barnhart, C.L. (1961) *Let's Read: A Linguistic Approach* Detroit: Wayne State University Press.
Crystal, D. (1975) *'Linguistic Perspectives in Reading'* In *Reading* Vol. 9. No. 2.
Crystal, D. (1976) *Child Language, Learning and Linguistics* London: Edward Arnold.
DES (1975) *A Language For Life* (The Bullock Report) London: HMSO.
DES (1988) *Report of the Committee of Inquiry Into The Teaching Of English Language* HMSO.
Fries, C.C. (1964) 'Linguistics and the Teaching of Reading' *The Reading Teacher* May.
Gattegno, C. (1962) 'Words in Colour' *Reading: Educational Explorers.*
Goodman, K.S. (1967) 'Reading: A Psycholinguistic Guessing Game' *Journal of the Reading Specialist* Vol. 6, May.
Gray, W.S. (1956) *The Teaching of Reading and Writing* Paris: UNESCO.
Hunter-Carsch, M. (ed) (1987) *Language and Literacy: Recent Research and its Implications for the Classroom* Occasional Paper, University of Leicester School of Education.
Mackay, D. et al. (1970) *Breakthrough to Literacy* London: Longman.
Morris, J.M. (1959) *Reading in the Primary School* London: Newnes.
Morris, J.M. (1970) *Teacher Training: Teaching of Reading* Minutes of evidence taken before the Select Committee on Education and Science (Sub-Committee B) London: HMSO.
Morris, J.M. (1973) 'You Can't Teach What You Don't Know' In M. Clark and A. Milne (Eds) *Reading and Related Skills* London: Ward Lock Educational.
Morris, J.M. et al. (1974–83) *Language in Action* London & Basingstoke: Macmillan Education.
Morris, J.M. (1977) *Development of Language and Reading* (microfiche) ERIC.
Morris, J.M. (1984) 'Phonics 44 for initial Literacy in English' *Reading* Vol. 18. No. 1.
Morris, J.M. (1985) 'Before a byte, the LITE approach to literacy in J. Ewing, (ed.) *Reading and the New Technologies*. London: Heinemann Educational Books.
Morris, J.M. (1987) 'Memories of John Downing: A Personal Reminiscence' UKRA Newsletter. Autumn.
Mountford, J. (1967) 'Linguistics and Reading and Writing' in John Downing and Amy L. Brown (Eds) *The Second International Reading Symposium* London: Cassell.
NCLE (1984) *Language Awareness: A Bibliography of Materials for Pupils and Teachers* National Congress on Languages in Education.
Perfetti, C.A. (1985) *Reading Ability* Oxford University Press.

Smith, Henry Lee (1956) *Linguistic Science and the Teaching of English*
    Inglis Lecture 1954. Cambridge Mass: Harvard University Press.
Watts, A.F. (1944) *The Language and Mental Development of Children*
    London : Harrap.
Wijk, A. (1959) *Regularized English* Stockholm: Almquist & Wiksell for the
    University of Stockholm.

22 Speech and writing: the development of a model with a functional sentence perspective

George M. Young

This article explores the differences between the media of speech and writing and the need to incorporate the differentiating features of the latter in any model of the production of written texts. Critical to any such model is what is termed a functional sentence perspective which accounts for the complex sentence as an efficient information-processing device.

Teachers lack an explicit model of the production of written text. A consequence of this is the lack among teachers of an appropriate vocabulary for talking about writing and the absence from their instructional plans of any principled rules of engagement to develop writing skills. Most are aware that writing involves a complex and specific set of motor skills but the process of production is opaque to introspection and, in the present deficit state of empirical research, must remain a mystery. Failure to understand writing as a linguistic process in turn prevents the teacher from fully understanding the problems that written text presents to the young reader. It is often assumed that listening and reading are essentially similar and differ only in the aural and visual nature of their input. At the root of this assumption is the belief that speech and writing are merely symmetrical mirror images of a common code and that whatever is said of one is, mutatis mutandis, true of the other. Yet what people write and read is organised linguistically in a way which is quite different from the patterning of speech. There are features of the context of writing which distinguish it from that of speech and which are always influences that operate to create the very distinctive pattern of the written text. These features require incorporation in any model which purports to account for the specific characteristics of written text. They are the visibility of the text, its autonomy, the graphic nature of the medium and the topic focus of its content. Each of these features carries certain implications for the process of production and demands a different set of skills for its control.

The visibility of the written text

Let us take, to begin with, the visibility of the text. Where speech fades rapidly, the written text remains on the page as a potential focus of attention. The words of speech are thus difficult to conceive as entities in isolation from their context of use. They are experienced as elements inseparable from the stream of apperception. In writing, the visibility of the text frees it from both the act of communication and the producer. A distance is placed between the word and the writer who can stand aside, comment upon, correct, even erase the text on the page. The word is released from the irrevocability which, at least until the invention of mechanical recording, afflicted all spoken text. There need be no Freudian slips on the written page. Even error can be eliminated. Inconsistency, even contradiction, gets submerged in the plosive flow of speech. Only writing has traditionally offered the possibility of extended critical examination. Thought which is written can be clarified and objectified in isolation from the connotations of the eliciting context. Written words are thus infinitely more abstract than the words of speech. They offer an ideal of definable truths with an inherent autonomy and permanence beyond the flow of the spoken word. It is arguably no accident that the first appearance of the phonemic alphabet in Ancient Greece preceded, by no more than a couple of generations, the beginnings of Western science and philosophy.

Yet there is a price to pay for permanence. The survival of the text ensures that the writer, unlike the speaker, is not allowed to forget. He or she is confronted with the permanent record of what has been written. Not only does this give the text a special juridical status in Western culture; it also affects the nature of the text itself. Expectations of order are created which demand the global planning of syntactic cohesion with the unfolding text. A good measure of these expectations is the tense cohesion, traditionally known as 'sequence of tenses', maintained by the skilled writer over often very wide stretches of narrative text. Such text-wide rules of procedure require a response set, a behavioural tension in the form of a metalinguistic span of scanning vision over the preceding text which is alien to the inexperienced writer accustomed to the fading and therefore forgettable text of speech.

The autonomy of the written text

The writer, like the speaker, must constantly pose the question: what can I assume to be the knowledge which I share with my addressee? The answer is determined by what the writer perceives to be in the immediate conciousness of the addressee. In speech what is presented as known or unknown will generally be derived from perceptions of knowledge shared with an immediate audience of utterance. Much of this, of course, will be world knowledge, culturally shared by all the participants. Writing draws upon the same world knowledge but the nature of the audience is more problematic for the writer interacts not with a live presence but with an abstract entity in the synmbolic world of the text. Awareness of such an audience can only be sustained by the external prompts of the author as he or she monitors the text. Unfamiliar with this reflexive process, the unskilled writer may lose awareness of audience and form unprecedented anaphoric connections throughout the text. This is why pronominal cohesion is such a useful indicator of children's writing development. The writing of young children is often heavily dependent upon knowledge assumed to be shared but which cannot be traced by the reader to the text. The child has to be taught that the referent of a pronoun must ultimately be located somewhere in the text. The textuality of presumed knowledge has to be learned.

Speech is a transparent code. Its meaning lies in the assimilability of the text to the context. It is predominantly a contextual implication of the text. In fact, only a fraction of it is explicitly represented in the text. Its complexity tends to be one of condensation of inference and association conveyed as much by intonational and paralinguistic systems as by the actual denotata of the words used. But the whole object of written language is to free the act of communication from the immediate context and transport it elsewhere. It is therefore driven inexorably towards the explication of meaning through lexis and syntax which provide the only available modality of communication. The extra semantic load that syntax is compelled to carry has caused it to generate structures that are clearly substitutes for the modalities of speech. In speech, for example, new information with a specific presupposition attached to it is conveyed by a marked turbulence in the tonic, the point of major change in the intonation contour, or its movement to an unexpected position in the clause or phrase. Thus in speech we might say, variously, 'WEBB swam the channel today'. 'Webb swam the CHANNEL today', or

'Webb swam the channel TODAY' with in each case the highlighted tonic carrying a different implication. The absence of this facility in writing has led to the higher frequency of what is known as the 'cleft sentence construction' which redistributes clause patterns to create syntactic echoes of the presuppositions of speech in such structures, as 'It was WEBB that swam the channel today'. 'It was the CHANNEL which Webb swam today', and so on. Meaning can clearly be conveyed by implication in writing but the isolation of the text and the consequent remoteness of the audience will mean that it is much more likely to be raised to an explicit presupposition in the surface of the text.

The graphicity of the medium

Speech is realised in phonic and kinesic patterns, Such is the immediacy of the medium that even the planning of speech is reflected in the text in hesitation phenomena. The graphic substance of writing is more viscous in flow. The act of writing is thus slower and more effortful. It involves long delays which are particularly noticeable in the inexperienced writer. The greater time this affords for verbal planning allows a considerable increase on the condensation of meaning but whereas in speech, as we have seen, the condensation is one of layered implications in the context of utterance, in writing the complexity is created layer upon layer in the surface of the text. The layering is achieved by devices of syntactic embedding that make one phrase or clause part of another, allowing us to produce structures of considerable length such as, for example, *'the three water board manhole covers in the truck parked at the intersection of the motorways'*. Embedding of this order allows a rapid processing of information but only to the reader whose eye is attuned to it, for it contains a complex 'nesting' of structures normally unattainable in speech.

All language is, in a sense, an epistemological model that breaks up the natural unity of the perceptual world. Phonemes, morphemes, words and phrases are organised discontinuously. Writing crystallises this discontinuity through spatial location. The units of graphology do not elide like those of speech. They are devices of sequentation unfamiliar to the inexperienced writer and alien to the accumulative nature of speech. It was for this among other reasons that the *Bullock Report* (DES 1975: 11.21) recommended explicit instruction in the graphological medium. Weak control of the medium creates blockages that take up short-term memory storage which might otherwise be available for the rehearsal of syntactic structures prior to transcription. Yet with developing technology the significance of graphicity may be exaggerated. Written texts of all kinds can be produced from dictation to a tape recorder or a shorthand typist. Experimental evidence suggests that good authors are good authors whether dictating or writing (Hartley, 1980). Finally, the innovation of the wordprocessor has enabled authors to overcome many of the constraints upon production caused by the previously irrevocable spatial linearisation of the written page.

The topic-centredness of writing

Writing is finally distinguished from speech by the extent of its topic-centredness for whereas the conceptual connectivity of speech derives ultimately from the world of its eliciting context that of writing devices almost entirely from the world of its developing topic. The topic is a mere channel of shared meaning in speech. It is the very source of shared meaning in writing. The linearisation of the topic in writing contrasts with the cyclical or spiralling of speech which follows a pattern of continual return to the world of shared meaning in the situation of utterance. The topic is thus a more powerful determinant of the nature of the text in writing than in speech. The unit of speech is the utterance, which is essentially a pragmatic concept, a move in a language game. It generally picks up some aspect of a conversational topic. It is distinguishable at its boundaries by alterations in intonation and contour and key. But attempts to find syntactic correlates have been largely abandoned. An utterance may be a phrase or a clause or, indeed, a larger number of usually topically-related clauses strung together. In writing, on the other hand, successive clauses are paired, separated and embedded within each other according to the strength of their connectedness to distinguishable aspects of the topic as these unfold. These aspects form the integrating concepts of sentences, for the sentence is the unit in which the choice of connectedness is made. In the text of the skilled writer the integrating concept is a discrete and separable unit. That of the child writer often still reflects the logic of the utterance in speech. It is much looser and more multi-dimensional. It is more like a paragraph which, if anything, is the closest analogue to the spoken utterance. Without a true analogue in speech the significance of the sentence has got to be learned. Its acquistion is of paramount importance for it is the only road to the world of the written page.

The function of the complete sentence in writing

It is interesting to consider why developing child writers ever move beyond sentences of this primitive type. The answer may lie in the role of the complex sentence as a more efficient information-processing device. The processing consists of foregrounding and backgrounding the flow of propositions that relate to the topic in accordance with the perceived states of knowledge of the receiver. Two types of communicative foreground are particularly significant. These we might term the *logical* and *informational* foregrounds of the text. In the logical foreground are placed those propositions that form an independent dialogic move in the development of the topic, whether in the shape of an assertion, question, wish or whatever. In the logical background are those causes, conditions, contexts, etc which constitute the supporting moves which enable the independent moves in the discourse to have rhetorical force. The informational foreground we have already encountered in part in our brief review of the cleft sentence construction. In this foreground is placed information which is presented as 'new' in the sense that it is regarded as not within the immediate consciousness of the receiver. By the same token, information which is 'given' or 'old' since it is perceived to be part of the immediate taken-for-granted knowledge of the receiver is assigned to the informational background. As every text unfolds in discourse, the information encoded is distributed between those two quite separate communicative foregrounds.

In speech, particularly the more informal kind, what is foreground and background is often conveyed by association and inference and, where signalled at all, is frequently imparted by a delicate combination of intonation and sequence. Transferred to the written page the result is the chains of clauses strung together that form the earliest sentences of the unskilled writer. Such structures are serviceable so long as the sequence is chronological and the propositional material low in density. The system breaks down where a number of propositions compete for the foreground in the form of discourse that demands that they be martialled to achieve a rhetorical effect.

In writing the congestion can only be controlled effectively by grammaticalising the foregrounds and embedding them within the structure of the complex sentence. The logical foreground is located in the main clause of the sentence with its background moves in the qualifying and subordinate clauses. The informational foregound consists of syntactic focusing devices that convey background presuppositions in their syntactic structure. The example we saw was the cleft sentence construction. The process by which these two syntactic foregrounds combine to form the complex sentence and the way in which they are used by children in their first hesitant moves beyond the simple sentence have been studied by the author and reported in a series of papers that purport to present a model of syntactic control in written language development (cf Young, 1982, 1983, 1985). At the core of this model is what can only be described as a functional sentence perspective. Without such a perspective the process by which a writer moves from the simple to the complex sentence must always remain a mystery both to the teacher and the child.

References

DES (1975) *A Language for Life* (The Bullock Report) HMSO.

Hartley, J. (Ed) (1980) *The Psychology of Written Communication* London: Kogan Page.

Young, G. (1982) 'The Elaborated Code: A New Formulation Within a functional Framework' *Language & Speech*, 25, 1. Pp. 81–93.

Young, G. (1983) 'A Systemic Model of the Elaborate Code' *Language & Speed* 26, 2. Pp. 171–190.

Young, G. (1985) 'The Development of Logic and Focus in Childrens' Writing' *Language & Speech*, 28, 2. Pp. 115–127.

23 Genre and register: implications for reading

Alison B. Littlefair

The term 'genre' is used very widely and generally indicates things which have a good deal in common. Some systemic linguists, however, are looking a little more closely at genre for it may be seen as a meaning system. It is not an independent meaning system as is music, since it is dependent upon language for its expression. The language patterns which realise genre are those of its particular register.

In the course of their school careers, pupils read a variety of genres: the major genre categories of books used in school would seem to be literary, expository, procedural and reference. Each is characterised by a structure which is realised by flexible register patterning. If the majority of pupils are to understand the meanings which different genres represent, they must be made aware of the implications of different register patterns. Research has been undertaken to investigate how far some 3rd year junior school pupils and some 1st and 4th year secondary school pupils of varying reading ability perceive register factors of books of different genres and how far the development of this perception would seem to be a significant factor in the development of reading skills.

Introduction

The linguistic basis of my research follows the systemic model of language which considers the patterning of language in use.

Initially, I used the two terms 'genre' and 'register', synonymously. However, it became more appropriate to regard them as individual perspectives of language variety: thus 'genre' indicates the categories of books and 'register' indicates the flexible linguistic patterning used within each genre.

I became aware that some systemic linguists in Sydney University had developed the notion of 'genre' and further have begun to have considerable influence on some language curricula and some initial and in-service teacher training in Australia. In addition, I noted that the discussion about genre is continuing quite dynamically.

This discussion is based on the view that all language, be it spoke or written, is expressed within a context of culture. Culture is made up of all kinds of meaningful, purposeful activities. There has been considerable research (Halliday and Hasan, 1980, Ventola, 1987) into the linguistic patterning which structures these activities. The most usual example is that of service encounters, such as a visit to the doctor or to the greengrocer. There seems little question but that as we engage in an activity, we follow a structure which we have become aware of as participants in our particular culture. By contrast, it is obvious that buying and selling within a culture which uses a system of bargaining will be structured differently.

An abstract meaning of genre is now given by some systemic linguists to indicate a purposeful activity within a context of culture. The form of the activity is named 'generic structure'. The genre structure is not inflexible since another variable has to be considered, that of the immediate context of situation.

Halliday and Hasan (1980) have suggested that the context of a situation can be analysed in terms of its field (which is concerned with the subject area); its mode (which is concerned with the manner of communication), and its tenor (which is concerned with the relationship between the participants). The resulting patterning indicates the register. The interaction of the field, mode and tenor indicate the meaning which is expressed through language; the ideational meaning of language is expressed through the field, the textual meaning of language through the mode, and the interpersonal meaning of language through the tenor.

Thus it may be said that a particular genre has a generic structure whose meaning or purpose is realised through register patterning.

It follows that the categories of books in school may be considered as genres. I have suggested that there are four major genres of books: literary, expository, procedural and reference. Each major genre category has a flexible structure which enables the purpose or meaning of that genre to be realised through register patterning. Thus books in the literary genre aim to narrate or describe; books in the expository genre aim to explain, to describe facts; books in the procedural genre aim to instruct; and books in the reference genre aim to describe decontextualised facts concisely.

My concern has been to inquire into the perception of pupils of the register of books used in school. If we declare that reading is taught in order that pupils may gain meaning and not just decode printed language, then we must consider how they perceive the two aspects of coherent text: cohesion within the text and register which relates text to context. Chapman (1987) has produced research which indicates that pupils' perception of cohesive ties within texts relates to their development as readers. It was therefore reasonable to inquire whether their perception of register has similar significance.

The study

I worked with 72 pupils drawn from two secondary schools and four junior schools. There were four groups of six 3rd year junior pupils, two groups of twelve 1st year secondary school pupils and two groups of twelve 4th year secondary school pupils. Each group contained an equal number of readers of low, average and able reading ability, although by the 4th year secondary school stage, the term 'readers' was replaced by the term 'pupils' since their ability was assessed on the basis of their language performance across the curriculum. The sample did not contain non-readers or pupils who spoke English as a second language.

The research methodology was mainly based on individual pupils trying to match pages taken from books of different genres with one of four 'master' pages taken from books representing the four major genres. Individual pupils described to me the reasons for their choices. These discussions were taped.

Later transcription of the tapes suggested that the responses of the pupils could be categorised as giving indication of some awareness of field, or mode, or tenor, or of their meaningful interaction in the text. The response of a pupil to a single matching task was considered as falling into a single category. This meant that the number of responses in each category could be reasonable compared and trends noted.

A brief description of the positive responses suggests there is an initial general awareness of the topic involved in the text (field). This is not surprising but it seems very significant that responses indicating pages as belonging to a subject specialisation were made by all ability groups but particularly by less able and average readers in the 1st year of the secondary school. No doubt this was a response to a more subject-dominated timetable and the books associated with this. The less able groups in the 4th year of the secondary school continued predominantly to note this aspect while the responses of readers in the more able groups were concerned with more complex aspects of register.

There was some awareness of simple aspects of the patterning within texts (mode) shown by pupils in all the age and ability groups. A more detailed awareness was most significant in the able groups, both in the 1st and 4th year of the secondary school. It may be that these readers, even in the junior school, quickly become aware of the patterning within texts and continue to develop perception of the difference in the register patterning of the genres of the books they read in the secondary school.

There was very little awareness of tenor but this perhaps reflects the fact that the linguistic devices which realise personal tenor in text are not easily accessible to pupils without the teacher indicating their significance in considerable detail.

An awareness of the obvious purpose of a text was indicated by all groups although the able and average readers gave most of the responses which fell into this category. However, the beginning of more perceptive awareness of the interactive meanings of the texts on the page was only noted from the responses of the average and able 4th year secondary groups which suggests that autonomous reading for meaning is only just being accomplished by more capable pupils towards the end of their compulsory education.

Concluding discussion

The trends of the responses seem to indicate that awareness of the register of books is developmental. Whilst it is difficult to distinguish between cognitive and linguistic development in reading, there would seem to be evidence that linguistic awareness plays a large role in the development of this perception. The question should therefore be asked as to how far teachers can help pupils to increase their awareness of linguistic features of the books they read. Such teaching would not be directed towards decontextualised grammar work but rather towards helping pupils become more aware of the linguistic patterning of register which relates text to context and realises the meaning of the writer.

Relevant teaching strategies would involve even quite young pupils hearing texts from different genres in order that they might subconsciously develop their awareness of the textual patterns. As pupils develop their reading abilities, teachers might well help them to compare books of different genres so that they may perceive beyond the subject area of a book and be more able to grapple with its meaning through its register patterning. There might also be teacher awareness of the balance of genres which their pupils are reading and have previously read.

Such suggestions can, of course, only be undertaken by teachers who have themselves an understanding of language patterning. This research suggests that it is not until towards the end of compulsory education that even able and average pupils are really able to grapple with the meanings of different genres of books used in school. If this is so, then it is essential that teachers have that understanding.

References

Chapman, L.J. (1987) *Reading From 5–11 Years* Open University Press.
Halliday, M.A.K. & Hasan, R. (1980) 'Text & Context: Aspects of Language, in a Social-Semiotic Perspective' *Sophia Linguistica (Working Papers In Linguistics)* 6. pp. 4–91.
Ventola, E. (1987) *The Structure of Interaction* Pinter.

24 Word processing and literacy skills

Frank Potter

'Word Processing and Literacy Skills' is a research project concerned with the applications and implications of word processors for reading and writing.

It is sponsored by the Commission of the European Communities, Edge Hill College of Higher Education, The United Kingdom Reading Association and the Department of Education and Science.

Introduction

The objectives of the project are:

- to increase contacts and eventually collaboration between educational researchers;
- to organise a seminar to explore key issues;
- to publish a handbook for teachers and educators.

For the first stage of the project the European working group produced an interim report which included a register of current projects throughout the European Community, and a position paper outlining our current stage of knowledge.

A summary of this outline is presented below:

While there seems almost unanimous agreement among teachers that word processors can substantially improve children's writing, the research evidence is not so easily interpreted. Despite this, it does seem possible to draw certain tentative conclusions. First, it should be empasised that word processors do seem to have a significant role to play in improving children's literacy skills. The question therefore is not whether word processors should be used, but how they should be used.

There is a certain 'standard' way of using a word processor, in which the writer, sitting alone at the keyboard, composes directly at the keyboard. He/she then reviews the text on the computer screen, revises and then prints out another draft of the text.

One of the most important conclusions is that, because of certain limiting factors, this 'standard' way of using word processors may be the least effective. It is interesting to note that teachers have not only independently come to a similar conclusion, but have also managed to think of other ways of using the word processor so as to take advantage of its unique facitilies.

The value of of word processing seems to depend upon the stage of the writing process for which it is used – word processers facilitate revising, redrafting and editing, but composing and reviewing are only facilitated under certain special circumstances.

Certain factors are responsible for this, namely:

• whether changes are identified on screen or on hard copy;
• children's familiarity with the word processor;
• whether associated peripherals and facilities are used.

As would be expected, it also seems that word processers are especially beneficial for some individuals.

Recognising these problems, different teachers have arrived at different ways of making effective use of word processors – for example to demonstrate and encourage redrafting, to facilitate collaborative writing, and to emphasise the communicative function of writing, by making writers more aware of the importance of audience (through the printout, the VDU screen and the potential of electronic mail).

25 Teaching English in Japan

Yoshihiko Sugano

Professor Sugano briefly outlined the context in which Japanese pupils learn English. He drew attention to the limitations of a traditionally grammar based approach to teaching. The lively discussion which ensued made reference to the Kingman Report's recommendations within the context of teaching English in England and explored the possible impact, in the Japanese school situation, of the 'language experience approach' as a means of increasing pupils' involvement in formulating their own questions and actively exploring topics of their choice rather than solely book-based programmes or expensive langauge laboratory approaches.

Current approaches to teaching English to children in England whose first language is other than English were discussed. Examples of teaching Japanese children in Japan, using such techniques, were illustrated by Dr Joyce Morris, one of the participants in the workshop, who had actually talked with Japanese children who had, at that time, been reading and writing about London. As a resident of London she was able to invite questions about everyday life there. There appeared to be both interest and easy involvement in spoken English in such a 'lesson'. Issues arising included the scarcity of 'people resources' in terms of those fluent in spoken English. There was reportedly limited use of the range of published resources, in the sense that teachers' dependence on programmed instructions was widespread and traditionally 'culturally patterned' within schools.

The value of the audio tape recorder was emphasised and modifications of 'story approach' in stories taped at normal and slower speaking rates suggested on the basis of the editor's classroom experience in Canada teaching English to 'New Canadians'. Professor Sugano's short paper is included as follows. There was generally expressed appreciation and interest in continuing the 'International Exchange'.

Japanese Formal Education

After kindergarten at the age of six there is primary school, then three years in lower secondary. The combined nine years are compulsory but at age 15 it is possible to go on to upper secondary as some 95% of students do. Three or four years later about 35% of the graduates enter University (for four to six year courses) or junior colleges (for two years).

Pupils learn English for six years through lower and upper secondary and for four years in University, thus totalling ten years of learning English on the basis of three to four hours per week. One 'school hour' is defined as a class period of 50 minutes in school but at University the 'school hour' becomes 90 minutes.

Even after that long period of learning, pupils' spoken communication in English is still weak and confidence lacking in attempting to answer any questions if asked by an English-speaking visitor. The difficulties may be explained as follows:

1 In Japan very few people have the chance to speak to foreigners. Only a few are able to travel and live for some time in English-speaking countries. In my own case I have had the chance to speak English only three or four times in Japan during the last five years. There are more opportunities to communicate with speakers of Chinese, Korean and Formosan language, all of which are different in construction from Japanese and are more difficult than English.

2 The problem may also include the national characteristics of the Japanese. Historically they are, on the whole very shy and reticent with foreigners, partly because of the obstacle of the foreign language. This has been pointed out since the Meiji era (1870) as constituting a kind of 'inferiority complex'.

3 The most important problem is the method of teaching in schools. Traditionally the main emphasis in the compulsory English lessons is on the teaching of grammar. Literacy includes reading, writing, listening and speaking, however, teachers of English begin with a few words and grammar first. Many pupils attempt to learn English grammar by heart. At University students may translate English sentences into Japanese, holding a dictionary in one hand. They can read or write English sentences, yet have great difficulty understanding and speaking English despite the length of time spent in formal learning of the language. Very few can read write, listen and speak equally well in English.

As a response to this widespread situation in Japan, and since the Second World War, many teachers of English have been devising ways of solving the problem. Despite attempts to improve things the problem still requires attention. Suggestions and advice are welcomed.

Acknowledgement

With thanks to Tepo Din, a 15-year-old friend from Leicester and to Japanese-speaking colleagues all of whom assisted with the presentation and discussion. Thanks also to Mrs Hunter-Carsch and to the UKRA for the opportunity to present the short-paper.

PART 5

Literacy Difficulties

26 Less proficient readers and retelling: learning to re-create text

Elizabeth Goodacre

Young children spontaneously retell stories that have been read to them and seem to obtain much enjoyment from doing so. Miscue analysis makes use of retelling as a measure of the meaning that pupils have gained from their reading. Experiments and studies in reading comprehension have used retelling as a way of assessing readers' comprehension, but few have considered whether retelling as a strategy can be used to improve reading comprehension. However, some studies have been concerned with how the teacher can model retelling and use it as part of reading instruction, explaining to learners how retelling can be of practical use in everyday life by helping the reader to check whether they have understood what they have read.

The paper also describes how the Conference workshop provided members with an opportunity to try out the strategy themselves and to evaluate these ideas, particularly as to how they might be used to help less proficient readers.

Young children's re-creation of text

In the light of the conference title, 'Reading and Re-Creation' I would like to consider the recreation of text involved in the telling of what has been read. The reader not only remembers the text but reproduces it in retelling. I have been interested in retelling since one of my children was very small. Most parents are familiar with the stage when young children memorise a favourite story and want it read again and again. If a parent tries to condense the story or omit a portion of the text, the young listener can get very annoyed indeed. The child may often be able to repeat, word for word, whole sections of a story and won't have the reader skip any part of it. My son loved the Reverend Awdry's stories about *Thomas the Tank Engine*, and there was a short period when he would delight in listening to me read them aloud and would interrupt at regular intervals to repeat phrases and quite long sections of the text. I was interested in the differences between what was in the text and what he reproduced from memory. The material which he heard read aloud was processed selectively and encoded into memory storage and then produced at his current level of linguistic competence, eg

> The text read as:
> *Don't go so fast grumbled the coaches; but James did not listen. He wanted to run away before the Fat Controller could call him back.*

> My four-year-old reproduced it as:
> *Don't go so fast, said the coaches; but James didn't listen. He wanted to run before the Fat Controller can call after him.*

Shortly after this, I came across Don Holdaway's studies of young children's recalled or memorised book language (1976, 1979). He described young children's spontaneous attempts to retrieve pleasurable book experiences and produced (from taped sessions) samples of their reconstructions of texts read to them.

Using retelling to assess reading comprehension

I was also interested in the Goodmans' ideas about miscue analysis and noted that in *The Reading Miscue Inventory* (Goodman and Burke, 1972) retelling was recommended as a *broader and deeper measure of the meanings that the student has gained from the reading*. The RMI Manual provides details of how the retelling should be organised, the teacher asking the pupil to review in his own words what he has read. The retelling is said to indicate the reader's ability to interrelate, interpret and draw conclusions from the content read aloud. The teacher has an outline of the material read, which indicates the characters, events, plot and theme of the story. It is suggested that the teacher does not interrupt the reader in their retelling but can question the reader afterward, focusing on the elements in the retelling outline. The Manual provides a somewhat arbitrary marking scheme for what has been recalled, which can be used for retelling both story or informational material.

I used miscue analysis, developing my own coding system and sometimes asking for a retelling. I didn't make use of a marking scheme but rather used the retelling as a way of trying to understand what the reader had made of the particular text in the light of their experience and knowledge of the world and their linguistic competence. In the Conference workshop I used an example of an eight-year-old girl (RA 7.4) reading a story composed by a teacher, which showed how a particular miscue influenced the reader's recall of the story.

Recent research on reading comprehension and retelling

During the last decade there has been a marked increase in reading research which focuses on reading comprehension, both in this country and in the United States. I carried out a survey of the sections on 'comprehension research' and 'oral reading research' in the *Annual Summary of Investigation Relating to Reading* for the period 1982–86. The latter section provided some information about retelling, as much of this research was based on miscue analysis. In the comprehension research, various ways of assessing readers' understanding of what they had read (aloud or silently) were cited. References were made to the reader retelling, reviewing or recalling text and to the retention of what had been read. Such retelling or reviewing could be in oral or written form. The researcher might use prompts or probe questions to elicit more information. Sometimes experiments even involved some form of intervention between the reading and the retelling, such as the reader being asked to repeat a string of numbers or the alphabet before they commenced the recall.

When it came to analysing what had been retold, most of the research seemed to concentrate on how the reader had organised what they had recalled. Some studies were concerned with the extent to which the reader had struck to the author's structure, and the nature and the extent of their divergence. Some researchers described the retelling or recall as at a 'high' or 'low' level. It was not always clear what this meant and one would have to consult the actual study to find out the criteria used to determine such 'levels' in the reproduction of texts.

A number of the studies also varied as to the unit of analysis used. The original text would be divided into propositions and the retelling would be analysed for the number and type of propositions recalled which were in the original. Sometimes the comparison was quantitative – what proportion of the original text was recalled in the retellings; sometimes qualitative – the numer and type of omissions and additions, or what distortions. In some studies the original text was divided into main or important ideas and supportive details, and then the researchers analysed the extent to which the main ideas were apparent in the retelling.

If we look at what the reader was being asked to recall, there are considerable differences in the types of text used in such studies. Quite apart from whether the reader is asked to read aloud or silently, recall orally or in writing – often related to the age of the reader – the texts may be different in type or genre; eg narrative or folk tale (complete or incomplete) or information or expository texts. Sometimes text was altered to discover the effect of cohesiveness – by having the reader read and recall text with or without connectives. The influence of illustrations was studied by using text with or without pictures. From the point of view of the 'subjects' involved in the studies, there are variations in the age of the learners, their reading ability, their prior experience or knowledge, their cultural or racial background.

Because of the differences in the samples used, the nature of the task for the reader, and the types of texts used, it is difficult to draw valid conclusions about the relationship between retelling and reading comprehension. Some of the relationships may only exist at particular stages in the learner's acquisition of reading. There is also the question of the interrelationship of variables and their effects. For instance, Rusted and Hodgson (1985), trying to find out about the effect of pictures, found that pictures facilitated recall in retelling (that is, recall of pictorial features) but this only applied in relation to factual passages and not to fiction. Hartson (1984) found that young readers in their retelling comprehended 'well-formed versions' of a story better than variant versions but this did not apply when the material they read was a folktale.

Modelling retelling as a strategy for developing reading comprehension

The most recent research seems to suggest that it may be necessary for readers themselves to understand something about retelling as a strategy. Johnston (1985) cites recent research describing instruction strategies and stresses that pupils need to be helped to understand *why* they are doing what they are doing and to extend that beyond the immediate task. Learners need feedback and a focus on the process of understanding rather than simply stressing the amount that has been understood at a particular point in time.

Most studies have used retelling as a means of assessing reading comprehension. As Koskinen, Gambrell, Kapinus and Heathington (1988) point out, only a few studies have focused on using retelling as a means of improving reading comprehension. Studies by Gambrella, Pfeiffer and Wilson (1985), Rose, Cundick and Higbee (1984) and Kapinus, Gambrella and Koskinen (in press) taken together suggest that encouraging pupils to engage in the verbal rehearsal of what they have read results in improved reading comprehension. Koskinen and her colleague (1988) claim retelling is both effective and time efficient. They suggest a sequence to help less proficient readers use retelling as a strategy for enhancing their reading comprehension. They consider it is important that a rationale for retelling should be shared with the learners.

> *Tell them they will be retelling a story to develop storytelling skill and that retelling also will help them check to see if they understand what they have read . . . We often want to tell friends about something that has happened or something we have seen or read. Practising retelling will help make such accounts more accurate and interesting.*

The teacher should model retelling, and the children and the teacher can discuss whether the points recalled by the teacher are the most important. After the teacher models retelling the learners should be provided with opportunities to practise it for themselves, and given guidance as to how to use prompt questions. Also it can be suggested to them that they can retell stories 'in their heads' (silent verbal rehearsal) as an independent strategy when they want to remember what they have read.

Koskinen and her colleagues consider the important features of this approach are that the learner is provided with guidance and modelling of how to retell and a rationale for the development of such a strategy. They warn that teachers, when they begin to use retelling, find they need to consider the level, type and length of the reading materials used. Materials used for initial experiences need to be short and well structured – as the reader grows in proficiency she can move on to retelling longer and more complex text information. Koskinen et al suggest that children can work effectively in pairs, taking turns to act as reteller or listener. The latter should be given a purpose for listening. One purpose is to have the listener tell their partner one thing they like about the partner's retelling: '*The listener learns to notice features of retelling that can enhance their own retelling, and retellers get to hear compliments about their work*'.

Conference workshop

The Workshop was organised so that members had the opportunity to try out retelling as a strategy for themselves. They worked in pairs, each taking in turn the role of reteller or listener; each having the opportunity to read and then retell a short narrative and then an expository text. Then in fours they compared notes about their experience and came together for a final session of lively comment. The texts were all based on material from the *Times Educational Supplement*. Members of the workshop were surprised by the selective nature of their recall and particularly about the additions and omissions they made in their retellings. Partners recalled and reconstructed quite different text. Pairs went on to discuss the reasons for this and to reflect on differences in their prior knowledge, and also the extent to which they visualised or made use of images as they read and recalled.

It was suggested that not only might this be a useful approach to try out with less proficient readers, but that a variant might be for individual learners to read a text and then retell the material onto a tape recorder. They could then compare their retelling with the original text reflecting on the differences between the original and the retelling. The same positive feedback could be encouraged as with pairs, so that the individuals would be learning not only to be an active learner but to give themselves praise and positive self-evaluation. The general view was that the workshop had been a worthwhile experience, and an opportunity to rethink the place and value of retelling, not only for assessing reading comprehension but as a means to improve it.

References

Gambrell, L., Pfeiffer, W. & Wilson, R. (1985) 'The Effect of Retelling upon Comprehension, and Recall of Text Information'. *Journal of Education Research* 78, pp. 216–220.

Goodman, Y. & Burke, C. (1972) 'Procedure for Diagnosis and Evaluation'. *Reading Miscue Inventory Manual* Macmillan.

Hartson, E. (1984) 'The Effects of Story Structure in Texts on the Reading comprehension of 1st and 2nd Grade Students'. *The California Reader*, 17, (3) pp. 6–10.

Holdaway, D. (1976) *New Horizons In Reading* 'Self-Evaluation and Reading Development'. ed. by Merritt Fifth World Congress on Reading in Vienna', Newark: International Reading Association, pp. 181–192.

Holdaway, D. (1979) *The Foundations of Literacy* Ashton Scholastic.

Johnston, P. (1985) 'Teaching Students to Apply Strategies that Improve Reading Comprehension'. *The Elementary School Journal* 85, pp. 635–645.

Kapinus, B., Gambrell, L. & Koskinen, P. (in Press) 'The Effect of Practice in Retelling upon the Reader.' *Thirty-Sixth Year Book of the National Reading Conference* Rochester, N.Y.: National Reading Conference.

Koskinen, P., Gambrell, L., Kapinus, L. & Heathinton, B. (1988) 'Retelling: A Strategy for Enchancing Students' Reading Comprehension'. *The Reading Teacher.*

Rose, M., Cundick, B., & Higbee, K. (1984) 'Verbal Rehearsal and Visual Imagery: Nnemonic Aids for Learning Disabled Children.' ' *Journal of Learning Disabilities* 16, pp. 353–54.

Rusted, J. & Hodgson, S. (1985) 'Evaluating the Picture Facilitation Effect in Children's Recall of Written Texts.' *British Journal of Educational Psychology* 55, pp. 288–294.

Weintraub, S. et al. (1984 *Summary of Investigations Relating to Reading* July 1, 1982 to June 30, 1983.

—— (1985) *Summary of Investigations Relating to Reading* July 1, 1983 to June 30, 1984.

—— (1986) *Summary of Investigations Relating to Reading* July 1, 1984 to June 30, 1985.

—— (1987) *Summary of Investigations Relating to Reading* July 1, 1985 to June 30, 1986. Newark: International Reading Association.

27 A comparison of three community reading projects

Margaret Litchfield

Leicestershire Literacy Support Service (LSS) has a well-established tradition of devising and resourcing parental/volunteer programmes to nurture reading interest and attainment from pre-school age to secondary level. However, after initial controlled trials to ascertain an individual project's effectiveness, most time (perhaps inevitably) has been concentrated on implementation and evaluation, with little opportunity for cross-project comparison. An opportunity arose, during the academic year 1986–1987, for the following small comparative study to be undertaken.

Introduction

Mary Linwood School is a co-educational secondary school, with an intake, in September 1986, of 840 students aged 11 to 16, from two large council estates on the edge of Leicester. Its catchment area could be broadly described as lower socio-economic. All the students speak English as a first language. In the summer of 1986, the Literacy Support Service was asked to help organise the Special Educational Needs Department with a specific remit to look at the needs of poor readers. Along with many other suggestions the school kindly agreed to operate community involvement programmes.

The Projects

The three projects undertaken were:

1 Paired reading. This was the traditional model explored by Morgan et al (1979) and developed by Topping (1986) in Kirklees.
2 A parent/volunteer helper scheme.
3 Cross-age tutoring using fourth and fifth year volunteer students.

The method for the last two derived from the work of Glynn (Clarke & Glynn 1980). It was adapted by LSS and the framework which was taught to helpers is reproduced in Appendix 1 on page 210. The timing of the work coincided with a complete restocking of the SEN department of Mary Linwood School. The book-buying policy was in line with current thinking about 'real' books and where schemes were included they were chosen for their natural language, strong story line and interest content. In all three projects, as in all aspects of the department's work, students were given free or guided choice and no student was ever pressed to continue with a text which, after consideration, was found to be boring. In all cases a member of the school staff was responsible for training and in-school organisation but was provided with videotapes, extensive notes and information for helpers by the Literacy Support Service.

The objectives of the work were:

1 To improve the students' attainment in and attitude to reading.
2 To foster good home/school and in-school relationships.
3 To compare the efficacy of the three projects in terms of
   • students' reading attainment,
   • students' attitude to reading,
   • students' attitude to 'lay' helpers,
   • parental and volunteer response in terms of initial willingness to take part and post project reflections.
4 To consider the organisational implications for the school.
5 To examine any effect on the reading attainment of the fourth and fifth year tutors.
6 To continue evaluating how a support service can give optimum help to schools.

The students

Forty-two students were identified who were deemed suitable for the projects. This extra help would be an addition to that ordinarily supplied by the SEN department, not a substitute. The sample comprised 12 girls and 30 boys with an average chronological age of 12 years (from 11 years 1 month to 13 years 11 months) with an average Reading Accuracy of 8:1 to 9:2 (from No Score to 9:5 – 10:6) and an average comprehension score of 8:3 to 9:10 (from 7:2–8:9 to 10:4–10:11) in September 1986. The test used was the *New Macmillan Reading Analysis* (Vincent & de la Mare 1985). All

students were interviewed pre- and post-project using the questionnaires reproduced in Appendix 2 (page 211).

Personnel and organisation

It was decided to undertake Paired Reading for six weeks in the
Autumn term, to allow for the possible Hawthorne effect that previous trials had shown and which could then be gauged at the final
assessment in June 1987. Nine parents responded positively and
undertook the work. Nine members of the school staff volunteered
to undertake the home visiting element. Parents were again can-
vassed in January 1987 and a further nine agreed to undertake the
'Helping Children Read' model (Appendix 1). These were joined by
12 school staff (not all teachers) who also wanted to help, so that 21
students were catered for. The fourth and fifth year students were
then asked if they would like to help the remaining 12 children,
using the same method. 24 of the students were assessed using
Gapadol (McLeod & Anderson 1972) and were randomly allocated
to project and control groups. Projects 2 and 3 involved the helpers
and students working together for a maximum of 15 minutes of
three times per week from the middle of January 1987 to the beginning of May 1987 (with a two-week break at Easter). The paired
reading project lasted six weeks, but the pairs worked together
for a maximum of 15 minutes for six nights per week. This made a
maximum of 36 sessions possible for paired reading and 39 for the
other two. All helpers were invited to comment post-project (using
questionnaires reproduced in Appendix 3), as was the member of
staff who undertook to organise what proved to be a very hard-
working year! (see questionnaire in Appendix 4.)

Results and comments

Student questionnaires (Appendix 2) and assessments

For brevity, throughout this section the Paired Reading Group will
be designated P1, the Parent/Volunteer Group who undertook
'Helping Children Read' will be P2 and the Cross Age Tutoring
Group, P3.

The questionnaires were designed to examine attitudes and effective responses to reading. There is no empirical validity since
responses are based on self-estimation by the students. However, the

Table 1

NAME OF PROJECT	NUMBER OF STUDENTS
Paired reading	9
Helping children read	21
Cross age tutoring	12

contention was that if the final results yielded gains in positive views and self-esteem these would be 'real' gains – since the student who acts like a reader is far more likely to become one. Where possible, results are compared across all three projects following the order of the questionnaires.

1 Do you like reading?

Table 2

	START OF PROJECT			END OF PROJECT		
	yes	sometimes	no	yes	sometimes	no
P1	78%	11%	11%	100%	0%	0%
P2	43%	21.5%	28.5%	52.5%	38%	9.5%
P3	41%	25%	34%	92%	8%	0%

It would seem from Table 2 that many students in all three projects were more positive about reading at the end of the projects with the P3 students reflecting the greatest amount of attitude change.

2 What do you read?

The 'categories' of literature used in this question were those offered by students in previous interviews, with the exception of poetry.

At final interview there was a 100% response to stories/novels. Although 55% of P1, 76% of P2 and 67% of P3 said they read newspapers, further questioning revealed that this was usually to check the timing of television programmes or a cursory glance through the *Sun*, *Daily Mirror* or local evening paper. Responses to books/magazines for information, at final interview were P1–66%, P2–52% and P3–83%. This was usually related to hobbies such as football, fishing, knitting and 'pop' music. Poetry elicited the least interest, although there was a slight gain in P2 and P3 final responses.

3 How often do you read on your own?

This question was included since spontaneous , independent reading is an indication of real interest. The interviewers were very precise in their definition of this question and pointed out that library periods in school were not to be included. However, students were remined that magazines, comics, etc. are reading. This was felt to be necessary since many students equated reading with stories only, or at the most, information location in reference books. Is this a view that schools unconsciously foster?

Table 3

FREQUENCY	START OF PROJECT			END OF PROJECT		
	P1	P2	P3	P1	P2	P3
3–5 times per week	55%	38%	33%	67%	52%	59%
1–3 times per week	33%	41%	42%	33%	48%	25%
Once a week	12%	13%	17%	–	–	8%
1–3 times per month	–	8%	–	–	–	8%
Less than once per month	–	–	–	–	–	–
Never	–	–	8%	–	–	–

All three projects demonstrated independent reading with perhaps P3 showing greatest gains. Material chosen mirrored the responses to question 2 with stories heading the list. By far the favourite locations for reading was in bed or in the bedroom.

4 Is reading easy/hard?

This question was included from the commonsense view that all of us have a tendency not to pursue a task we find difficult. It could also be argued that any diminution in 'hard' responses would indicate increased confidence. The 'depends' category was included since some students sensibly pointed out that text difficulty and length would affect their response.

Table 4

RESPONSE	START OF PROJECT			END OF PROJECT		
	P1	P2	P3	P1	P2	P3
Hard	33%	43%	50%	0%	33%	42%
Depends	45%	48%	33%	89%	58%	50%
Easy	22%	9%	17%	11%	9%	8%

Although all three groups showed a decrease in 'hard' responses the greatest gains were made in the 'depends' category. It is interesting to speculate on the reasons for this. Are the students developing greater sensitivity to text levels? If so this would also indicate greater self-awareness which would minimise the frustration that too difficult a choice for independent reading can cause. The only reasons given for finding reading difficult were long words and small print.

5 Is it important to be able to read?
All students thought it was important to be able to read both pre- and post-project but only one student (post-project) mentioned a leisure/enjoyment factor. All other responses were utilitarian and included for employment, functional reading (advertisements, maps), social sight vocabulary and examinations.

6 What do you do when you come to a word you don't know?
This question was asked to try to explore students' problem-solving strategies. Specific interest focused on the 'miss out and re-read' category since the Service's experience is that poor readers seldom spontaneously use context cues. Many students offered more than one response so results are reflected as a percentage of all students who mentioned each strategy.

Table 5

STRATEGY	START OF PROJECT			END OF PROJECT		
	P1	P2	P3	P1	P2	P3
Ask someone	44%	81%	58%	55%	57%	58%
Split into syllables	22%	35%	33%	66%	57%	66%
Miss out and leave	55%	43%	50%	11%	5%	0%
Miss out and re-read	0%	9%	17%	33%	38%	42%
Sound it out	33%	33%	42%	22%	5%	8%
Write it down	11%	0%	0%	11%	0%	0%
Try to guess	22%	0%	0%	0%	0%	0%

All three projects showed the pupils using increased context cues. A greater awareness that text should make sense may, perhaps, be inferred from the decrease in responses to merely 'miss out the word'. P3 showed greatest gains here.

7 Who helps you to read?

At initial interview parents and teachers were mentioned equally (about 60% of responses) and 22%, 29% and 17% respectively for each project said no one helped them. At final assessment this figure had fallen to zero. All P1 students mentioned their parents, all P2 students mentioned their helper and 66% of P3 students mentioned their tutor.

8 Have you enjoyed reading with X?

9 Have you learnt anything from reading with X?

All the students reported that they had enjoyed the projects. Claims made across all three groups included the ability to read longer, harder words, improvement in reading speed and problem-solving techniques and greater observation of punctuation.

10 Do you prefer reading with X or a teacher in class?

11 Do you think you are a better reader now?

Table 6

PREFERENCE	P1	P2	P3
Parent/helper	78%	80%	50%
Teacher	11%	9.5%	50%
No preference	11%	9.5%	

Reasons given for parent/helper preference included

It's more comfortable/quiet,
I'm on my own so I don't get distracted.
I like X, s/he understands me.
We have a laugh, s/he makes a joke of it.
If you're stuck, s/he'll help, you don't have to ask.
S/he has more time.
I'm more confident, not so nervous.
It's enjoyable.
I don't feel so stupid on my own.

Reasons given for teacher preference by P3 students were 'they know all the words' and 'they know more about it'. All the students thought their reading had improved stating that they had read more than they would normally do and many expressed a spontaneous wish to carry on the work.

Student assessment

(In all cases the *New Macmillan Reading Analysis* was used)

Table 7
P1 – Paired Reading

	Chron. A	R.A.	Comp. A
Sept '86 (average)	12 yrs 4 mths	8.4–9.5	8.2–9.9
Dec '86 (average difference)		+ 6.1 months	+ 6.1 months
June '86 (average difference)		+ 3.3 months	– 3.3 months

Table 8

RANGE OF DIFFERENCE – *June '87*	
R.A.	Comp. A
– 4 to + 9	– 4 to + 9

The students were asked to record the title of books read. This varied widely according to text length – the span was between three and twenty books with an average of eight.

(Table 9) refers to the project in which parents or adult volunteers operated the techniques derived from Glynn.

Table 9
P2 – Helping Children Read

Sept '86	Sept '86		June '87	
Average	Average		Average Difference	
Chron. A	R.A.	Comp. A	R.A.	Comp. A
12 yrs 1 mth	8:4–9:5	8:8–10.2	+ 7.7 mths	+ 3.4 mths

Table 10

RANGE OF DIFFERENCE – June '87	
R.A.	Comp. A
+ 2 to + 17 mths	– 2 to + 19 mths

P3 reports on the Project in which paired fifth year volunteers worked with younger students, again operating the modified cueing technique derived from Glynn.

Table 11
P3 – Cross Age Tutoring

Sept '86	Sept '86		June '87	
Average Chron. A	Average		Average Difference	
	R.A.	Comp. A	R.A.	Comp. A
11 yrs 8 mths	7:7–8:8	7:11–9.6	+ 7.2 mths	+ 5 mths

Table 12

RANGE OF DIFFERENCE – June '87	
R.A.	Comp. A
+ 2 to + 17 mths	– 2 to + 19 mths

Percentage of students whose gains were greater than the 8 months difference between initial and final assessment.

Table 13

Project	R.A.	Comp. A.
1	11%	11%
2	36%	33%
3	25%	17%

b) Parent/helper/tutor questionnaire (Appendix 3) and tutor assessment.

Reflections

All the helpers in P1 and P3 enjoyed the work and thought it was worthwhile. Specific comments included:

- From parents – a closer understanding of their child's difficulties and closer personal relationships,
- From all helpers, students' greater confidence, enthusiasm, fluency, ability to read longer words and harder books, fewer errors and the indpendent application of reading strategies in P3.

While the helpers in P2 largely reflected these feelings there were two exceptions – both of whom were school staff members. Both these participants had felt frustrated by frequent absenteeism and organisational issues including students' forgetfulness in keeping appointments. No organisational difficulties were reported by any parents in P1 or P2 nor by the tutors in P3. Parents were particularly positive in this respect and comments spontaneously offered included: 'fifteen minutes soon passes', 'the commitment was easy and I really want S . . . to improve his reading and understand what he's reading' and 'I don't think it's too much to ask'.

All helpers thought their students had enjoyed the work and were satisfied with the techniques they were asked to apply. There were no suggestions for modification of projects' content. Many parents reported a 'knock-on' effect in the family since other siblings also began to want to read to them. P1 parents reported that they found the home visits helpful in terms of confidence-building and reassurance. One parent valued the ease and intimacy generated by a one-to-one home visit as opposed to what she felt was the more formal, detached parents' evening at school.

All helpers professed willingness to continue working with students. However, several P3 tutors pointed out that they were now leaving school. Perhaps one answer to this problem is that tutors should be primarily invited from the fourth year so that their expertise and goodwill can be utilised in the first term of the fifth year as well, before examination pressure becomes dominant.

P3 tutors, when asked what, if anything, they had gained from the work, mentioned personal qualities which included patience, tolerance and improved listening skills. More practical gains included the techniques to help someone else with their reading and the knowledge, to counterbalance previous assumptions, that even very poor readers can improve with help. In terms of the tutors' own reading, several mentioned increased fluency and work attack skills and one boy said it had helped his spelling since the slower pace of his student had made him look more closely at words.

Tutor assessment

As stated earlier both project volunteers and a control group were assessed in January and May using GAPADOL.

Table 14

Group	Jan '87		May '87	
	Av. Chron. A.	Av. R.A.	Av. R.A.	Av. Diff.
Project	15 yrs 7 mths	14 yrs 1.3 mths	14 yrs 10 mths	+ 8.7 mths
Control	15 yrs 10 mths	14 yrs 1.8 mths	13 yrs 8.9 mths	– 4.9 mths

These results tend to confirm previous firfdings which have reported positive effects on the tutors' own reading attainment.

Organiser's comments (Appendix 4)

The member of staff who was responsible for administering the three projects felt that all tutors and tutees enjoyed the work, with the exception of the P2 volunteers mentioned above. She reported positive observed gains in both student attitude and performance and felt that all helpers had gained more expertise in reading techniques. Her main problems were organisational. Since the work in school was done in students' own time, rather than being included on the timetable, such difficulties were perhaps inevitable. Her advice to any other school which was considering undertaking the work would be to check the attendance record of students and vet fourth/fifth year volunteers for reliability. She would repeat the three projects using fourth rather than fifth years for P3 and could envisage this work as part of regular school practice provided that time could be arranged successfully.

She stated that she preferred students to choose their own books but pointed out the necessity for sufficient time to be selective and for the presence of a supportive figure to give advice when necessary. Her concluding remarks mentioned the excellent help offered by many staff and stated her priorities which had been to maintain goodwill for time freely given and to sustain student interest in the projects.

The teacher was asked to grade the Projects in terms of personal impression and preference (1st, 2nd, 3rd) according to four criteria:

Table 15

Project	1	2	3
Ease of organisation	2nd	1st	3rd
Improved attitude to reading	1st =	1st =	3rd
Improved reading performance	2nd	1st	3rd
Would you repeat the project	yes	yes	yes

It is interesting that while the organiser's first choice mirrors the formal assessment results, her second preference does not. This may be because of the work although these were not reflected in the tutor/student responses.

Conclusion

To return to the objectives of the work. It would seem that in general, students' attainment in and attitude to reading did increase. Although formal assessment gains may seem slight it must be remembered that the sample contained many students who, after six, seven and eight years of formal schooling, had gained as little as three years in reading attainment and comprehension. Forty-three per cent of parents accepted the invitation to help their child and all these were very positive about the work so that good home-school relationships have been fostered. The reading attainment of the fourth and fifth year student volunteers increased.

The teachers' questionnaire reflects the importance of organisational issues on the final impression of a project. Thus cross-age tutoring was rated lowest as an effective process even though both test results and students' views do not confirm this.

The work presents an example of how a balance can be achieved between the strengths of a school and the strengths of a support service. The projects have enabled more book sharing experiences to be made available to a larger number of students, on a one-to-one basis, than either school or support service staff could possibly provide, without this extended volunteer involvement.

There is no clear preferred project in overall terms since so many more issues than a formal reading score are involved. However, the author would be interested to hear of more work replicating the technique derived from Glynn since it does seem to generate greater independent problem-solving strategies than the helper-reliant Paired Reading technique.

References

Clark, M.M. & Glynn, T. (1980) 'Reading and Writing for the Child with Difficulties'. *Parent Child Interaction In Remedial Reading* University of Birmingham.

McLeod, J. & Anderson, J. (1972) *Gapadol* Heinemann.

Morgan, R. & Lyon, E. (1979) 'Paired Reading: A Preliminary Report On a Technique for Parental Tuition of Reading With Retarded Children' *Journal of Child Psychology and Psychiatry*, 20.

Topping, K. & Wolfendale, S. (1986) *Parental Involvement In Children's Reading* Croom Helm.

Vincent, D. and de la Mare, M. (1985) *New Macmillan Reading Analysis* Macmillan.

Appendix 1 Guidelines for helpers suggesting strategies
Discuss cover, title, possible contents and any other areas of interest prior to reading.

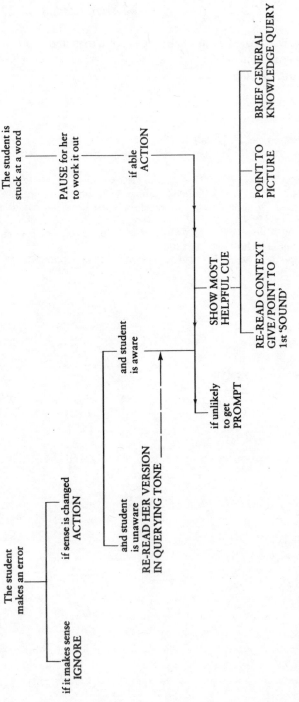

small letters indicate the situation
CAPITALS indicate HELPER'S ACTION

After reading, discuss what the book has been about and the student's reactions. If the book has not been completed the student can be asked to predict what happens next.

Based on Clunn's model in Clark, MM and Glynn, 1980

Appendix 2 Students' questionnaire

1 Do you like reading?   Why/why not?
2 Do you read – story books/novels, comic/newspapers, magazines, annuals, books/mags. for information, poetry?
3 How often do you read on your own?
  3 to 5 times per week
  1 to 3 times per week
  once per week
  1 to 3 times per month
  less than once per month
  never
  (the child should be reminded that newspapers, etc. are 'reading'
  – do not include library periods)
  What do you read?
  Where do you read?
4 Is reading easy/hard?
5 Is it important to be able to read?
6 What do you do when you come to a word you don't know? (List
  all responses but do not prompt.)
7 Who helps you to read? (query teacher, people at home, friends
  if omitted)
8 Have you enjoyed reading with X?
9 Have you learnt anything from reading with X?
10 Do you prefer to read with X or your teacher in class?
11 Do you think you are a better reader now?

  At initial interview, questions 1 to 7 were asked and at final
interview questions 1 to 11 were posed.

Appendix 3 Helpers' questionnaire

1 You've been helping X with reading. Has it been worthwhile?
  Have you enjoyed it?
2 Do you think X enjoyed the work?
3 Did you find the time commitment too much?
4 Were there any organisational problems?
5 Have you noticed any difference in
  a) X's attitude to reading?
  b) X's reading performance?
6 Would you be willing to help again?
7 Are there any alterations you would make in the way you were
  asked to help?

8 Did you encounter any problems it would be useful for others to hear?

9 Any other comments?

In addition Paired Reading parents were asked:

10 Has the work affected any other member of your family?

11 While the project was in progress you were visited several times by a member of school staff. Was this helpful to you? Why/why not?

In addition the Cross Age tutors were asked:

12 Have you learnt anything from taking part in the project?

Appendix 4   *Organiser's responses*

1 Have the helpers and students enjoyed the project?

2 Have you observed any difference in
   a) reading performance?
   b) attitude to reading?

3 What, if anything, do you think the tutors learnt from the project?

4 Were there any organisational difficulties?

5 What advice would you give to another school which was considering undertaking any/all of these projects?

6 Would you repeat any/all of the projects?

7 Are there any changes you would make?

8 Do you see a place for this kind of work as part of normal school practice?

9 How do you feel about children choosing their own books?

10 Please grade the projects 1st, 2nd and 3rd in terms of ease of organisation, improved attitude to reading and improved reading attainment.

11 Any other comments?

28 Reading achievement, hearing impairment and deafness

Jean Palmer

Controversy exists over methods of communication with deaf children and methods for teaching them to read have been labelled, 'confused eclecticism'. Research studies cite low achievement in reading and a 'deficit model of deafness' abounds. This chapter explores reasons for these views and makes suggestions for improvement in the light of knowledge of language acquisition and text linguistics.

Introduction

Research studies into the reading achievements of deaf children in many parts of the world, over a number of years and in different educational environments, have consistently shown that such children leave secondary school with a mean reading age of about nine years (Wrightstone et al 1963; di Francesca, 1972; Conrad, 1979). Several researchers have concluded that severely hearing-impaired children reach a plateau in reading development, some kind of ceiling beyond which the child cannot progress. However, identification of this plateau at a reading age of about nine is based on the use of traditional reading measures designed for normally hearing children (Brimer's Wide Span, Southgate Sentence Completion Test). More recent research has shown that deaf children in fact use different strategies from normally-hearing children to perform these tests and achieve their reading age scores differently (Webster (1981); Wood et al (1981); Beggs and Breslaw (1982). The so called 'deficit-model' abounds in the evaluative and descriptive literature described above, so that children are felt to fail because of their disability, their hearing loss.

Most of these studies have included at least some children who are reading at a level commensurate with their chronological age. It is surely time that such children were studied in more depth to establish factors which may have contributed to their achievement. The focus should move from the deficit-model approach to examine the proven strengths of some hearing-impaired readers. What deaf children can do is important, and studies which obscure more than they reveal by not showing differences between children and schools are somewhat unhelpful. It is important, too, to look at teachers and their perceptions of language acquisition and reading development. What is the effect on adults (teachers and parents) of knowing that one is dealing with hearing-impaired children/or a hearing-impaired child?

Reading and methods of teaching reading

However, it is first necessary to give some definition of what is understood by the term 'reading'. We read because print communicates in a meaningful way . . . or should do. Reading is an active, thinking process . . . or should be. But what happens in schools may not give a child (hearing or hearing-impaired) this view. The hearing-impaired child may indeed be said 'not to know what reading is about' (Wood, 1986). His bewilderment may be reinforced by conventional tests and teaching strategies which tend to promote word-by-word reading of material that is beyond the linguistic competence of the child.

It is agreed that reading is an important ability for deaf children to acquire because it is the only complete pattern of language they can receive (van Uden, 1965). A plethora of studies indicates the **product** of teaching, but very few address the **process** of reading. Fewer still concern themselves with **teaching** reading. Yet a stated main aim is to teach deaf children to read in the 'generally understood language' (Quigley, 1982). The last phrase highlights another concern of the educators of the hearing-impaired. Should education be by auditory-oral methods (residual hearing, lip-reading, reading, writing) or by so-called total communication methods (auditory-oral and manual methods of communication)? To many it seems obvious to use manual methods with the hearing-impaired. Pressures exist for children to be educated in this way – pressures from the deaf community and organisations such as the British Deaf Association (BDA). Sign-languages referred to include BSL, Signed English, Signs Supporting English and others. Research shows, however, that children educated by auditory-oral methods do as well (or better) than children in other programmes. The 1982–83 Gallaudet College survey which reported on the reading attainments of 55,000 deaf children revealed a significant decline in attainment since the switch to total communication (Delany, M., Stuckless, E. and Walter, G., 1984). Children who have acquired a sign language as a means of communication may be at no advantage when it comes to reading – natural sign systems (eg BSL) have different grammatical principles from spoken or written English.

Signed English (with signs based on BSL and including some finger spelling) presented in English word order, has a distorting effect on the accompanying speech. Signs Supporting English (or Pidgin Signed English) is characteristically a succession of content words. Most adult users of these systems are unlikely to be fluent – the language produced cannot be said to give adequate exposure to the gradually inceasing complexity of language needed if the child is to have access to 'generally understood language'. ('Perceptual and cognitive overload' – the brain cannot cope.)

There is evidence that in this country confusion exists in schools and units about different methods. Markides (1988) has reported substantial discrepancies between actual and reported practices. Few schools exhibited a consistent policy regarding methodology of instruction. There remains, of course, the question of transfer to conventional written English.

Effects of hearing disability and teaching methods on language development

The implication of the above is that the use of total communication affects deleteriously the language input to the child. Likewise, knowledge that a child is deaf may affect normal mother-child interaction of turn-taking, mutual eye-gazing, and mother-infant voicing, which are precursors to speech (Gregory and Mogford, 1981). The process by which adults and children normally 'negotiate' understanding is interfered with. Deafnesses seems to affect the intuitive skills which parents posses, such as timing the complexity of language used in response to the child's own. Similarly, teachers may and do react in a non-facilitative way when working with hearing-impaired children (Wood, 1986; Huntington and Watton, 1984). Griffiths (1983) has commented on the failure of teachers to expose deaf children to complex structures. Ongoing research on 120 children in the Greater Manchester area, however, shows that they can develop well linguistically, given good parental guidance and effective use of aids. (I have a video of some of them reading.) Management of the hearing loss is a crucial factor.

In considering reading and hearing impairment, another confounding variable is the educational placement of children. Changes in philosophy reflected in the 1981 Education Act have resulted in many more hearing-impaired children (including the severely and profoundly deaf) being placed in ordinary schools either fully integrated or in units. (About 80% are in mainstream education and 12% in special units.) In theory, this has been made possible by early diagnosis and the provision of FM-wireless aids. There is as yet no hard evidence as to how well these children are achieving, socially, emotionally, or educationally. Observation in schools while supervising students on teaching practice leads me to believe that some children are not faring well. Although this view would not be shared by all, I have observed that many children are unable to read worksheets and have poor study skills. Markides (in press) also notes that the use of hearing aids is not good.

Implications for research and teaching

Hearing-impaired children are a heterogeneous group and therefore a case-study approach involving detailed observation of individuals may well be more productive than solely quantitative measurements of attainment. There should not be a rigid and stereotyped response to the needs of hearing-impaired children. Neither should there be 'confused eclecticism' (Clarke, 1982) in methods of teaching reading. The locus of learning difficulty may well lie in the teaching environment. While linguistically overwhelming materials will defeat a child's expectation of getting meaning from text, deliberately restricted language materials run the risk of preventing the child from meeting language which he is actually capable of understanding. It has been shown, for example, that hearing-impaired readers can by-pass syntactic structures and proceed directly to the meaning of a story (Ewoldt, 1978); that children get more sense from a paragraph than from a sentence or a phrase (Marshall, 1970); that much of the re-writing done for deaf children in fact destroys many of the factors that support the reading process . . . and that difficult structures do not present difficulties when sufficient background knowledge and context are present (Ewoldt, 1986); that simplified text is not always easier to read (Voit, 1979).

In summary, the implications are as follows:

1 There is a need to go beyond word and sentence level in the study of the charateristics of written text which may be difficult for hearing-impaired children. Recent developments in text linguistics need to be utilised.

2 Assessments/tests should be chosen with the above in mind.
3 Reading instruction needs to have a language-base (language cannot initially be taught through reading).
4 There needs to be an examination of the ways in which the hearing-impaired child's environment is unneccessarily restrictive and insufficiently challenging.
5 Teachers need to be better informed about the reading process and the fact that the total is greater than the sum of the parts.

References

Beggs, W.D.A. & Breslaw, P.I. (1972) 'Reading Retardation or Linguistic Deficit? III' *Journal of Research in Reading.*

Clarke, B.R. (1982) 'How Hearing-Impaired Children Learn to Read Theoretical & Practical Issues' *Volta Review* 1982. Vol. 8.

Conrad, R. (1979) *The Deaf School Child* London: Harper & Row.

Delaney, M., Stuckless, E. & Walter, G. (1984) *Total Communication Efforts: A Longitudinal Study.*

di Francesca, S. (1972) Academic Achievement Test Results of a National Testing Programme For H.I. Students Series D. North Gallender College, London.

Engen, E. (1986) 'A Study of Comprehension of Cohesive in Written English By H.I. Unwin In *Aspects of Language: The Reading Process* Symposium.

Ewoldt, C. (1978) 'Reading For the Hearing of Hearing-Impaired: A Single Process' *American Annuals of the Deaf*, 123, 945–948.

Ewoldt, C. (1984) *American Annuals of the Deaf.* Vol. 129, No. 1.

Ewoldt, C. (1986) 'The Influence of Context on The Reading of Deaf Students' *Language Aspects in Reading.*

Gregory, S. & Mogford, (1981) 'Early Language Development with Deaf Children in *Perspectives on British Sign Language & Deafness.*

Griffiths, A.J. (1983) *The Linguistic Competence of Deaf Primary School Children.*

Huntington, A. & Watton, F. *Language & The Education of Hearing Impaired Children* Croom Helm.

Markides, A. (1988 in press) 'Speech Intelligibility' *American Annuals of the Deaf: Oral Approach to Total Communication.*

Quigley, S.P. & Kretschmer, R.E (1982) *The Education of Deaf Children: Issues, Theory and Practice* London: Edward Arnold.

Voit, H. (1979) *Proceedings of Oslo Congress on Reading.*

Webster, A. et al (1981) 'Reading Retardation or Linguistic Deficit? II. *Journal of Research in Reading.*

Wood *et al.*

29 Seminar report: specific learning difficulties and dyslexia some botes on current issues in teaching and research

John Bald, Kjeld Johansen, David Moseley

The seminar reported here was one of a number of conference sessions on this theme, and several of those taking part also read prepared papers. The following notes are not intended either to duplicate the papers or to provide a comprehensive account of the discussions, which ranged over three days. They do, however, raise issues which are relevant to the design of research studies which are concerned either with the nature of reading and learning difficulties or with the evaluation of teaching methods. Abstracts of the papers by Johansen and by Moseley are included in the following notes.

Designing research in the field of dyslexia: a note by David Moseley.

Large-scale research is problematic because the number of variables is so great. In 1967 I undertook a study including 1604 children but this was too small to provide sufficiently large sub-groups especially if boys and girls were to be looked at separately. One would need a parent population of at least 2500 at a particular age level from which to select, maybe, 400 children for individual assessment. This has never been done because it would be too costly and time-consuming, especially if a longitudinal study were contemplated. An alternative would be to identify maybe 50 children conforming to a predetermined pattern and to follow them through. This should be done not only with clinical samples where selective referral bias operates but also with children from the general population.

Small scale studies, even individual subject designs, can be of value if they include frequent repeated measures with instruments of known reliability.

Treatment studies should always be replicated by independent workers before public claims are made and financial benefits sought. The magnitude of gains can be evaluated by reference to existing published research and in relation to previous rates of progress. It is not always necessary to include controlled groups or to use an ABA design. Where ethical considerations permit, controls for the placebo effect are desirable.

Tests used in intervention studies should match the full range of skills which the study aims to explore or improve. Ceiling effects of tests should be anticipated, and appropriate additional measures used where necessary. Where benefits are claimed which are not detectable through tests, they should be described, and if possible fully documented, not simply mentioned briefly.

Dr Chasty (see also Chapter 5) identified three broad but distinct groups among pupils referred to the Dyslexia Institute. The first comprised verbally able pupils, typically with an IQ of 125·+, who had difficulties in one or more of the areas of short-term auditory memory, visual perception and motor skills. The pupils of the second group tended to have a weaker overall profile and lower verbal IQ, and were often well-adjusted socially, although they were not literate. Those of the third group had much more fragmented and heterogenous pattern of abilities and problems which had little in common with the other two. Dr Chasty said that '*dyslexia*' was '*an unhelpful word for describing these separate groups*' and argued that longitudinal studies ought to take account of their differences. Other participants argued that emotional, social and environmental factors should also be investigated.

The research of Dr Lynette Bradley and Professor Peter Bryant was noted with interest, although it appeared to contain no indication that pupils with weak sound categorisation who had been helped by their teaching methods could be considered to have specific learning difficulties.

Participants had mixed views and experiences with reference to Dr Helen Irlen's tinted lenses. Some had known users who had reported long-term benefits, but others had known wearers stop using the lenses after relatively short periods of time with no apparent benefit to their reading. Dr Chasty had consulted the heads of four specialised schools, who had reported no positive experience. There was extensive debate on the value of the research to date, and agreement on the need for a thorough academic investigation of the technique and its underlying theory.

Dr Kjeld Johansen reported that work with '*reading disabled*' pupils in Denmark had revealed that a substantial number relied more heavily on information from their left ear than from their right. He had developed training tapes designed to help pupils make more use of their right ear by means of stereo-headphones. These, he said, had resulted in positive effects on reading performance, and provided grounds for the inclusion of more precise auditory testing than was often employed in the assessment of learning difficulties. Dr Johansen saw a parallel between his work and studies of ocular dominance (see below).

David Moseley pointed out that there is a need for further research in the area of ocular suppression and muscle imbalance. He also noted, on the basis of his extensive review of studies concerning dominance and reading and spelling, that *'theories linking cerebral dominance with dyslexia are at present little more than speculation'* (see below).

Ear-preference, auditive-dominance and reading problems (Kjeld Johansen)

Children and adults with severe reading and spelling difficulties are often labelled as dyslexics by educators and psychologists on the basis of classroom and psychological tests where clear dyslexic behaviour is observed (slow reading, poor spelling, characteristic types of errors, left/right confusion).

From research with some two hundred children and from a survey of several hundred files from Danish audio-therapists it appears that some difficulties are primarily related to hearing.

Careful tests of the hearing (audiometry) may diagnose this kind of (semi) dyslexia and special audio-therapy is shown to have beneficial effects.

Dominance, reading, and spelling (David Moseley)

The following types of 'dominance' have at various times been thought to be associated with performance in reading and spelling, especially in theories put forward to account for specific learning difficulties or dyslexia:

- dominance of minor hemisphere function (eg spatial visualisation ability) over major hemisphere language functions;
- hand dominance (writing and other fine motor skills);
- visual field dominance;
- eye dominance (as in sighting, scanning or suppression).

Large-scale surveys (as opposed to clinical studies where referral biases are likely to operate) have failed to find clear-cut associations between measures of dominance and reading.

These issues were explored in a study involving 650 boys and 604 girls aged 8–9 years attending 16 state schools in a predominantly working-class area of London. Group tests of receptive vocabulary, two-dimensional spatial ability and spelling were given to all children and a battery of individual tests (including reading and dominance measures) to selected sub-samples. The test battery included a number of psychoneurological measures which had not previously been applied in a large-scale project. A group of 71 children with specific learning difficulties in spelling was compared with a group of 69 average spellers.

Some of the above measures (and some new ones) were at a later date applied to an additional sample of 44 dyslexia boys.

The main findings are summarised below:

1 The different measures of hand, visual field and eye dominance used in this study showed little or no concordance, with the exception of reading speed and scanning speed.
2 The incidence of high spatial ability in children with vocabulary scores in the average range was no greater among those retarded in spelling than in those of average attainment. Moreover, the evidence did not support Geschwind's theory of a sex-linked association between dyslexia and superior right-hemisphere function. The spatial visualisation scores of 12 girls with specific spelling problems did not differ significantly from those of 59 boys matched for receptive vocabulary and spelling attainment.
3 The incidence of left-handedness among children with specific spelling problems and among the dyslexic boys was not significantly different from the norm. No difference was found between the low-attaining and average subsamples on a finger-lifting test scored for lateral performance (absence of associated movements in other fingers).
4 Three putative measures of visual field dominance were obtained from subsamples of poor and average spellers. Perception of apparent movement and the illusion of figural after-effect to the left and to the right of fixation point proved to be unrelated to spelling ability. The third measure (the direction in which drawings faced) also failed to discriminate between the groups.
5 Low-attaining and average sub-samples did not differ in score distributions on the Asher sighting test, nor on a retinal rivalry

suppression measure of eye dominance. However, a significantly greater proportion of right-eye-suppressors was found in the dyslexic sample. It was also found that these children tended to be the poorest and slowest readers. A positive advantage associated with suppression of the left eye was also found in a sub-sample of children of high spatial ability.

6 None of the indices of mixed and crossed laterality used showed any potential as diagnostic indicators.

The predominantly negative findings of this study suggest that both parents and professionals should take care not to be influenced by 'clinical myths' concerning the causative role of 'cerebral dominance' in dyslexia.

Further research is needed in the area of ocular suppression and eye muscle imbalance.

References

Bryant, P. & Bradley, L. (1987) *Children's Reading Problems* Basil Blackwell Ltd.

Clark, M.M. (1970) *Reading Difficulties In Schools* Penguin. (2nd ed. Heinemann).

Ellis, A.W. (1984) *Reading, Writing & Dyslexia: A Cognitive Analysis* Lawrence Erlbaum Associates Ltd.

Gordon, N. & McKinlay, I. (1980) *Helping Clumsy Children* Churchill Livingstone.

See also: Roberton, G.L. & Miles, J. (1987) 'The Use of Coloured Overlays To Improve Visual Processing' *A Preliminary Survey. The Exceptional Child.* Vol. 34. March 1987. pp. 65–70.

Johansen, K. (1987) *Ear-Preference, Auditive Dominance & Reading Problems*.

Quin, V. & Macauslan, A. (1986) *Dyslexia: What Parents Ought to Know* Penguin.

30 Developmental dyslexia: issues for theory and practice

Maggie Snowling and Harry Chasty

In recent years, two different approaches to the study of developmental dyslexia have emerged within cognitive psychology. The first approach has focused on the cognitive deficits which underlie specific learning difficulties, the second has been concerned more directly with the reading and spelling strategies which dyslexics are forced to adopt. In this paper, we shall argue that both lines of evidence must be taken into account if we are to understand the educational needs of 'dyslexic' children. It is also important to adopt a developmental perspective (Snowling, 1987). The first part of the paper reviews some recent research on the language skills of reading-disabled children to include problems with naming and phonological processes and, in the second part, the implications for children in the classroom and also for the specialist teacher are discussed.

Introduction

The concept of dyslexia has had a chequered history. For far too long its critics have opposed the 'medical flavour' of the condition and have argued, rightly, that many of the problems experienced by dyslexic readers, (for example, reversals) have been exaggerated. Certainly, myths surround the term 'dyslexia' and these have done little to further the cause of children with specific learning difficulties. A common misconception, for example, is that dyslexic children have reading problems in the absence of any of the cognitive or language difficulties which usually accompany school failure. This view not only misrepresents the nature of the dyslexic's learning difficulty but wrongly prescribes the type of educational treatment required. More properly, dyslexia can be considered to be a learning difficulty associated with specific cognitive and linguistic deficits not predicted on the basis of age and intelligence. These deficits undoubtedly vary between children and may account for the specific patterns of reading and spelling deficit seen at the individual level (Hulme and Snowling, 1988). Practitioners must be aware of the nature of these cognitive deficits, of how they affect the course of literacy development and, more generally, of the constraints they place upon the child's ability to learn.

Experimental psychologists working in this field have attempted to elucidate the 'causes' of dyslexia by comparing the processing skills of normal and dyslexic readers. Two consistent findings have emerged: dyslexics are subject to verbal memory deficits and to problems with phoneme segmentation. The extent to which these two types of problem are associated is not clear but it is unequivocal that they both affect the acquisition of reading and spelling skills. Verbal memory is required at an initial stage when letters must be associated with their names, and more so for the acquisition of letter-sound correspondences. Further, it is required to support the development of early whole-word reading strategies whereby sight words are associated with their verbal labels or names. At a later stage of development, a child must understand the alphabetic principle, that is, how speech sounds map onto letters within words, if he or she is to develop a flexible reading system which allows unfamiliar words to be tackled. Children with phonological problems are unable to segment the speech stream and therefore find it difficult to make this developmental advance (Frith, 1985). The effect on spelling development is even more detrimental.

Phoneme segmentation and dyslexia

It is widely held that disabled readers are subject to phoneme segmentation problems but the possibility that these stem from difficulties with speech perception has been less well explored. A notable exception can be found in the work of Brady, Shankweiler and Mann (1983) who observed that poor readers made more errors in a repetition task than good readers when high and low frequency words were presented in a noisy environment. They therefore argued that poor readers require a higher quality of speech signal for accurate perception than normal readers. If true, this finding is of considerable importance for it could explain why dyslexics are slower than expected to acquire spoken language, and why they can flounder in noisy classroom environments. It would also go some way towards an explanation of why they have difficulties with phonological reading and spelling strategies. To elucidate the nature of the dyslexics' repetition deficit, Snowling, Goulandris, Bowlby and Howell (1986) compared the ability of dyslexic and normal readers to repeat familiar words and unfamiliar nonwords under different levels of noise masking. The 19 dyslexic subjects all attended a specialist school for dyslexic children. Their mean age was 10 years 8 months but they were reading at the 8 year level. They were compared with 19 normally developing 10-year-olds (chronological age controls) and, more importantly, with 19 normal 8-year-olds who were reading at the same level as the dyslexics. These were the Reading Age-matched controls (RA-controls).

To examine an early (input) stage of auditory processing, the experimental stimuli (words and nonwords) were presented in clear surroundings or with noise masking. The rationale was that if dyslexics have difficulty at an early stage of processing, they would be affected more by noise than normal readers. To examine functioning of the lexical system, single-syllable words of high and low frequency of occurrence were (to be) repeated. If dyslexics have problems with lexical access or retrieval, then they should respond differently to these words than normal readers. Finally, to examine functioning of a nonlexical processing route, presumably used in language learning, subjects were asked to repeat nonwords which were compiled from the high frequency items by changing the initial phonemes.

The results differed in a number of ways from those of Brady et al (1984). First, there was no differential effect of noise masking. The performance of all subjects deteriorated when there was noise and dyslexics did not differ from normal readers in this respect. Thus, dyslexics have no difficulty with input processing. Turning to the effect of word frequency, this was significant for all groups, indicating that high frequency words were easier to process than low frequency words. Dyslexics made more errors than their chronological age controls; in fact, their performance was similar to that of younger Reading Age-matched controls, even though this was an auditory task, not one involving written words.

The group differences for the repetition of nonwords were striking. Here dyslexics made significantly more errors than both control groups. Furthermore, dyslexics were the only group for whom nonword repetition was significantly harder than the repetition of low frequency read words. In short, the dyslexics showed a 'nonword repetition deficit'. This could not be attributed to problems with acoustic analysis for they were not differentially affected by the addition of noise masking. A problem with output phonology could also be ruled out or else a more general articulation problem would have emerged. Hence, the most likely locus of their difficulty was within nonlexical procedures involved in speech processing, namely phoneme segmentation and blending processes.

Of particular interest for present purposes are the developmental consequences of this phonological processing deficit. It is likely, for example, that a child who has difficulty in repeating unfamiliar words will be slow to learn 'new' spoken vocabulary – foreign language learning would be particularly affected. It is interesting in this respect that the dyslexics were no better than younger Reading Age-matched controls when repeating low frequency words. Certainly they made more errors than the age-matched comparison group, suggesting that they had access to fewer articulatory-motor programmes that their age and IQ would predict. The suggestion was borne out when the same subjects were required to distinguish spoken words from nonwords in an auditory lexical decision task. Again, dyslexics performed like younger Reading Age-matched controls and less well than age-matched peers.

Object naming deficits in dyslexia

If the hypothesis that dyslexics are slower to acquire lexical knowledge than normal readers is true, it should be possible to show that they have unexpected naming difficulties. Moreover, if these lexical difficulties are attributable to underlying problems with phonological analysis, the laying down of phonological rather than semantic specifications of spoken words will be affected, thus, naming deficits may exist in dyslexics even when they have adequate knowledge of word meanings. Studies by Denckla and Rudel (1976) and Katz (1986) which point to word finding difficulties amongst dyslexics, in the absence of receptive vocabulary deficits, are consonant with this view.

In a recent extension of this work, Snowling, Van Wagtendonk and Stafford (1988) carried out an object-naming task in which subjects names 33 objects from pictures, 33 following their spoken definitions. The performance of dyslexic children ranging in age from nine to 11 years was compared with that of a comparison group of eleven-year-olds and a younger group of eight-year-olds, all reading at age-appropriate levels. The dyslexics made more errors, both in picture naming and in naming objects from their spoken definitions, than their chronological age controls. Importantly, the dyslexics' naming problem could not be attributed to inadequate word knowledge per se. It was not predicted by verbal ability as measured by a receptive vocabulary test and, furthermore, every subject could define more of the object names than they could produce. Since comparisons between the dyslexics and the eight-year-old comparison group were in no case significant, it can be concluded that the dyslexics performed only as well as normal readers some two years their junior on the object naming tasks. This points to a difficulty in retrieving the phonological forms of object names which they know, which is out of step with age and intelligence.

Hence, while dyslexics may be able to define words accurately by reference to sematic knowledge, they have difficulty in retrieving the object names from long-term memory. This matches up with clinical experience, particularly the high incidence of circumlocutions in dyslexic speech. Interestingly, in the present experiment, when the dyslexics accessed names from pictures, they subsequently remembered the names better when they retrieved them following a spoken definition. In this way they performed differently from normal readers whose recall of names was similar regardless of how they were elicited. This may have implications for the way in which dyslexics are taught.

So far, we have focused upon two arguably related language deficits in dyslexia: phonological processing problems and object naming difficulties. Short-term verbal memory problems can confidently be added to this list. It now falls to us to show how these difficulties can affect the acquisition of written language skills. We shall do this by reference to a single case study, that of J.M., a dyslexic boy of superior intelligence.

When first seen, aged eight years, J.M. had specific reading and spelling problems associated with the following processing problems: difficulties with rhyme and auditory organisation, repetition difficulties and a reduced short-term memory span (Snowling, Stackhouse and Rack, 1986). Four years later, his reading and spelling skills had improved as had his segmentation ability. However, he had obvious naming difficulties, scoring less well than would normally be expected on the naming test mentioned above, and persisting memory deficits. To investigate the nature of his memory impairment further, he was administered two verbal memory and one visual memory test. When asked to remember series of words of short, medium and long spoken duration, his performance was severely depressed. In fact, his memory span and speech rate for these words was roughly comparable to that of normal five-year-olds. Similarly, his memory for acoustically similar and dissimilar words was at the five-year level. In marked contrast, his memory span for abstract shapes which are difficult to name was normal, if not above average (Snowling and Hulme, in preparation). Considering his profile of cognitive strengths and weaknesses, it can be anticipated that in reading and spelling he would rely upon visual skills and experience phonological difficulties. This is precisely the pattern which was seen both at initial assessment and at follow-up. Here we shall discuss briefly the results of the first assessment at which J.M.'s reading and spelling strategies were compared with those of younger normal readers of the same reading age.

First, to examine J.M.'s reading of words and nonwords, he was asked to read a mixed series of 31 regular (dance, cash) and 31 irregular (choir, vase) words, matched for frequency. In each case, 19 were of one syllable, 12 were of two syllables (market, litre). In addition, he attempted 31 nonwords which were compiled from the irregular items by changing the first phoneme. On this test, normal R.A. controls (reading at the seven-year level) read approximately 50% of single syllable nonwords correctly and some 30% of the two syllable items. While J.M.'s reading of words was not significantly different from that of controls, unlike them, he had no success whatsoever with nonwords. Many of his attempts were 'lexicalisations', eg he read *plood* as 'pool', *hign* as 'high', *swad* as 'want' and *wamp* as 'warm'. These results suggested that although J.M had a sight vocabulary, he could not use a nonlexical route to phonology. In other words, he had difficulty with a phonic reading strategy. Further support for this view came from his reading of the regular and irregular words. Here an advantage for regular items would indicate the development and use of phonological reading strategies. However, when asked to read matched lists of regular and irregular words, J.M. did not show a regularity effect. He did as well as Reading Age controls when reading irregular words, but he did not reap the same advantage as them when attempting the regular words. Moreover, his reading errors resembled their targets visually. They included *sign* as 'sing', *bowl* as 'blow', *organ* as 'orange'. Further, one category of error that was present in the normal sample but absent from J.M.'s data was that of 'regularisations'. These occur when irregular words (eg broad) are read by grapheme-phoneme translation (eg to arrive at 'brode'). Nineteen per cent of normal readers' errors on single syllable words were regularisations, but J.M. made none of these.

To assess J.M.'s alphabetic competence further, he was asked to spell a series of one, two and three syllable words. He spelled significantly fewer of these words correctly than normal children who were reading at the same level as him. Moreover, examination of his spelling errors showed that they were all dysphonetic eg SAG for sack, TPIT for trumptet, SIKEOLEG for cigarette and CODTER for contented. In contrast, the normal readers made similar proportions of phonetic and nonphonetic mistakes.

To conclude, the results of the above tests confirmed that J.M. was, at that time, functioning at an early stage of literacy development. He was relying upon his visual skills and had not developed phonological strategies, presumably because of his segmentation and auditory memory problems. As a consequence, when compared with Reading Age-matched controls, his reading errors were primarily visual, he had difficulty in reading nonwords and his spelling errors were dysphonetic. This pattern of performance in fact persisted four years later despite a significant improvement in reading and spelling competence.

The case of J.M. illustrates at least two important points. First, dyslexia is more than a failure to learn to read. Accompanying perceptual, cognitive and linguistic difficulties may account to a large extent for the pattern of learning difficulty which we see. Second, and of crucial importance, dyslexics can and do learn to read and spell, in spite of persisting cognitive deficits (Snowling, 1987). It is most likely that they do this by relying upon their strengths. We turn now to consider how the teacher can translate these theoretical ideas into practical terms, with the dual aim of extending the skills of children with specific learning difficulties and of increasing their learning options.

The teaching challenge

If, as teachers, we are prepared to accept the perspective outlined above, and to use the term 'specific learning difficulties', we must meet the challenge the concept brings with it. The major implication of what we have discussed so far is that children do not all bring the same body of skills to the reading task. There are individual differences in the extent to which the skills necessary for reading have developed. Awareness and sensitivity to these individual differences must be part of the professionalism of the 'reading' teacher.

Differences in learning-skill raise questions such as, 'If this child doesn't learn the way you teach, can you teach him the way he learns?' and, perhaps more significantly, 'Can you, in your teaching, extend his learning strategies and capabilities?'. These children can be viewed as having difficulties:

- in the initial acquisition of the sub skills of learning;
- in linking the sub skills together to build an overall 'schema' which allows the skill to be controlled automatically.

The difficulties can be observed not just in reading but across the range of the curriculum. They are discussed below, together with the provision which should be made.

Teaching provision for dyslexics

We should like to dispense immediately with the narrow view that dyslexic children must be taught to read. No one would argue against their receiving such teaching, but this falls short of the provision they require. To varying degrees, depending upon the individual's cognitive profile, attention must be paid to the following areas:

1 Fine motor skills development (train the hand)
2 Laterality-sequence training (where do I start?)
   It is estimated that 81% of children in ordinary classrooms are right-handed, 6% are left handed, (Groden, 1969); this leaves the thought-provoking conclusion that some 13% do not know which hand they prefer. This must affect their sequencing, control of fine motor skills, and application of learning strategies requiring these components. Direct teaching of sequencing and fine motor skills is necessary for these children if they are to cope with classroom demands.
3 Memory training to extend capacity and to develop organisational skills.
   Some 75% of children assessed at the Dyslexia Institute have serious working-memory deficiencies. Awareness of the information storage competencies available to the student, the relative capacity in each register, and the range of strategies available in recall is the most important information for the teacher in determining the approach to teaching. Working memory capacity is limited at any one moment. So, if the task in hand is a complex one such as reading, the child may fail to carry out all the elements of that large skill successfully. On the other hand, decoding may be possible but not comprehension. So, rather than teaching reading as a unitary skill, the teacher should train memory to make reading more efficient. Memory strategies can be taught

using a skill-directed precision-teaching approach. They will not develop spontaneously in dyslexic children through normal curricular practice.

4 Visual perceptual training to develop skills for recognising shapes consistently.

5 Auditory perceptual training to develop skill in recognising sounds consistently, and sound categorization (Bradley and Bryant, 1983).

Training in visual and auditory perceptual skills usually forms the basis of so-called 'pre-reading programmes'. Such training is essential for the satisfactory application of structured multi-sensory teaching approaches. In addition, the teacher should facilitate spoken language development as this is the foundation upon which classroom learning (and literacy) is built. So, to our list we can add:

6 Language development through talk:

- getting sounds and words right
- getting sentences right
- concept/idea/labelling
- creating an organisation for talk (Klein, 1985).

7 Structured mult-sensory training to develop simultaneous skills in reading, spelling and writing.

8 Number language training: using structured multi-sensory methods.

9 Expression of ideas in writing (Goulandris, 1985).

Structured mult-sensory learning methods were initially developed, and are most frequently used, to facilitate literacy learning. However, the procedures are applicable across the curriculum.

In applying structured multi-sensory teaching techniques to literacy learning, the teacher is aware that the child cannot handle the text in the way that a competent reader does. To compensate for this, it is necessary to build clear links between the shape of the text unit seen, the sound it makes, its meaning, and the movement pattern to be written on paper to represent the idea. Principles of structure and order are adhered to, so that the child is not taken beyond present knowledge or competence and, by assuring success, motivation is guaranteed. A structured multi-sensory system is not just a means of teaching reading. It recognises that reading is only an intermediate step on the way from talk to continuous writing. This procedure builds the necessary skills to enable the child to read 'real books' and record the sense required from them. In turn this is only one aspect of reading training. There are problems in the use of reading skills which stem from the insensitive use of a 'books' approach.

Perry (1969) was concerned by the limitations in the use of reading skills shown by undergraduates at Harvard and Radcliffe Colleges. This academic e! .ce undoubtedly had very high levels of reading skill as measured on any test of reading attainment. They could handle any book they came across. Yet, within the context of the reading demands placed upon those students at that level of university education, they were struggling. This was clearly demonstrated by the fact that some 1500 of these students turned up for Perry's reading course, which met at the unsocial hour of 8 am. He provided them with a demanding chapter 'The Development of the English State, 1066–1272', part of an advanced course: *The Growth of Western Institutions*. He indicated that they should 'read' the chapter and be prepared to answer a written text at the end. After twenty minutes he examined their strategies. The vast majority (ie some 90%) were reading from the beginning, word by word, line by line, page by page. While Perry acknowledged their competence in this limited skill, he questioned their strategies, a sense of purpose in reading is not acquired directly by experience with books, but must be taught in a structured way.

If this was important for students with the high level basic reading skills of the Harvard group, how much more important is such fundamental teaching for students who lack that competence, and experience specific learning difficulties?

The distinction between a student's ability to carry out a skill, and his ability to see the most effective use for that skill in a range of circumstances must be the concern of every reading teacher. This vital process of applying a skill, whatever its competence, with the highest possible level of efficiency is really a question of **learning** rather than **reading**. We must ensure that the student with specific learning difficulties applies all his thinking competences with the maximum efficiency. Hence, we can make our final prescription:

10 Study skills training to facilitate the application of skills mentioned in 1 to 9.

Even from the earliest stages the child should be taught to analyse each task, as follows:

Why am I doing this?
What do I expect at the end? What outcome is required?

What strategy should be used?
Was it successful?
How can it be improved?

Children must learn to apply the system which is most relevant in relation to their particular learning needs. Hence, the teacher is aiming to develop 'metacognitive' skills: 'awareness of one's mental processes, the capacity to reflect on **how** one learns, how to strengthen memory, how to tackle problems systematically – reflection, awareness, understanding and perhaps ultimately control'. So we are teaching the child not just reading, but learning to learn.

The *Hale Report* (1964) on university teaching methods stated:

> *The aim of the course should not be primarily to equip the student with facts or knowledge, but to teach him to think for himself and work on his own.*

Should this not be the aim of all education?

To return to the challenge made earlier; if that child doesn't learn the way you teach, can you teach him the way he learns, and more importantly, can you extend his knowledge and control over his own learning skills? That is the challenge of teaching children with specific learning difficulties.

References

Bradley, L. & Bryant, P. (1978) 'Categorising Sounds & Learning to Read: A Causal Connexion?' *Nature* 201, 419.

Brady, S., Shankweiler, D. & Mann, V. 'Speech Perception & Memory Coding in Relation to Reading Ability.' *Journal of Experimental Psychology* 35, 345–367.

Denckla, M.B. & Rudel, R.G. (1976) 'Naming of Object Drawings by Dyslexic, & Other Learning-Disabled Children.' *Brain & Language* 3, 1–15.

Frith, U. (1985) 'Beneath the Surface of Developmental Dyslexia' In Patterson, K., Marshall, J.C. & Coltheart, M. (eds) *Surface Dyslexia* London: Routledge & Kegan-Paul.

Goulandris, N. (1985) 'Extending the Written Language Skill of Chilren with Specific Learning Difficulties.' In Snowling, M.J. (ed.) *Children's Written Language Difficulties* Windsor: NFER-Nelson.

Groden, (1959) 'Laterality Preferences in Normal Children.' *Journal of Perceptual & Motor Skills*, 28, 213.

Hale Report (1964) *Advisory Report On Teaching in Scottish Universities.*

Hulme, C. & Snowling, M. (1988) 'The Classification of Children with

Reading Difficulties.' *Developmental Medicine & Child Neurology.*

Katz, R.B. (1986) 'Phonological Deficiencies in Children with Reading Disability: Evidence from an Object Naming Test.' *Cognition* 22, 225–257.

Klein, H. (1985) 'The Assessment of Persisting Language Difficulties in the Language-Disabled' In Snowling, M.J. (ed.) *Children's Written Language Difficulties* Windsor: NFER-Nelson.

Perry, (1969) *Harvard Education Review* Report to Faculty.

Snowling, M. (1987) *Dyslexia: A Cognitive Developmental Perspective* Oxford: Basil Blackwell.

Snowling, M., Goulandris, N., Bowlby, M. & Howell, P. (1986) 'Segmentation & Speech Perception in Normal & Dyslexic Readers.' *Journal of Experimental Child Psychology* 41, 489–507.

Snowling, M.J., Stackhouse, J. & Rack, J.P. (1986) 'Phonological Dyslexia & Dysgraphia: A Developmental Analysis.' *Cognitive Neuropsychology* 3, 309–339.

Snowling, M., Van Wagtendonk, B. & Stafford, C. (1988) 'Object Naming Deficits in Developmental Dyslexia.' *Reading Research Quarterly.*

31 The puppet theatre: a forum for innovation and inspiration

David Lloyd

Puppets play an important part in the life of the special class at Merrydale Junior School in Leicester. Essentially they give children the opportunity to communicate more effectively than they can on paper. Children who may be withdrawn come to life using puppets, those children with behaviour difficulties benefit through sharing and co-operating, although the demands made upon the children are exacting.

Introduction

A 15 minute video (supported by a small grant from UKRA and made by the Leicester University AVS Department) was shown to the conference delegates. It highlighted the four stages involved in making and performing a play and the ways in which each stage seeks to meet the needs of the individual children.

1. Creating the story
2. Familiarisation exercises
3. Rehearsal in small chunks
4. Performance

Each stage acts as a therapy for the children in a number of ways.

1 Creating the story

The puppet theatre itself is big enough to accommodate all the children in the class, should they wish to be involved. Many of the children have fertile imaginations which often remain untapped because they are unable to work or feel unable to express themselves without feeling desperately inhibited. As a result all stories are tackled informally. The children suggest a theme: Ghostbusters; Monkey's Birthday Party; The Wicked Witches. Once the theme has been chosen democratically the children each choose one puppet for the play. There is a wide choice and so arguments are rare. The chosen puppets provide a framework from which a story will evolve and from which creative interaction will arise.

The story is divided into a beginning, a middle and an end. Work on creating the story never exceeds 20 minutes but completion can take several weeks. With the puppets in mind ideas begin to flow. The children learn to listen and appreciate the value of each others' comments. They learn to organise their thoughts and think in greater detail. I act as mediator and provide the necessary balance with the dynamics of the theatre always in mind.

Throughout this exercise, I make notes of every suggestion made so that everyone's offering may be included wherever possible. These notes form the basis of the story, which the children then listen to and alter as they see fit. An illustrated book is made which will include words and illustrations made by the children.

2 Familiarisation

Before the children enter the puppet theatre they first'work with a partner in our television studio (an old TV set). Small sections of the story which involve particular puppets are used for this. Children who normally despise working co-operatively in any way can perform and interact positively on the TV set. This has been a powerful therapy for children with severe behavioural difficulties. I am looking to sharpen their awareness of the audience – ie encouraging projection of voice and more clearly-defined movements in a small space. For the more withdrawn children, pairing them with a confident child often helps them to become more confident and relaxed.

3 Rehearsal in small groups

Once the children have begun to gain confidence behind the television it is possible to begin rehearsing sections of the play within the theatre itself. This is achieved best by working in groups of four or five. The story is carefully pieced together and welded into something dynamic and meaningful. This setting gives me an opportunity to 'negotiate' with the children – encouraging them to speak clearly, interact with others effectively and respond to the necessary cues. This places rigorous demands upon each child taking part. Frequently disputes arise between individual children. Aggressive outbursts have been known to occur during rehearsal because someone is poking someone else in the back! Similarly, differences between children evident in such settings as the playground can spill over into a rehearsal simply because the children are so easily incensed and often so quick themselves to tease and exploit their peers. On one occasion, one boy refused to work with another, tearing up his puppet.

However, the majority of children never allow this disruption to persist; their own keenness to complete the show and perform it acts as a powerful lever against those who might seek to disrupt proceedings. The result is a series of rehearsals that ultimately teach self-control and composure as well as the fundamentals that any such play demands. Parents are always welcomed and they frequently attend rehearsals – this in itself promotes a sense of purpose in the children involved.

One is always conscious of the dangers of over-rehearsal; full run throughs are limited as the children are unable to sustain their concentration. Now time is spent assembling props and constructing any necessary scenery which the children try to make colourful and eye-catching and to provide a chance for the children to manoeuvre within the theatre between scenes.

4 The performance

A performance is usually given to the whole school and will last 10-15 minutes. The children sit in rows of three and while the music is playing they alter positions so that they are ready at the front when required. This demands patience, co-operation and cohesiveness – features not common in an ordinary setting. Those performing must remember their lines and the directions given, so that the audience benefits. Self-discipline and precision timing are essential ingredients of any successful play. The sense of achievement and fulfilment is immense despite the demands of the performance itself and the challenges of preparation.

Afterwards children of all ages convey their appreciation to all who took part. They feel good about themselves and accepted by their peers in the school as having something positive to offer. This means a great deal.

Wider implications

There are times during the week when children from other classes come and use the theatre. Again this serves to open up the class and help break down any stigma that might exist between these 'special children' and the rest of the school.

In September two new ideas will come into force. Children from neighbouring infant schools will be welcomed for performances and children from a local senior school will assist me in directing a play.

The puppets can be used to bring a great deal of pleasure to many.

32 Seminar report: adult basic literacy

Martin Good, Margaret Herrington, Darryn Holland, Sue Houlton, Norma Mudd and Janet Swinney

The seminar reported here ran for one full day and included additional preparatory discussion workshops. The aim was to provide an exchange of views on current developments in the field of adult basic education, with particular reference to literacy. Some of the papers are published in full elsewhere.

1 Self-assessment in reading and writing for adult learners (Martin Good and Darryn Holland)

In the past, many adult educational centres used 'reading age' tests devised for use with children. This method was of limited validity with adults; there was a need for monitoring progress in terminology which would be easily understood both by student and tutor. Recent methods involve tutor/student discussion in which short-term goals are negotiated. As these are gradually achieved they are recorded by student and tutor. The student gains confidence and has a meaningful, personal, potentially diagnostic, record of assessment and progress.

2 Partners in reading (Sue Houlton)

There has been considerable interest in parents becoming involved in their children's literacy development. However, such trends assume that parents who become involved are literacy-competent. Parents who are students in local Adult Basic Education are often motivated, like others, to help their children's literacy development. With workshop support, they are able to make a valuable contribution to their children's learning.

3 Distance learning in adult basic education. (Margaret Herrington)

Over the past four years Margaret Herrington has been involved in developing a system of 'distance learning' in literacy and numeracy for adults in rural areas who are unwilling or unable to go to Adult Basic Education (ABE) groups. Paid tutors (volunteer tutors would seem inappropriate in distance learning) facilitate such learning by exchanging tapes and making telephone calls in addition to visits – these being made every four to six weeks.

Great self-discipline is required by these students in terms of organising study-time and completing set work. Thus, tutors often need to help students with such organisational difficulties.

4 Introducing students in ABE to modern literature using previewing techniques (Norma Mudd)

Once ABE students have achieved some of their immediate aims in reading/writing/spelling, some express a desire to move 'outwards' to learn more about another subject in this case, modern literature. However, such an undertaking seems a far cry from the generally rather narrow range of books provided for Basic Skills learning.

Writers attempt to communicate with their readers in a wide variety of language, styles, and registers. For successful learning, adults in ABE needed to be given clear guidance before attempting to interact **with**, enjoy and understand modern literature.

Suggestions were provided as to how a poem and an extract from a novel could be previewed so that the students' existing knowledge could be linked to the new knowledge – and so that new vocabulary and concepts could also be discussed and introduced before adults tackled the text itself.

5 Working with adults in the community (Janet Swinney)

Adult Literacy in England and Wales is becoming increasingly 'employment orientated'. In Scotland however, the concept of 'work in the community' is still strong. Literacy work has been undertaken with, for example, travelling people and the wives of striking miners in Scotland. The group looked at a wide range of booklets *actually* written by adults from varying backgrounds and with varying levels of literacy.